C

T
of
se
th
o
ri

a
m
b
i
t
o
s

b
i
f
p
a
t
a
t

I
I
s
S

Julio Cesar Donadone is currently a Full Professor at the Federal University of São Carlos, Brazil, and coordinator of the Center of Studies on Economic Sociology and Finance NESEFI -UFSCar. He has experience in sociology, especially in economic sociology, working mainly on the following topics: intermediaries, financialization, and field dynamics.

Routledge Frontiers of Political Economy

Innovation, Complexity and Economic Evolution
From Theory to Policy
Pier Paolo Saviotti

Economic Growth and Inequality
The Economist's Dilemma
Laurent Dobuzinskis

Wellbeing, Nature and Moral Values in Economics
How Modern Economic Analysis Faces the Challenges Ahead
Heinz Welsch

Why are Presidential Regimes Bad for the Economy?
Understanding the Link between Forms of Government and Economic Outcomes
Richard McManus and Gulcin Ozkan

Critical Theory and Economics
Philosophical Notes on Contemporary Inequality
Robin Maialeh

Corporate Financialization
An Economic Sociology Perspective
Marcelo José do Carmo, Mário Sacomano Neto and Julio Cesar Donadone

For more information about this series, please visit: www.routledge.com/Routledge-Frontiers-of-Political-Economy/book-series/SE0345

Corporate Financialization

An Economic Sociology Perspective

Marcelo José do Carmo,
Mário Sacomano Neto and
Julio Cesar Donadone

TRANSLATION BY

JANE GODWIN COURY

Routledge
Taylor & Francis Group
LONDON AND NEW YORK

First published 2023
by Routledge
4 Park Square, Milton Park, Abingdon, Oxon OX14 4RN

and by Routledge
605 Third Avenue, New York, NY 10158

Routledge is an imprint of the Taylor & Francis Group, an informa business

British Library Cataloguing-in-Publication Data
A catalogue record for this book is available from the British Library

Library of Congress Cataloging-in-Publication Data
Names: Do Carmo, Marcelo José, 1973- author. | Sacomano Neto, Mário, author. | Donadone, Julio Cesar, author.
Title: Corporate financialization : an economic sociology perspective / Marcelo José do Carmo, Mário Sacomano Neto, Julio Cesar Donadone.
Description: New York, NY : Routledge, 2023. |
Series: Routledge frontiers of political economy | Includes bibliographical references and index. |
Identifiers: LCCN 2022047630 (print) | LCCN 2022047631 (ebook) | ISBN 9781032313955 (hardback) | ISBN 9781032313962 (paperback) | ISBN 9781003309536 (ebook)
Subjects: LCSH: Corporations—Finance. | Financialization.
Classification: LCC HG4026 .D576 2023 (print) | LCC HG4026 (ebook) | DDC 658.15—dc23/eng/20221128
LC record available at https://lccn.loc.gov/2022047630
LC ebook record available at https://lccn.loc.gov/2022047631

ISBN: 9781032313955 (hbk)
ISBN: 9781032313962 (pbk)
ISBN: 9781003309536 (ebk)

DOI: 10.4324/9781003309536

Typeset in Bembo
by codeMantra

Contents

Figures

Figures

Tables

About the Authors

Marcelo José do Carmo has a PhD in Production Engineering from the Federal University of São Carlos, São Paulo, Brazil (2020). He holds a BSc in Social Sciences, majoring in Political Science, from the Federal University of São Carlos (1999) and an MSc in Production Engineering (2017) from the same institution. He was a visiting researcher at PMO Alliance Manchester Business School under the supervision of Professor Dr. Ismail Erturk (2020). His interests lie in politics, sociology, and economy, particularly economic sociology, organizations, stakeholders, and financialization. He is now a university lecturer at the Production Engineering Department at the Polytechnic School of the University of São Paulo (USP).

Mário Sacomano Neto is currently an Associate Professor of Organizational Studies at the Federal University of São Carlos, UFSCar, Brazil. He holds a BSc in Business and Management from the Pontifical Catholic University. He has a PhD in Industrial Engineering from the Federal University of São Carlos and an MSc in Industrial Engineering from the University of São Paulo (USP). He was a visiting scholar at the University of California, Berkeley (2018), under the supervision of Neil Fligstein (Department of Sociology) and a visiting scholar at the University of Chicago (2001) under the supervision of Professor Gary Herrigel and John Padgett (Political Science Department). He has experience in organizational studies, economic sociology, corporate control, strategy, field theory, and financialization.

Julio Cesar Donadone is currently a Full Professor at the Federal University of São Carlos, Brazil, and coordinator of the Center of Studies on Economic Sociology and Finance NESEFI -UFSCar. He was a visiting researcher at the University of California, Berkeley, USA (1998 and 2018) and EHESS – École des Hautes Études en Sciences Sociales – Paris, France (2005). He has experience in sociology, especially in economic sociology, working mainly on the following topics: intermediaries, financialization, and field dynamics.

About the Authors

Acknowledgments

We would like to thank CAPES (Coordination for the Improvement of Higher Education Personnel, the Brazilian government educational agency) for the financial support, through a three-year doctoral scholarship awarded to the author Marcelo José do Carmo, without which it would not have been possible to develop this research work. We would also like to thank the Routledge team who helped us share our research with a broader audience: our editor Andy Humphries, Emma Morley, Christiana Mandizha, Angharad Fearn, and Navin from Newgen Publishing UK, who are also the team responsible for publishing our first book *Financialisation in the Automotive Industry: Capital and Labour in Contemporary Society*, released in July 2021. We are grateful to the anonymous reviewers, who posed important questions and made reflections on financialization. Special thanks to Professor Dr. Ismail Erturk from the Alliance Manchester Business School, who was very important for this work, helping to identify the financialization indicators that form the basis of this research. From Brazil, we would like to thank Professors Dr. Silvio Eduardo Alvarez Candido, Dr. Martin Mundo Neto, Dr. Raphael Jonathas da Costa Lima, Dr. Marcelo José Carrer, and Dr. Felipe Cavenaghi, whose contributions to this work were very helpful and significant. Thank you to our families and friends, and everyone who has contributed to this work in some way.

Acknowledgements

1 Introduction

According to Van der Zwan (2014), financialization of the economy, companies, and society is considered a multidimensional process. It is both a new regime of accumulation and the rise and predominance of principles to maximize shareholder value and even the financialization of daily life, incorporating everyday practices specific to financial institutions in people's daily lives. An example of this is life insurance, which in its early days was frowned upon for dealing with the expectation of death and monetizing life, but today is perfectly accepted and practiced. According to other authors, the financial sector in the economy is increasingly growing in importance (Epstein, 2002; Palley, 2008; Davis & Kim, 2015).

Klinge et al. (2021) stipulate three levels of corporate financialization analysis: "(1) the national-level and macro-comparative analysis, (2) the sector- and firm-level analysis, and (3) econometric studies" (...). They "argue that corporations should be studied in their spatial organization", adding that the geographic dimension is fundamental to the study of corporate financialization (Klinge et al., 2021, p.1). In our book, we aim to join these three levels in a unified and systemic analysis.

Following Thomson and Dutta (2015), financialization includes the development of financial instruments such as securitization, derivative contracts, foreign exchange markets through the so-called carry trade, investment banks, shadow banking, growing financial assets, and unprecedented expansion of the average daily value traded by financial markets compared with the daily trading of goods and services (Thomson & Dutta, 2015, p.11).

On the other hand, according to other authors, we are facing an economic phenomenon that resembles marketing (Godechot, 2015), whereby actors capture key assets of economic production for their benefit, thus increasing economic inequality between social strata (Piketty, 2014). However, some authors consider the concept of financialization as an exaggeration and full of limitations (Christophers, 2015). Irrespectively, the term financialization seems to be an attempt to conceptualize an abstract economic phenomenon that has been occurring for almost forty years and certainly has many gaps to be filled.

DOI: 10.4324/9781003309536-1

The question of power is fundamental in the study of financialization, insofar as it is through power individuals decide where profit sharing should be destined. According to Bebchuk and Fried (2004), power has everything to do with the decisions made by and in favor of CEOs, and their high gains are, according to the authors, the "smoking gun" or the unequivocal proof that the high compensation paid to managers is related to power within the organization. In their study on payment and performance, these North American authors discuss the relationship among the internal power of executives, dispersed shareholders as a support point for the accumulation of internal power and the degree of independence that the Boards acquire, all in the interest of the powerful shareholders and senior executives (Bebchuk & Fried, 2004, pp.21–30). The issue of dispersing/concentrating shareholders also attaches importance to the debate on financialization because it shows that few large shareholders hold significant shares under their control and accumulate considerable decision-making power, while most shareholders, dispersed in thousands of small investors, have little or no influence on companies' decision-making processes.

1.1 Two conceptions of control

Neil Fligstein (2001) states that financialization consists of a change in the concept of corporate control, whereby shareholders specialize in maximizing return based on the increase in the value of companies' shares. This process marks the transition from the financial concept of corporate control to the concept of maximizing shareholder value, where the company is not only used as an asset to be the subject of mergers and acquisitions but is used to value the share price through dividend payment, stock repurchases, and valuation on stock exchanges (Fligstein, 2001, p.149).

This movement starts by managers failing to be able to value the firm only through mergers and acquisitions, which did not immediately allow desirable returns, and which maintained the diversification and the current model in large corporations, of vertical integration. With the advent of orientation aimed at maximizing shareholder value, there was a tendency to divest themselves of sectors that were considered unprofitable, to focus on core businesses and to raise the share price of companies in the financial markets (Fligstein, 2001, p.148).

According to Fligstein, the shareholder value conception of control is also a financial conception, but it is criticized in terms of what is considered a failure to increase the share price. The author quotes Davis and Thompson (1994), who consider the development of the maximizing shareholder value conception as a kind of social movement, consistent with the political–cultural approach (Fligstein, 2001, p.149). In addition to this view, there are also approaches to financial economics, which considers this change in corporate control as an efficient reallocation of assets, and sociological approaches, considering the growing dominance of banks and financial institutions over companies, a factor of vulnerability of companies and financial manipulations. Fligstein points out that the role of the state is also fundamental in creating this new financial reorganization, as in the United States, with the relaxation policies of antitrust laws and tax cut laws in Ronald Reagan's government (1981–1988), which produced legal and political conditions that led to the financial reorganization of firms (Fligstein, 2001, p.150).

Analyzing the current situation, Fligstein's (2001) propositions are correct, as the role of the state in terms of financialization remains decisive. The recent corporate tax reduction laws, passed at the US Congress on the initiative of the Donald Trump administration, have greatly favored large financial groups, such as Berkshire Hathaway, which had an accounting valuation of US$ 65 billion in 2017, of which US$ 36 billion came from operating activities and US$ 29 billion "was courtesy of Donald Trump's tax cut" (Alpher, 2018).

1.2 Marxist and regulation theory

The debate on financialization derives from the theses on the valorization of capital through activities that do not need to go through the sphere of production, as was discussed by Chesnais (1999). It happens that the production and productive processes of work are still important for goods to be produced to be sold later (Cushen & Thompson, 2016). This is where financialization takes on more challenging shapes. If capital appreciation occurs using the M-M′ formula (money that generates more money), without the intermediation of production, and if production decreases, because its activity generates little or no capital appreciation in the long run, what money will be generated? If goods are not created, there would consequently be no more money to be generated and more free flow of money created by productive operations. And how would the dividends be paid? With more shares? We do not know, because it is speculation on our part, but the important fact here is that over the last forty years, a movement of intense development of the so-called fictitious capital, one that is based only on contracts, papers, and future income promises, has been occurring.

Domination of finance over real economic activities has persisted and grown, and therefore, "financialization has increased inequality, slowed down investment in 'real' production, mounted pressures on indebted households and individuals, and led to a decline in democratic accountability" (Thomson & Dutta, 2015, p.5). These authors point out that the speed of growth of financial assets over the world's GDP has been enormous. In 1980, they represented 120% of the world's GDP, or US$ 12 trillion; in 1990, they represented 263% of the world's GDP, or US$ 56 trillion; in 2000, they started to represent 310% of the global GDP, accounting for US$ 119 trillion; and in 2010, they had a ratio of 316% of the world's GDP, with a value of US$ 219 trillion. For a global GDP of US$ 80 trillion in 2013, that is, financial assets are three times greater than the entire production of goods and services on a global scale (Thomson & Dutta, 2015, p.7).

To have an idea of these numbers, the average daily value of financial market transactions in April 2013 was of the order of US$ 5.3 trillion, while the average daily value traded in goods and services in 2012 was US$ 58.9 billion, ninety times less. The value traded in the financial markets in less than a week is greater than the amount sold in goods and services in an entire year (Thomson & Dutta, 2015, p.11).

1.3 Mainstream economics

In this debate about component categories or financialization indicators, we would like to oppose the mainstream theory, as it considers that maximizing shareholder value has always existed and is not the product of a transformation in the conceptions of control. We will see in our empirical data that observable reality does not always match many theories, which, in the desire to be general and highly explanatory, in practice overlook reality data.

There are authors who claim that there is a tendency toward the disappearance of dividend payments to shareholders (Fama & French, 2001, p.2). It is not what the numbers show. Based on extensive documentation on the history of dividend payments in the United States, Fama and French studied the period from 1926 to 1999 and found that "in 1973, 52.8% of publicly traded non-financial non-utility firms pay dividends. The proportion of payers rises to a peak of 66.5% in 1978. Then, it falls rather relentlessly. In 1999, only 20.8% of firms pay dividends" (Fama & French, 2001, p.3). The fact is that this number has certainly increased today, and the drop from 66.5% of firms in 1978 to 20.8% of firms in 1999 has to do with the merger and acquisition process, which has reconcentrated corporate ownership in large companies and economic groups (Davis, 2008; Fichtner et al., 2017) and does not indicate a drop in dividend payments in absolute numbers, as this has been increasing to billions of dollars every year.

Fama & French (2001) attempt to explain this phenomenon by saying that companies follow at least three requirements to pay dividends: profitability, investment opportunity, and size. Larger firms are more likely to pay dividends, which seems correct. Moreover, companies that invest heavily in Research & Development (R&D) have little propensity to pay dividends (Fama & French, 2001, p.3). This is not true. We will see below that companies such as Apple, Microsoft, and Johnson & Johnson distributed billionaire dividends to shareholders and are companies that invest heavily in R&D, exactly the Achilles heel of the development and success of these companies. Apple spent US$ 18.7 billion on R&D in 2020, Microsoft US$ 20.7 billion, and Johnson & Johnson spent US$ 12.1 billion in the same year (Nasdaq, 2021a, 2021b, 2021c).

The idea of the low propensity of current companies to pay dividends to shareholders did not materialize, although there are cases of Google, Facebook, Amazon, and Berkshire Hathaway, which have not been paying dividends to shareholders, but some of these companies practice stock repurchases. In addition, these companies are a tiny minority. In our study, it can be observed that in only four years, from 2013 to 2016, only the ten largest companies in market capitalization spent almost US$ 500 billion in dividends, either in cash or stock repurchases, contrary to the thesis put forward by Fama and French (2001) on the propensity for the "disappearance" of dividend payments by contemporary companies. For this reason, we would like to question the theoretical assumptions of the economic mainstream about financialization: that there would be no financialization, but only a natural process that has always occurred in the economy, with only different, larger quantities. That is, where mainstream economics theorists see only continuity in the process, we see a break in the pattern and the subsequent development of another conception of control and functioning of the economy and society.

1.4 Purpose and democracy

Patriotta (2021) analyzed the controversies concerning the future of corporations, reviewing two other articles for the same issue of the *Journal of Management Studies*. In the article, the author introduces Mayer (2021) and Davis (2021), who have different views on the future of corporations.

> Colin Mayer advocates a view of the corporation as a purpose-driven institution that can become a vehicle for economic and social prosperity. The counterpoint by Jerry Davis emphasizes the declining role of contemporary corporations, and argues for the need to develop both internal and external corporate democracy.
>
> (Patriotta, 2021, p.879)

There would be a "shareholder/stakeholder dichotomy", in which Mayer is a critic. Patriotta states that "according to Mayer, this is a false dichotomy that should be overcome by shifting the analytical focus from the main beneficiaries of a corporation's activity to its commitment to its stated purpose (...) (Patriotta, 2021, p.880).

Mayer (2021) questions why businesses exist and what their purpose is, and states that many companies had already abandoned Milton Friedman's doctrine, according to which the company's only social function was the search for profit. He declares that

> many of the largest corporations have discarded the conventional Milton Friedman (1962, 1970) doctrine that there is one and only social purpose of business to increase profits so long as it stays within the rules of the game in favor of the view that corporate purpose should reflect the interests of stakeholders as well as shareholders.
>
> (Mayer, 2021, p.888)

In other words, Mayer (2021) believes that it is possible to reconcile the well-being of all stakeholders if the company is imbued with such a purpose.

The definition that all stakeholders must have equal attention and equal importance must be expressly stated as a firm purpose of the corporation.

Contrary to what Mayer thinks, Davis (2021) highlights how modern corporations have succumbed to greed and corruption, seeking profit above all and everyone. The author remembers pharmaceutical companies and opioid addiction, sugar and obesity and other companies that cause damage to health and more problems than solutions to people. According to Patriotta "for Davis, shareholder capitalism fuels corporate greed and induces corporations to pursue profit at the expense of public well-being" (Patriotta, 2021, p.881). Davis proposes reforms from above, through state regulation, and from below, through the democratization of corporations, with greater power and participation for all stakeholders, not just shareholders. Patriotta resumes that

> in recent years, the US stock market has become increasingly concentrated, largely identifiable with the S&P index, dominated by tech giants, and heavily influenced by large investors. The combination of unethical behavior and corporate failure in the face of crises demonstrates the necessity to revive and update existing government regulations and strengthen state intervention.
>
> (Patriotta, 2021, p.882)

Based on empirical data, it can be stated in this work that we are closer to Davis' skepticisms than to Mayer's optimism. While we agree that it is necessary for the company to have a strong purpose of serving all stakeholders, merely a declaration of intent has not been enough to ensure this happens. This is what Froud et al. (2006) classified as *narrative and numbers*, and the concrete reality has been very different from what is advertised. Regarding this, Patriotta (2021) argues that "to paraphrase Argyris and Schon (1978), one could argue that purpose might merely provide an *espoused theory*, while shareholder primacy acts as a *theory-in-use* that informs actual corporate behavior" (Patriotta, 2021, p.881).

The authors we discuss in this book have been developing categories of analysis on financialization for some time, each of which emphasizes an aspect of this process. We believe that the combination of some of these categories would give us the opportunity to create a broader picture of the financialization processes of society, the economy, and companies. That is why the choice of indicators/categories of analysis that are being debated by internationally renowned authors, high academic productivity and influencing current debates, can help to build on the literature regarding this topic in an enriching way. It is important to note that no indicator is more important than the other, there is no hierarchy, but we seek to organize these financialization indicators *pari passu* to develop this research. We recall that such categories of analysis were already used in a master's dissertation (Carmo, 2017) when financialization in the automotive industry was studied through the five largest automakers worldwide. These categories proved to be useful, and empirical data were found to strongly support the theoretical constructions that gave rise to the indicators. In other words, it was not reality that suited the precepts of the theory well, but the theory on financialization using these categories of analysis/indicators only confirms on a theoretical level what happens in practice. That is why this study is useful in terms of testing financialization theories and reinforcing them, drawing important conclusions from them, based on the study of the empirical data obtained in the investigation process.

1.5 Financialization indicators

1.5.1 Sources of profitability

The first indicator is the comparison between the sources of profitability. Froud et al. (2006) considered that one of the characteristics of the financialization process is the development of financial segments of companies, obtaining greater proportional profitability than the productive segment of firms. Services, in addition to valuing companies through stock exchanges, among other financial instruments, lead to proportionally higher profits than the production area. This was confirmed in the book *Financialization and Strategy: narrative and numbers* (2006), which studied the case of Ford, General Electric, and the pharmaceutical company, GlaxoSmithKline. In a master's dissertation (Carmo, 2017), when the five largest automakers were studied, the same reality was found as what occurred in these other companies. Ford continued its process of expanding profits through Ford Credit, while production profits declined, and the sector even made a loss. In the other automakers, the growth of the financial segment also occurred, although with different dynamics. In summary, this indicator created by Froud et al. (2006) is of paramount importance for those who want to analyze the financialization processes of large contemporary companies.

1.5.2 Shareholding composition/corporate control

The second indicator refers to the shareholding composition of the companies and the shareholding acquisitions that the groups carry out in the companies' shares. Useem (1996) was one of the first to detect the transition process from managerialism to the predominance of shareholders. The managers' revolution was followed by the shareholders' revolution, such as those actors who would lead the management of companies, even if far from the boards, gaining enormous influence in the management of modern firms' strategies. Therefore, Davis (2008) addressed the concentration of ownership in the hands of a few investment funds and banks, which meant that few financial institutions participated in the vast majority of company boards. And now, more recently, Fichtner et al. (2017) circumscribed their research in the power of just three gigantic investment funds, The Vanguard Group, BlackRock Inc., and State Street Corp., which together are present in 88% of the companies listed on the S&P 500 and are the largest shareholders by 40% of all North American companies (Fichtner et al., 2017, p.322). In short, this indicator is also very important in the study of financialization processes.

1.5.3 Mergers and acquisitions

Mergers and acquisitions of companies are an old phenomenon in industrial capitalism, and they do not exactly concern financialization itself. Since the beginning of the twentieth century, companies have merged, concentrating the market more on fewer companies and buying others, working toward vertical integration. In the case of company acquisitions, although the time for vertical integration has apparently passed, focusing on core businesses, the fact is that the practice of acquiring companies that are competitors or complementary to the business has been recurring in the largest companies in market capitalization. Our study will show that the ten largest companies analyzed here, all of them, regardless of the sector in which they operate, acquired smaller companies, start-ups, or even already large companies, which grew fast and could become an obstacle for these business giants.

In the case of information and communication technology companies, the phenomenon of acquisitions occurs intensely. Currently, "Google and Apple are the pillars of the mobile ecosystem and have been very active in acquiring companies in recent years" (Yang et al., 2018, p.15).

That is, company acquisitions strengthen financialization as it concentrates ownership in fewer hands, decision-making power and the number of dividends that will be paid and shares that will be repurchased in smaller decision circles.

1.5.4 Origin of company managers

The fourth indicator refers to the origin of company managers. According to Fligstein (1991), analyzing the professional and educational trajectory of company executives is a clue to understanding their current decisions as their trajectory speaks volumes about who they are and the environment in which they were formed. Although this is true, and Fligstein's text, from 1991 onward, has faced real changes in the configuration of financialization, i.e., more intense and aggravated, it is no longer possible to judge whether the origin of the leaders has directly to do with the decisions taken today. When Fligstein wrote about it in 1991, the different conceptions of corporate control were studied as tight periods and perfectly delimited from each other (production, marketing and sales, and finance, the latter comprising two moments, mergers and acquisitions and maximizing shareholder value, our focal period), and this was valuable because it raised the question for changes in corporate control concepts. However, nowadays, in this second moment of financialization, the simple origin and trajectory of the executives does not sufficiently explain their current decisions, as both the members who came from the industrial world and those who participated in financial institutions, make practically equal decisions as all decisions are frankly favorable to shareholders and top executives.

1.5.5 Compensation payment to executives

The fifth financialization indicator to be analyzed in this book is the compensation payment to executives. Several authors, such as Bebchuk and Fried (2004); Erturk et al. (2005); Lazonick (2016); and Hopkins and Lazonick (2016), assert that millionaire compensation payment to the main executives has nothing to do with performance, but rather with the internal power that managers acquire. While there is a slight correspondence to the performance itself (if there is ample profit, there are more payoffs; if there are losses there may even be a cut in compensation payouts), in general, there is no direct relationship between pay and performance. In addition, millionaire compensation payment to executives, through stock options, aims to increase share prices on stock exchanges, a mechanism that helps to increase the company's market capitalization. It also helps in the concentration of income, as most of the compensation to executives is not subject to income tax, and only a small part of the managers' earnings is taxed.

1.5.6 Dividend payments to shareholders and stock repurchases

The sixth indicator analyzed is dividend payments to shareholders, one of the most important indicators that reveal the most striking characteristic of current capitalism: making production a mere means of generating wealth and distributing it to shareholders. While some advocate that there would be a tendency to end dividend payments to shareholders (Fama & French, 2001), this is not what we see in the current literature and in the numbers and empirical data (Lazonick, 2011, 2012, 2013). Increasingly, large annual dividends are being paid to shareholders, whether in cash or in stock repurchases or stock buybacks, whereby the company repurchases stocks from itself, causing a rise in stock prices as a result of a large buying movement.

1.5.7 Employee salaries

The seventh indicator is that of company employee salaries. One of the characteristics of the financialization process is that the financial hubs of the business (shareholders and executives) are benefited while the financial hubs of the productive pole (workers, jobs, factories, and other physical assets) are impaired. Shimizu (2014, 2015) studied the issue of wages in Japanese automakers and concluded that a progressive dismantling of labor and remuneration relations was underway. Ohnoism, which became known for its ability to reward workers and groups of workers in Toyota's plants, was giving way to the establishment of more individualistic criteria, which made work precarious and devalued. In a master's dissertation (Carmo, 2017), we demonstrated that the average wage of workers at Ford and GM was below the average level of all American workers, and now, we have obtained preliminary data that place salaries at Apple, for example, at an equally low level, lower than the average of all American workers' wages.

1.5.8 Employment

The eighth and final financialization indicator is employment. Several authors have been debating that employment has been made more flexible, precarious, and outsourced (Marx & Mello, 2012; Shimizu, 2014, 2015; Pardi, 2016; Lepadatu & Janoski, 2017). Moreover, a stable job with social rights and fair pay will no longer exist in the medium term. In the United States, the end of good jobs was analyzed by Wartzman (2017), and we have seen how jobs are increasingly threatened in the current economic moment at an international level (Carmo et al., 2021). The case of Ford's departure from Brazil, Russia, and India exposes how the short-term valuation strategies of business have prevailed over employment, income, and job stability concerns, which concerns everyone.

Financialization is an economic process that presents several indicators that we aim to discuss to expand knowledge on the topic, contributing to this important point on the research agenda of economic sociology. This agenda has been developed by sociologists and economists who understand the economic sphere not as something separate from the rest of society, but as something *embedded* in social relations (Granovetter, 1985). Multiple interactions between the various political and economic institutions, organizations, states, and countries cross the entire society, and their understanding requires using a broader tool, including several disciplines, such as sociology, economics, political science, administration, engineering ,and even law and psychology. This multidisciplinarity is what provides conditions for a more holistic and systemic analysis of today's complex and diverse society.

The text structure will be divided into ten cases through which we will discuss eight indicators in each case using tables, charts, graphs, and respective texts that analyze the data and dialogue with the existing theoretical production. An appendix will be presented showing how these companies are today, five years after the data were first collected in 2017. The ten largest companies in market capitalization in December 2017 were Apple, Google, Microsoft, Amazon, Berkshire Hathaway, Facebook, Johnson & Johnson, JPMorgan Chase & Co., Tencent Holdings, and ExxonMobil.

1.6 The first research results

Table 1.1 shows the ten largest companies in market capitalization and dividend payments, in addition to stock repurchases over four years, from 2013 to 2016.

Table 1.1 Market Capitalization, net income and % of net income distributed to shareholders. 2013 to 2016 in billions of US$

	2013	*2014*	*2015*	*2016*	*Net profit and distributed profit*
Market Capitalization in billions of US$ 12/15/2017					
Apple	37,037	39,510	53,394	45,687	Net Profit
US$ 752 Bi	33,954	56,856	47,357	42,367	Distributed Profit
	91,67	143	88,69	92,7	%
Google	12,210	13,620	15,830	19,480	Net Profit
US$ 579.5 Bi	0,00	0,00	0,00	0,00	Distributed Profit
	0	0	0	0	%
Microsoft	21,863	22,074	12,193	16,798	Net Profit
US$ 507.5 Bi	21,863	22,074	20,807	23,612	Distributed Profit
	100	100	170	140	%
Amazon	0274	−0241	0596	2371	Net Profit
US$ 427 Bi	0,00	0,00	0,00	0,00	Distributed Profit
	0	0	0	0	%
Berkshire Hathaway	19,480	19,870	24,080	24,070	Net Profit
US$ 409.9 Bi	0	0	0	0	Distributed Profit
	0	0	0	0	%
Facebook	1491	2925	3669	10,188	Net Profit
US$ 407.3 Bi	0,00	0,00	0,00	0,00	Distributed Profit
	0	0	0	0	%
Johnson & Johnson	13,830	16,320	15,410	16,540	Net Profit
US$ 338.6 Bi	13,830	16,320	15,410	16,540	Distributed Profit
	100	100	100	100	%
JPMorgan Chase & Co.	17,886	21,745	24,442	24,733	Net Profit
US$ 306.6 Bi	16,557	20,077	22,406	22,583	Distributed Profit
	92,56	92,32	91,67	91,3	%
Tencent Holdings	2700	3200	6600	7100	Net Profit
US$ 277.1 Bi	2700	3200	6600	7100	Distributed Profit
	100	100	100	100	%
ExxonMobil	n/a	32,520	16,150	7,840	Net Profit
242.2	n/a	11,400	16,150	12,900	Distributed Profit
	n/a	35	100	164	%
Total of distributed dividends/stock repurchases					2013 to 2016 billions of US$
Billions of US$	86,231	129,927	128,730	125,102	469,990

Source:https://www.statista.com/statistics/263264/top-companies-in-the-world-by-market-value/and www.nasdaq.com

From the data presented in Table 1.1, it can be observed that the amounts of net income distributed to shareholders or stock repurchases represent a significant portion of the resources generated by companies that are distributed to their controllers. It shows situations in which 170% of net income was distributed, as in the case of Microsoft in 2015, when it profited US$ 12 billion and distributed US$ 20 billion to shareholders, due to the accumulation of cash that these gigantic companies were able to produce. An interesting fact is the case of JPMorgan Chase & Co., one of the largest US banks, which always distributes less than 100% of its net income to its shareholders, leaving a reserve in the organization's cashiers.

1.6.1 Non-financial companies paid more dividends than financial ones

It can be observed that the prediction made by Fama and French (2001) about the propensity to no longer pay dividends to shareholders is not generally verified. It should also be mentioned that non-financial companies paid more dividends to shareholders than financial companies. Berkshire Hathaway, for example, does not pay dividends to shareholders, providing an interesting element in the study of financialization as one of the assumptions of this phenomenon is maximizing shareholder value and therefore periodic payments to investors.

JPMorgan Chase bank paid an average of 92% of net income to its shareholders from 2013 to 2016, leaving some reserve, more than US$ 1 billion a year. Why would a financial company be less committed to maximizing shareholder return than a non-financial company? Why did a bank pay fewer dividends than a manufacturing company? This is an issue to be debated in more depth and can pave the way for studies in the research agenda on financialization and economic sociology.

The fact is that today's large companies are financial centers with an industrial predominance, as noted by Chesnais (1999) and even banks have been gradually adhering to financialization practices, and as such dividend payments are a corollary maximum. However, as Erturk (2015) analyzed, even in banks the financialized mentality is the result of a progressive inculcation and not a natural and applicable process with equal intensity in all companies in the same way.

To sum up, the ten companies we discussed here distributed an amount of US$ 469.9 billion to their shareholders, including dividends and stock repurchases, in just four years (2013–2016), which shows enormous investor influence. Apple alone distributed around US$ 180 billion in dividends or stock repurchases to shareholders in these four years, from 2013 to 2016, representing 40% of the total of the top ten, as we will see later. In fact, Apple, Microsoft, and ExxonMobil have even distributed more than 100% of their net income in dividends and stock repurchases in a few years.

This trend of distributing more and more dividends to shareholders, through cash or stock repurchases, has been occurring in almost all companies with a higher market capitalization. The exceptions are Google, Facebook, Amazon, and Berkshire Hathaway, which have not been paying dividends to shareholders. However, some of them practice stock repurchases, which is even more thought-provoking and challenging for our research, because it raises the question of heterogeneity of this economic phenomenon when we study each company.

1.6.2 Major shareholders are large financial groups

One of the aspects that led to the emergence of the liberalized and deregulated finance regime was the "entry of relatively new, but particularly powerful agents, of money capital or concentrated money capital, which were pension funds and investment funds, that gave rise to the notion of 'institutional investors'" (Farnetti, 1999, p.183).

These funds have become the most decisive private institutions in the context of globalized finance, according to Farnetti (1999), who studied the role of Anglo-Saxon pension funds and collective investments. According to the author, other categories of institutional investors were added to the pension funds, "such as insurance companies and the various collective investment funds, which considerably increased the supply of capital in search of net investments" (Farnetti, 1999, p.188).

The companies that we will analyze have in common the fact that their largest shareholders are the same financial groups. In our recent studies on the financialization of the automotive industry (Carmo, 2017; Carmo et al., 2018, 2019, 2020, 2021), we analyzed the five largest automakers worldwide according to the volume of production. We found in them (especially in the North American ones, such as Ford and GM, but also in the others) the largest shareholders who are billionaire investment funds and banks, and these same groups are also the largest shareholders in these large companies now studied. The Vanguard Group, BlackRock Inc., State Street Corp., and Berkshire Hathaway, among others, are the largest shareholders of both the automakers, as well as these other companies that we now introduce in the debate.

Table 1.2 shows the five largest shareholders of the ten largest companies in market capitalization worldwide.

As was seen in Table 1.2, it is practically the same shareholders that lead the ranking of the largest in all ten companies analyzed. All are large financial-type organizations, which increasingly hold significant shares and decisions within these analyzed companies. We believe that this may be a striking feature of financialization: the shareholding control of large financial groups over manufacturing companies, to create value to pay dividends to shareholders, typical of the current era.

Table 1.2 Largest shareholders of the ten largest companies by market capitalization

Apple – 6/30/2017

	Shares held	*Amounts in thousands of US$*
The Vanguard Group Inc.	342,197,877	59,029,134
BlackRock Inc.	313,366,448	54,055,712
State Street Corp.	212,361,715	36,632,396
FMR LLC	157,165,510	27,111,050
Berkshire Hathaway	130,191,960	22,458,113

Google – 6/30/2017

	Shares held	*Amounts in thousands of US$*
The Vanguard Group Inc.	20,440,038	21,103,930
BlackRock Inc.	18,058,006	18,644,530
FMR LLC	13,971,679	14,425,479
State Street Corp.	11,923,667	12,310,948
T. Rowe Price Associates Inc /MD/	10,068,751	10,395,784

Microsoft – 6/30/2017

	Shares held	*Amounts in thousands of US$*
The Vanguard Group Inc.	564,052,011	47,459,336
BlackRock Inc.	477,160,372	40,148,274
Capital World Investors	334,919,849	28,180,156
State Street Corp.	307,965,955	25,912,255
T. Rowe Price Associates Inc /MD/	187,181,584	15,749,458

Amazon – 6/30/2017

	Shares held	*Amounts in thousands of US$*
The Vanguard Group Inc.	26,863,386	29,861,340
BlackRock Inc.	23,925,821	26,595,943
FMR LLC	18,468,693	20,529,799
T. Rowe Price Associates Inc /MD/	17,521,863	19,477,303
State Street Corp.	16,228,565	18,039,673

Berkshire Hathaway – BRK B - 9/30/2017

	Shares held	*Amounts in thousands of US$*
The Vanguard Group Inc.	122,389,425	25,721,362
BlackRock Inc.	102,620,861	21,566,800
State Street Corp.	81,358,344	17,098,270
Bill & Melinda Gates Foundation Trust	68,569,972	14,410,665
SFMG, LLC	45,594,752	9,582,193

Facebook – 6/30/2017

	Shares held	*Amounts in thousands of US$*
The Vanguard Group Inc.	162,530,760	29,080,004
BlackRock Inc.	138,877,313	24,847,929
FMR LLC	131,431,757	23,515,770
State Street Corp.	91,999,973	16,460,635
T. Rowe Price Associates Inc /MD/	66,868,292	11,964,075

Exxon Mobil– 6/30/2017

	Shares held	*Amounts in thousands of US$*
The Vanguard Group Inc.	309,411,379	25,736,839
BlackRock Inc.	256,590,217	21,343,174
State Street Corp.	208,886,675	17,375,194
Northern Trust Corp.	55,832,375	4,644,137
Bank of New York Mellon Corp.	54,169,811	4,505,845

Johnson & Johnson – 9/30/2017

	Shares held	*Amounts in thousands of US$*
The Vanguard Group Inc.	201,821,086	27,851,310
BlackRock Inc.	168,417,318	23,241,590
State Street Corp.	155,054,539	21,397,526
State Farm Mutual Automobile Insurance Co.	37,878,592	5,227,246
Bank of New York Mellon Corp.	36,594,054	5,049,979

JP Morgan Chase & Co. – 9/30/2017

	Shares held	*Amounts in thousands of US$*
The Vanguard Group Inc.	251,791,483	28,369,346
BlackRock Inc.	228,636,034	25,760,422
State Street Corp.	164,811,927	18,569,360
FMR LLC	93,138,233	10,493,885
T. Rowe Price Associates Inc /MD/	76,451,129	8,613,749

Tencent Holdings – 6/30/2017

	Shares held	*Amounts in thousands of US$*
Naspers Ltd.	3,151,201,900	n/a
Hua Teng Ma	819,507,500	n/a
The Vanguard Group Inc.	188,695,177	n/a
BlackRock Fund Advisors	113,658,800	n/a
Norges Bank Investment Management	73,248,214	n/a

Sources: http://www.4-traders.com/TENCENT-HOLDINGS-LTD-3045861/company/ and http://www.nasdaq.com/symbol/aapl/institutionalholdings

1.6.3 The Big Three of Wall Street

Fichtner et al. (2017) consider the three main US passive investment funds as the Big Three of Wall Street. The Vanguard Group, BlackRock Inc., and State Street Corp. have trillions of dollars in assets under management. They have stakes in thousands of companies around the world and great power to influence global investment and disinvestment decisions. These funds are the major shareholders of the companies we review in this book.

According to data from Nasdaq.com, the largest of all these organizations was The Vanguard Group Inc. Based in Valley Forge, Pennsylvania, United States, this financial group had an estimated market capitalization of US$ 2.243 trillion on September 30, 2017. In 2017, it invested in 4,025 different companies and different branches of the economy. Technology (21.29%) and financial services (21.23%) were the largest sectors in which this giant aimed to expand its business. Health (12.15%), industries (11.63%), and energy (5.62%) were also part of its portfolio. It is the largest shareholder in Apple, Google, Microsoft, Amazon, JPMorgan Chase & Co., and ExxonMobil, among others (Nasdaq, 2021d).

Second in the ranking of the largest financial groups is BlackRock Inc., valued at US$ 2.037 trillion in September 2017. Represented in New York City, this group invested in 4,837 companies in 2017. Its main investments were in the following sectors: financial (21.94%), technology (21.14%), health (12.92%), and industries (11.02%), and concentrated two thirds of its investments in these four sectors, as seems to be the pattern of diversification of these large groups (Nasdaq, 2021e).

Another giant investor is State Street Corp. Headquartered in Boston, Massachusetts, the group had a market capitalization estimated at US$ 1.194 trillion on September 30, 2017, ranking third among major financial groups. It invested in 3616 companies, mainly divided into technology (20.55%), financial services (20.24%), industries (12.83%), and health (12.82%), all adding up to two thirds of all its investments in these four major sectors of the economy (Nasdaq, 2021f).

In addition to these large groups, dozens of others gather the bulk of US private capital and a large part of world capital, and their influence is felt in thousands of manufacturing companies, which, under the growing dependence on massive capital to invest, has been radically changing its governance, its market strategies, and its business models.

1.7 Valuation of companies' stock price

We will now introduce the appreciation of the stock price of five companies analyzed, in the period of one year, from November 2016 to November 2017 (Ycharts, 2017). The appreciation of the stock price of Apple, Amazon, Google, Facebook, and Microsoft is significant. This growth ranged from 35.63% in Google's shares to 57.30% in Apple's shares. No other business or productive activity has experienced this appreciation in the world financial market in just one year. However, in the companies analyzed here, appreciation increased from an average of 45% in one year.

These companies also manufacture products, such as smartphones, computers, Internet providers, computer programs, social networks, and automated retail sales; that is, they are companies that have billionaire revenues, but the growth in the value of their shares and, consequently, their market capitalization does not follow the same proportion as the growth in their revenues. The appreciation of their shares in the stock market grows much faster than their revenues. We will see that Amazon's stock price growth was 595% in just five years, from 2014 to 2019, while other stock indices grew by much smaller percentages, such as 74% in the case of the S&P 500, 112% in the case of Morgan Stanley Technology Index, and 149% on the S&P 500 retailing index. Table 1.3 shows Amazon's stock price growth.

Whoever invested US$100 in Amazon stock in 2014 had a spectacular result in 2019, reaching US$ 595, which is almost 600% appreciation in just five years, or 120% a year. It is much higher than the increase in revenues, which were also significant, but did not reach the level of the appreciation of the shares. Table 1.4 shows Amazon's revenues growth.

Table 1.3 Amazon's incredible stock price performance

Year	*Amazon.com, Inc.*	*Morgan Stanley Technology Index*	*S&P 500 Index*	*S&P 500 Retailing Index*
2014	US$ 100	US$ 100	US$ 100	US$ 100
2015	US$ 218	US$ 107	US$ 101	US$ 126
2016	US$ 242	US$ 120	US$ 114	US$ 133
2017	US$ 377	US$ 167	US$ 138	US$ 173
2018	US$ 484	US$ 154	US$ 132	US$ 197
2019	US$ 595	US$ 212	US$ 174	US$ 249

Source: Amazon *Annual Report*, 2019, p.77

Table 1.4 Amazon's revenue growth

Year	*Total net sales in billion dollars*
2015	107,006
2016	135,987
2017	177,866
2018	232,887
2019	280,522
2020	386,064

Source: Amazon *Annual Report*, 2019, p.18 and Amazon *Annual Report*, 2020, p.39

From 2015 to 2019, Amazon's revenues grew at an annual average of approximately 30% over the previous year. Only in 2020, because of the new coronavirus pandemic, in which e-commerce was greatly benefited by social isolation, did revenues grow from US$ 280 billion in 2019 to US$ 386 billion in 2020, 40% less increase in revenue over the previous year, while share price growth was 120% per year. In other words, these numbers confirm that the speed of revenue growth was lower than the speed of growth of the company's share price, indicating that there must be other rationales to guide investment decisions and share purchases. We will look at the Amazon case in more detail later, and we can anticipate that the case of Amazon is of a heterogeneous nature, quite different from the cases presented by other companies. Amazon does not pay dividends to shareholders or practice stock repurchases. It also does not pay millionaire compensation to its main executives, showing a difference between earnings between CEO and other employees that are much smaller than the differences found in the other companies analyzed by us. However, such heterogeneity does not weaken the concept of financialization, but it is an exception that only confirms the rule: i.e., the overwhelming majority of large companies have been undergoing a financialization process, maximizing shareholder value as a primacy.

To sum up, large groups of institutional investors, banks, and other financial institutions have invested heavily in thousands of companies, largely manufacturing companies, which suggests that production is still important for creating a free flow of money that will be reversed in the form of dividends and stock repurchases. They are strongly interconnected, although there is room to affirm that the financial sphere has acquired enormous autonomy and preponderance *vis-à-vis* the sphere of production.

Taking into account the shareholding composition of these large companies, their increasing profits, dividend payments to shareholders and stock repurchases, relatively low wages for workers, and millionaire compensation for executives, we tried to create a framework for analyzing the financialization process that affects the current corporate world, in their multiple dimensions, using economic sociology tools to better explain economic phenomena that are often neglected by mainstream economics, for whom everything is a result of an optimal allocation of resources. For the worker who was laid off and whose factory was closed because of short-term strategies, there is nothing optimal or fair about these decisions; only sadness and the attempt to start life anew, in an extremely liquid, uncommitted, and rootless time.

References

Alpher, S. 2018. Tax cuts boost Berkshire Hathaway book value in 2017. *SeekingAlpha.com*. 24 February. Available at: https://seekingalpha.com/news/3333993-tax-cuts-boost-berkshire-hathaway-book-value-in-2017#email_link

Amazon.com. 2019. *Annual Report*, 2019. Available at: https://s2.q4cdn.com/299287126/files/doc_financials/2020/ar/2019-Annual-Report.pdf

Amazon.com. 2020. *Annual Report*, 2020. Available at: https://www.sec.gov/Archives/edgar/data/1018724/000101872421000004/amzn-20201231.htm

Bebchuk, L.A. and Fried, J.M. 2004. Pay without performance, the unfulfilled promise of executive compensation, part II: power and pay, draft of the book *Pay without Performance, The Unfulfilled Promise of Executive Compensation*. Available at: http://www.law.harvard.edu/faculty/bebchuk/pdfs/Performance-Part2.pdf. Accessed 09/10/2021.

Carmo, M.J. 2017. Análise do processo de financeirização do setor automotivo. *Dissertação de Mestrado apresentada ao programa de Pós-Graduação em Engenharia de Produção da Universidade Federal de São Carlos*- UFSCar, 135 f. Available at: https://repositorio.ufscar.br/handle/ufscar/8917

Carmo, M.J., Sacomano Neto, M., and Donadone, J.C. 2018. Análise da financeirização no setor automotivo: O caso da Ford Motor Company. *Nova Economia*. DOI: 10.1590/0103–6351/3469

Carmo, M.J., Sacomano Neto, M., and Donadone, J.C. 2019. Financialization in the automotive industry: shareholders, managers, and salaries. *Journal of Economic Issues*, 53(3), 841–862. DOI: 10.1080/00213624.2019.1646609

Carmo, M.J., Sacomano Neto, M., and Donadone, J.C. 2020. Multiple dynamics of financialization in the automotive sector: Ford and Hyundai cases. *Gestão & Produção*. DOI: 10.1590/0104–530x5173-20

Carmo, M.J., Sacomano Neto, M., and Donadone, J.C. 2021. *Financialization in the Automotive Industry: Capital and Labour in Contemporary Society*. London and New York: Routledge. Available at: https://www.routledge.com/Financialisation-in-the-Automotive-Industry-Capital-and-Labour-in-Contemporary/Carmo-Neto-Donadone/p/book/9780367751395

Chesnais, F. 1999. *A mundialização financeira: gênese, custos e riscos*. Coordenado por François Chesnais, Editora Xamã, São Paulo.

Christophers, B. 2015. The limits to financialization. *Dialogues in Human Geography*, 5(2), 183–200.

Cushen, J. and Thompson, P. 2016. Financialization and value: why labour and the labour process still matter. *Work, Employment and Society*, 30(2), 352–365.

Davis, G.F. and Thompson, T.A. 1994. A social movement perspective on corporate control. *Administrative Science Quarterly*, 39(1), 141–173. Available at: https://doi.org/10.2307/2393497.

Davis, G.F. 2008. A new finance capitalism? Mutual funds and ownership re-concentration in the United States. *European Management Review*, 5, 11–21.

Davis, G.F. and Kim, S. 2015. Financialization of the economy. *Annual Review of Sociology*, 41, 203–221.

Davis, G.F. 2021. Corporate purpose needs democracy. *Journal of Management Studies*, 58(3), 902–913. DOI: 10.1111/joms.12659.

Epstein, G. 2002. Financialization, rentier interest, and central bank policy. *Paper prepared for PERI Conference on "Financialization of the World Economy"*, 7–8 December 2001, University of Massachusetts, Amherst. This version, June, 2002.

Erturk, I., Froud, J., Johal, S., and Williams, K. 2005. Pay for corporate performance or pay as social division: re-thinking the problem of top management pay in giant corporations. *Competition and Change*, 9(1), 49–74.

Erturk, I. 2015. Financialization, bank business models and the limits of post-crisis bank regulation. *Journal of Banking Regulation*, 17(1/2), 60–72.

Fama, E. and French, K.R. 2001. Disappearing dividends: Changing firm characteristics or lower propensity to pay? *Journal of Financial Economics*, 60, 3–43.

Farnetti, R. 1999. O papel dos fundos de pensão e de investimentos coletivos anglo-saxônicos no desenvolvimento das finanças globalizadas. *A mundialização financeira: gênese, custos e riscos.* F. Chesnais (ed.), 183–210, São Paulo: Editora Xamã.
Fichtner, J., Heemskerk, E.M., and Garcia-Bernardo, J. 2017. Hidden power of the Big Three? Passive index funds, re-concentration of corporate ownership, and new financial risk. *Business and Politics*, 19(2), 298–326.
Fligstein, N. 1991. The structural transformation of American industry: an institutional account of the causes of diversification in the largest firms, 1919–1979. *The new institutionalism in organizational analysis.* Paul J. DiMaggio and Walter W. Powell (eds.), 311–336. Chicago, IL: University of Chicago Press.
Fligstein, N. 2001. *The Architecture of Markets. An Economic Sociology of Twenty-first-Century Capitalist Societies.* Princeton, NJ: Princeton University Press.
Froud, J., Johal, S., Leaver, A., and Williams, K. 2006. *Financialization and Strategy: Narrative and Numbers.* London: Routledge.
Godechot, O. 2015. Financialization is marketization! A study on the respective impact of various dimensions of financialization on the increase in global inequality. *MaxPo Discussion Paper*, 15(3), 1–20. Available at: https://econpapers.repec.org/paper/zbwmaxpod/153.htm.
Granovetter, M. 1985. Economic action and social structure: the problem of embeddedness. *American Journal of Sociology*, 91(3), 481–510.
Hopkins, M. and Lazonick, W. 2016. The mismeasure of mammon: uses and abuses of executive pay data. *Working Paper No. 49.* Institute for New Economic Thinking. Available at: https://www.ineteconomics.org/uploads/papers/WP_49_Hopkins_Lazonick_August_29.pdf
Klinge, T.J., Fernandez, R., and Aalbers, M.B. 2021. Whither corporate financialization? A literature review. *Geography Compass.* DOI: https://doi.org/10.1111/gec3.12588
Lazonick, W. 2011. How 'maximizing value' for shareholders robs workers and taxpayers. *Huffpost Business.* Available at: https://www.huffpost.com/entry/how-maximizing-value-for-_b_892396. Accessed 02/20/2017.
Lazonick, W. 2012. How American corporations transformed from producers to predators. *Huffpost Business.* Available at: https://www.huffpost.com/entry/how-american-corporations_b_1399500. Accessed 02/20/2017.
Lazonick, W. 2013. Robots don't destroy jobs; rapacious corporate executives do. *Huffpost Business.* Available at: https://www.huffpost.com/entry/robots-dont-destroy-jobs-_b_2396465. Accessed 02/20/2017.
Lazonick, W. 2016. The value-extracting CEO: how executive stock-based pay undermines investment in productive capabilities. *Working Paper No. 54.* Institute for New Economic Thinking. Available at: https://www.ineteconomics.org/uploads/papers/WP_54-Lazonick-Value-Extracting-CEO-2016.pdf
Lepadatu, D. and Janoski, T. 2017. Just-in-Time workforce: temporary workers as a structural aspect of lean production in the auto industry. *25° International Gerpisa Colloquium.* Paris, France.
Marx, R. and Mello, A.M. 2012. Automotive industry transformations and work relations in brazil. What is the next step? *20° International Gerpisa Colloquium.* Paris, France.
Mayer, C. 2021. The future of the corporation and the economics of purpose. *Journal of Management Studies*, 58(3), 887–901. DOI: 10.1111/joms.12660.

Nasdaq, 2021a. Apple R&D expenditures. Available at: https://www.nasdaq.com/market-activity/stocks/aapl/financials. Accessed 09/10/2021.

Nasdaq, 2021b. Microsoft R&D expenditures. Available at: https://www.nasdaq.com/market-activity/stocks/msft/financials. Accessed 09/10/2021.

Nasdaq, 2021c. Johnson & Johnson R&D expenditures. Available at: https://www.nasdaq.com/market-activity/stocks/jnj/financials. Accessed 09/10/2021.

Nasdaq, 2021d. Vanguard Group Inc. position statistics and sector weighting. Available at: https://www.nasdaq.com/market-activity/institutional-portfolio/vanguard-group-inc-61322. Accessed 09/10/2021.

Nasdaq, 2021e. BlackRock Inc. position statistics and sector weighting. Available at: https://www.nasdaq.com/market-activity/institutional-portfolio/blackrock-inc-711679. Accessed 09/10/2021.

Nasdaq, 2021f. State Street Corp. position statistics and sector weighting. Available at: https://www.nasdaq.com/market-activity/institutional-portfolio/state-street-corp-6697. Accessed 09/10/2021.

Palley, T.I. 2008. Financialization: what it is and why it matters. *IMK Working Paper*, n° 04/2008.

Pardi, T. 2016. The future of work in the automotive sector: scenarios for mature countries. *24° International Gerpisa Colloquium*. Puebla, México.

Patriotta, G. 2021. The future of the corporation. *Journal of Management Studies*, 58(3), 879–886. DOI: 10.1111/joms.12673.

Piketty, T. 2014. *O Capital no século XXI*. Rio de Janeiro: Editora Intrínseca.

Shimizu, K. 2014. The strategic behavior of Japanese carmakers and its impact on employment. *22° International Gerpisa Colloquium*. Kyoto, Japan.

Shimizu, K. 2015. The change in the wage system and its impact on the production management at Toyota: The End of Ohnoism? *23° International Gerpisa Colloquium*. Paris, France.

Thomson, F. and Dutta, S. 2015. Financialisation: a primer. *Transnational Institute*. Amsterdam, NL.

Useem, M. 1996. *Investor Capitalism: How Money Managers Are Changing the Face of Corporate America*. New York: BasicBooks.

Van Der Zwan, N. 2014. Making sense of financialization. *Socio-Economic Review*, 12, 99–129.

Wartzman, R. 2017. *The End of Loyalty: The Rise and Fall of Good Jobs in America*. New York: Public Affairs.

Yang, S.H., Nam, C., and Kim, S. 2018. The effects of M&A's within the mobile ecosystem on the rival's shareholder value: the case of Google and Apple. *Telecommunications Policy*, 42, 15–23.

Ycharts. 2017. Apple Inc. Available at: https://ycharts.com/companies/AAPL

2 Apple Inc.

Founded on April 1, 1976, in Cupertino, California, by Steve Jobs and Steve Wozniak to produce computer boards and then personal computers, Apple revolutionized technology and brought the best in information technology to the large masses of ordinary consumers. This multinational company is a true global industry phenomenon and an almost unprecedented innovator. In forty years, it has become the largest company in market value, with the highest profits, and is considered differentiated by the public in three main aspects:

> it's intriguing CEO Steve Jobs, who has achieved iconic status in life and death; its incredible iOS products, especially the iPhone and iPad, and their predecessor the iPod, which have literally placed sophisticated technology in the hands of the masses; and its stratospheric stock price ...
>
> (Lazonick et al., 2013, p.249)

In this paper, the authors discussed Apple's financial situation through the "theory of innovative enterprise", developed by William Lazonick, which is an alternative to the transaction cost theory. The theory of innovative enterprise states that companies that work in technology, with research and development, should take advantage of the economic and institutional environment that provides conditions for their growth and development. The theory states that innovation processes are collective, uncertain, and cumulative (Lazonick et al., 2013, p.250).

In addition to the broader environment surrounding the organization, in the "innovative enterprise theory", the relationship between strategic control, organizational integration, and financial commitment is also established. It is based on the trade-offs stipulated between these three spheres that an assessment of the economic performance of these innovative companies, such as Apple, is made. According to the authors who developed this theory, there is no economic justification at Apple for the billion-dollar dividend payments to shareholders and stock repurchases, at the levels we are seeing today, from the risk-reward perspective. It is a huge amount of money for shareholders and almost nothing for other stakeholders, such as workers and taxpayers, who

DOI: 10.4324/9781003309536-2

would have more rights to claim on these profits (Lazonick et al., 2013). This option of distributing almost all the profitability to shareholders and executives, that is, a minority, may have severe impacts on developing Research & Development and on the economy.

Montgomerie and Roscoe (2013) claimed that Apple's exceptional performance stems from the fact of "owning the consumer". According to the authors,

> the source of Apple's recent success is a business model that enables the company to exercise unparalleled control over its multi-channel platform. This business model relies on the integration of content (software, media and apps) and hardware (laptops, phones and tablets) to drive growth.
> (Montgomerie & Roscoe, 2013, p.292)

Furthermore, growth is steady and Apple is the leader in the smartphone ecosystem.

The concept of ecosystem appears in Yang et al. (2018), who emphasizes that "since the widespread adoption of smartphones, the rate at which innovative changes have been introduced in both mobile and other industries has accelerated". They studied the effects of mergers and acquisitions on business success. "(…) Currently, Google and Apple are the keystones of the mobile ecosystem, and they have been quite active in acquiring firms over the past ten years" (Yang et al., 2018, p.15).

Many studies on Apple's revolutionary character, financial success and business model have been conducted in many dimensions (Bergvall-Kåreborn & Howcroft, 2013; Haslam et al., 2013; Heracleous, 2013). The outsourcing of production was also investigated (Lo, 2011), and the novelty highlighted was outsourcing digital content, a successful brand of Apple's business model and an innovation in relation to the outsourcing only of manufactured technological components (Bergvall-Kåreborn & Howcroft, 2013, p.280).

In the field of financialization analysis, studies such as Lehman and Haslam (2013) point to doubts that Apple's business model could be sustainable over time. They explore the dysfunctional economic and social aspects of a company that seeks to fragment and expand the global value chain, to capture more and more value while reducing costs and risks (Lehman & Haslam, 2013, p.245). Along the same lines, Froud et al. (2014) argue that favorable cost conditions helped to develop productive power in Asia thirty years ago, and currently, US financial power goes there and benefits enormously from low labor costs in China, for example. Apple's partnership with Foxconn, the largest supplier, helped to greatly reduce smartphone production costs and increased profitability. Power in supply chains was crucial for financial success (Froud et al., 2014, p.46).

Following this line of reasoning, we want to analyze the financialization of Apple and other companies, based on eight categories of analysis and indicators that we will discuss below.

2.1 Comparison between the sources of profitability

We will now move on to the comparison between companies' sources of profitability. Apple's revenue has been growing year by year, at an average rate of 10% per year for at least the period between 2012 and 2017. The revenues increased 10% from 2012 to 2013; 15% from 2013 to 2014; 27% from 2014 to 2015; fell 7% from 2015 to 2016; and rose again 7% from 2016 to 2017. The data can be seen in Figure 2.1 and reflect a company in constant growth, although varied, which places it among the largest and most profitable in the world. What we will see next is that the company's service sector has been growing much more than the manufacturing sector, although this is still the flagship of the company's production of smartphones and other products.

Observing revenue alone does not inform one about the composition. Decomposition is needed to verify how much each item or segment contributes to a business. Table 2.1 shows that the iPhone is responsible for most of Apple's revenue, having gone from 50.3% of sales in 2012 to 66.3% in 2015 and 61.6% in 2017.

As the iPhone grows in its share of Apple's revenue, other products such as the iPad and the Mac personal computer are completely declining. The iPad fell from 19.8% of total sales in 2012 to 8.4% in 2017. Mac sales fell from 14.8% of revenues in 2012 to 11.3% in 2017. Services rose from 8.2% in 2012 to 13.1% of total revenues in 2017. Services represent digital content and include revenue from the iTunes Store, the App Store, the Mac App Store, the iBooks Store, AppleCare, Apple Music, Apple Pay, licensing, and other services (Apple *Annual Report*, 2014, p.27).

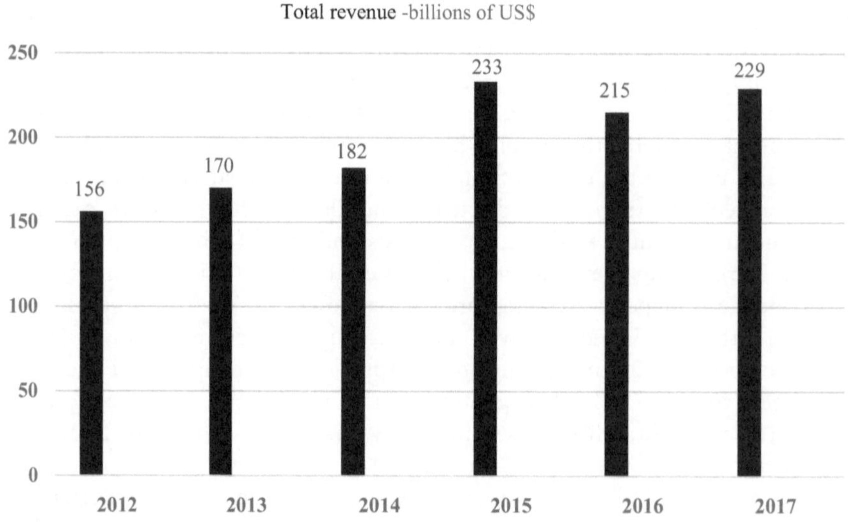

Figure 2.1 Apple's revenue in billions of US$
Source: http://www.nasdaq.com/symbol/aapl/financials?query=income-statement

Table 2.1 Apple's revenue by product, in billions of US$ and % of revenues

	2012	*2013*	*2014*	*2015*	*2016*	*2017*
iPhone	78,692	91,279	101,991	155,041	136,700	141,319
%	50.3	53.4	55.8	66.3	63.4	61.6
iPad	30,945	31,980	30,283	23,227	20,628	19,222
%	19.8	18.7	16.6	9.9	9.6	8.4
Mac	23,221	21,483	24,079	25,471	22,831	25,850
%	14.8	12.6	13.2	10.9	10.6	11.3
Services	12,890	16,051	18,063	19,909	24,348	29,980
%	8.2	9.4	9.9	8.5	11.3	13.1
Other products	10,760	10,117	8379	10,067	11,132	12,863
%	6.9	5.9	4.6	4.3	5.2	5.6

Sources: Apple Inc. *Annual Report*. Form 10-K. https://www.annualreports.com/HostedData/AnnualReportArchive/a/NASDAQ_AAPL_2014.pdf, p.27 and https://www.annualreports.com/HostedData/AnnualReportArchive/a/NASDAQ_AAPL_2017.pdf, p.23

Service revenues have represented the highest proportional growth compared with any other product in the company. While iPhone revenue grew from US$ 78.6 billion in 2012 to US$ 141.3 billion in 2017, an 80% increase in absolute numbers, service revenue grew from US$ 12.890 billion in 2012 to US$ 29.980 billion in 2017, an increase of more than 130% in the same period, as shown in Figure 2.2. This trend of service growth in manufacturing companies is a clear sign of the financialization process, through which the manufacturing area loses importance for the services and financial areas of companies. However, at Apple this does not happen so clearly as the manufacturer profits are high, requiring a more detailed analysis to detect such a movement, but it certainly expresses a strong tendency of servitization of operations, which is much more profitable than the manufacturing processes. This is one of main characteristics of the financialization process. The growth of services at Apple can be clearly seen in Figure 2.2

One aspect that proves our argument that services grow more in the participation of the business is that although revenues are growing year by year, fewer iPhones have been sold worldwide, at least between 2015 and 2017. In 2007, when it was launched, the iPhone sold 1.39 million units and grew steadily until 2015, when it sold 231 million units internationally. In 2016, it dropped to 211 million units, and in 2017, it rose to 216 million units sold. That is, services grow, iPhone prices rise for the consumer because of its exclusive brand, but the number of devices sold is lower than before. This is a classic form in which financialization is presented, that is, more value with less physical product produced. This means more money drained from the consumer to the company, more concentration of income, more dividends paid to shareholders, more compensation to executives, and so on.

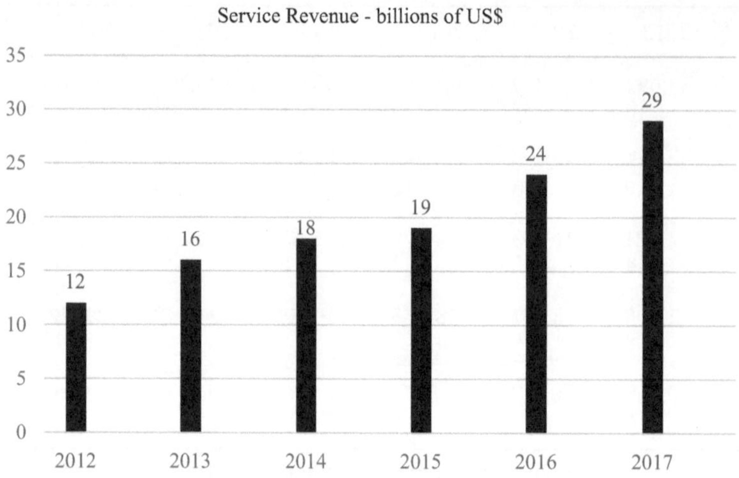

Figure 2.2 Apple's service revenue
Sources: Apple Inc. *Annual Report*. Form 10-K. https://www.annualreports.com/HostedData/AnnualReportArchive/a/NASDAQ_AAPL_2014.pdf p.27 and https://www.annualreports.com/HostedData/AnnualReportArchive/a/NASDAQ_AAPL_2017.pdf, p.23

Table 2.2 iPhone units sold between 2007 and 2018. Worldwide level in millions of units

2007	*1.390*
2008	11.630
2009	20.730
2010	39.990
2011	72.290
2012	125.050
2013	150.260
2014	169.220
2015	231.220
2016	211.880
2017	216.760
2018	217.720
12 years	1.468.140.000

Source: Statista.com. Available at: https://www.statista.com/statistics/276306/global-apple-iphone-sales-since-fiscal-year-2007/

Table 2.2 shows the number of iPhones sold between 2007 and 2018.

Although Apple sold almost 1.5 billion smartphone units in just twelve years, after 2015 (the year that had the highest sales in our historical series, which runs from 2007 to 2018), there was a drop in the number of devices sold, as shown in Table 2.2. However, revenues increased from 2016 to 2017, which was stronger than the increase in the number of handsets sold. Having sold fewer devices and having more money in their pockets, Apple Inc. is in paradise. In fact, the company's strength is the profit margin, one of the biggest in the world, considering manufacturing companies. Apple's gross profit margin and operating profit margin were 38.5% and 26.76%, respectively, in 2017, which are quite high compared with any other sector (Apple *Annual Report*, 2017, p.26). In the automotive industry, for example, these figures ranged from 3% to 4% at Ford to 11% to 14% at Hyundai (Carmo et al., 2021). There is a huge difference between the two sectors based on the production of goods. These margins were even higher, if we consider 2012, when Apple reached 43.9% of the gross margin (Apple *Annual Report*, 2014, p.32). In a company that is a manufacturer such as Apple, its productive sector is quite profitable compared with that of automotive companies, described by Carmo et al. (2021).

An explanation for the success of profitability from a quality product considered to be transcendental (Garvin, 1984) is that it can be sold at prices much higher than those of its competitors, as can be seen in Table 2.3.

> The iPhone maker saw its market share jump from 8.8% in 2014 to 13.4% in 2015, mainly thanks to the brand's strong appeal to Chinese consumers. Selling at an average price that is at more than three times as high as it is for most of its competitors, Apple's devices are still considered status symbols in China. In fact, when Chinese consumers were asked for their favorite luxury brand in 2015, it was Apple that took the top honors – ahead of Gucci and Louis Vuitton.
>
> (Richter, 2016)

The Chinese market represented 19.5% of Apple's revenues in 2017, reaching a value of US$ 44.7 billion, making it its third-largest market (Apple *Annual Report,* 2017, p.23). In China, Apple sells the iPhone at least three times more expensive than any of its competitors. While there were handsets sold for US$ 141, US$ 208, US$ 213, and US$ 231 in 2015, the Apple smartphone was sold for US$ 718 on average (Richter, 2016).

Of course, this has a strong impact on the revenue of the company, which uses transcendental quality to sell its products at prices absurdly higher than

Table 2.3 Average price sold by Apple and its competitors in China

Company	*Market share % 2014*	*Market share % 2015*	*Average selling price 2015 US$*
Xiaomi	12.4	15	141.00
Huawei	9.7	14.5	213.00
Apple	8.8	13.4	718.00
Oppo	6.1	8.1	231.00
Vivo	6.6	8.1	208.00

Source: Richter, 2016, from www.statista.com

those of its competitors. Furthermore, it would not be correct to say that Apple uses more sophisticated technology than that of its competitors because all the technologies used by Apple are already in the domain of its competitors (Mazzucato, 2014) and its products are mass-produced in China, at a low cost, by companies such as Foxconn, Pegatron, and Catcher, for example, which we will see next in the section on outsourcing. In fact, there is market exploration for a product similar to the others, but with aggressive marketing, strong political relations, the pioneer in creating the smartphone, presenting considerable beauty in design, colors, and other superficialities, but this would not justify in any way such prices and such profitability. Only a psychological explanation, which reveals irrational ways, could help to interpret the behavior of Apple consumers, who pay several times more for a product that has several similar cheaper products on the market. Table 2.4 illustrates this fact.

If we start discussing economic rationality, we will see that, although Apple products are indeed good, their consumption does not correspond, in practice, to what the neoclassical theory advocates. According to this, *Homo Economicus* always acts consciously to maximize its interests through the cost-benefit equation. That is, the consumer realizes his/her need by spending as little as possible. It is irrational, therefore, to spend much more on a product that, although is very good, has similar products on the market at much lower prices. Figure 2.2 shows that they are not inferior brands or products to those of Apple. For instance, Motorola, Google, OnePlus, and Asus are in a 50% price range, which is lower than that practiced at Apple. There is, as we have already mentioned, no rational explanation for such economic behavior. Only luxury and exclusivity may explain this.

Thorstein Veblen (1899) drew attention to this economic phenomenon, considering it as a product of conspicuous consumption, carried out by the "leisure classes" to differentiate themselves from the working classes. Hence, the more a product is consumed, the more expensive it becomes, and the more expensive it becomes, which may seem counter-intuitive, the more consumption it has. In the neoclassical theory of market equilibrium, when a

Table 2.4 Average smartphone prices worldwide – retail price in US$ 2017

Apple	*746.37*
Samsung	679.71
LG	649.33
HTC	624.50
Motorola	420.80
Google	400.00
OnePlus	349.00
Asus	284.00
Alcatel	280.00
Huawei	199.00

Source: Swappa.com. https://swappa.com/

commodity has a high price, its consumption usually falls, giving way to the consumption of its substitutes. In the case of Apple products, the so-called Veblen Effect occurs very clearly, as these are products have increased in price over time, and even so, there is a growing demand for them.

2.2 The valuation process at Apple Inc.

In addition to this manufacturing aspect of financialization, where the composition of profitability reveals an increase in services, in the price of products, and a decrease in sales on iPads and Macs, among other products of the company, we have the other side of financialization. This entails the search for valuating company shares in the stock market through stock repurchases and other artificial mechanisms that aim to value the company not through production, but in the financial market, as we will now see.

As we mentioned at the beginning of the Apple case, the dizzying share price of the largest company in terms of market capitalization worldwide has little to do with revenue growth, but it is very independent of production operations and has to do with prospects of long-term investors, although the current trend is for short-term appreciation in most cases. Table 2.5 shows the history of Apple's market capitalization in just three months when it went from US$ 777 billion on September 25, 2017, to US$ 904 billion on November 8, and then dropped to US$ 752 billion on December 25, 2017.

Table 2.5 Apple's market capitalization history. Sept/Dec 2017

Date	*Value in billions of US$*
Sept 25, 2017	777.63
Sept 26, 2017	791.00
Sept 27, 2017	796.63
Sept 28, 2017	791.73
Sept 29, 2017	796.06
Nov 1, 2017	856.87
Nov 2, 2017	863.13
Nov 3, 2017	885.67
Nov 6, 2017	894.65
Nov 7, 2017	897.53
Nov 8, 2017	904.87
Nov 9, 2017	903.02
Nov 10, 2017	896.81
Nov 13, 2017	893.22
Nov 14, 2017	879.71
Nov 15, 2017	868.11
Nov 16, 2017	878.48
Nov 17, 2017	873.60
Nov 20, 2017	872.73
Nov 21, 2017	888.95
Nov 22, 2017	898.30
Dec 25, 2017	752.00

Source: https://ycharts.com/companies/AAPL/market_cap

It should be mentioned that in just one day, from November 2, 2017, to November 3, of the same year, overnight, the company went from US$ 863.13 billion in market capitalization to US$ 885.67 billion, an appreciation of US$ 22.54 billion. That is, in a single day, Apple's market cap increased by more than US$ 22 billion. This meant that the shareholder who sold his/her shares in the very short term made a real fortune, which was paid out of the profits generated by production in the form of cash dividends and stock repurchases. It is clear that many shareholders continued their shares for months and years, without selling them, but benefited in the same way, as the share price rose by 57% in just one year, as we saw in the Introduction.

This is proof of our thesis that the valuation of shares does not have much to do with the reality of the production of iPhones and other Apple devices and services, but of speculative movements and investors' perspectives, in addition to stock repurchase movements, responsible for making stock prices rise artificially, without anything being done very differently in the sphere of production, as we will see later in the section on the dividend payments to shareholders.

In the stock market, Apple's shares were one of the most profitable investments to make everyone rich who had money to invest. Table 2.6 shows the valuation of US$ 100 invested in September 2015, year by year, until September 2020.

The reader will notice that the valuation of Apple's shares was much higher than any other index quoted on the US stock exchanges, notably the technology indexes, in which Apple participates. In just five years, the company's shares appreciated by 424%, far above the S&P 500 index, which returned 194%, and higher than other technology indices such as the S&P Information Technology and the Dow Jones US Technology Supersector, which gave returns of 333% and 325%, respectively, in just five years.

Thus, we must remember that Apple's revenues grew only around 50% from 2012 to 2017, at US$ 156 billion in 2012 and reached US$ 229 billion

Table 2.6 Valuation of US$ 100 invested from September 2015 to September 2020

	*Comparison of 5-year Cumulative Total Return**					
	2015	*2016*	*2017*	*2018*	*2019*	*2020*
Apple Inc.	100	100	140	208	204	424
S&P 500 Index	100	115	137	161	168	194
S&P Information Technology Index	100	123	158	208	226	333
Dow Jones U.S. Technology Supersector Index	100	122	156	205	218	325

Source: Apple *Annual Report*, 2020. Available at: https://annualreport.stocklight.com/NASDAQ/AAPL/201273977.pdf, p.18

* $100 invested on September 25, 2015, in stock or index, including reinvestment of dividends. Data points are the last day of each fiscal year for the Company's common stock and September 30 for indexes

in 2017. Apple's shares valuation grew eight times more than the revenues in a similar period, which is coincident with our assumptions that the valuation is not only related to the revenues and productive operations, but is much more independent from the real world, although financial markets are very real, and continue their struggle to extract value from the real production.

2.3 Shareholding composition

The largest shareholders of the ten largest companies by market capitalization are huge groups of institutional investors, banks, insurance companies, and other financial-type organizations.

In the case of Apple, this is not different. Table 2.7 shows the fifteen largest shareholders of the technological giant, and they are the same in the ten largest companies in the world. The three largest shareholders can be highlighted: The Vanguard Group, BlackRock, Inc., and State Street Corp., which together held 876,922,687 shares in 2017, estimated at US$ 154.17 billion.

Considering an equity structure that put the value of US$ 549.880 billion in issued shares in the hands of 2,826 institutional shareholders, 61.64% of Apple's structure was distributed among institutional investors in December 2017 (Nasdaq, 2018). The shares held by investors accounted for a total of 3,127,561,217. Only the three largest shareholders mentioned above held nearly 900 million shares or 28% of Apple Inc. shares.

Table 2.7 Apple's largest shareholders on December 31, 2017

Financial institutions	*Shares held*	*Amount in thousands of US$*	*% of Institutional shares*
The Vanguard Group	348,468,032	61,257,649	11.14
BlackRock Inc.	319,715,585	56,212,394	10.22
State Street Corp.	208,739,070	36,700,503	6.67
Berkshire Hathaway	165.333.962	29,069,017	5.28
FMR LLC	121,724,426	21,401,589	3.89
T Rowe Price Associates Inc./MD/	72,476,069	12,742,742	2.31
Northern Trust Corp.	65,664,289	11,548,612	2.09
Geode Capital Management LLC	56,447,158	9,924,539	1.80
Bank of New York Mellon Corp.	53,301,694	9,371,504	1.70
JPMorgan Chase & Co	51,621,255	9,076,049	1.65
Norges Bank	50,785,599	8,929,124	1.62
Invesco Ltd.	49,527,473	8,707,920	1.58
Morgan Stanley	41,230,512	7,249,149	1.31
Bank of America Corp/DE/	39,386,955	6,925,014	1.25
Goldman Sachs Group Inc.	35,376,782	6,219.946	1.13
Totals of 15 major shareholders	1,679,798,861	295,335,751	53.64%

Source: https://www.nasdaq.com/market-activity/stocks/aapl/institutional-holdings

The top five shareholders held more than US$ 200 billion in the company's shares. When we consider the 15 largest shareholders, they held 1,679,798,861 shares, which was equivalent to 53.64% of the company's shares, which was close to US$ 300 billion. This number corresponded to 0.55% of all shareholders. That is, half a per cent of Apple's shareholders owned more than 50% of the shares and the corresponding values. Compared to the automotive sector, previously studied by Carmo et al. (2021), the degree of concentration is even greater, as fewer shareholders are responsible for holding greater amounts of shares and cash, in a clear affirmation of the strength of financial institutions, in the property rights of the tech giant, increasingly merged with technology services and financial markets.

2.4 Shareholding acquisitions

Looking at the groups that most acquired Apple shares, we come across the same financial groups and banks, insurance companies and financial institutions, confirming the trend that more and more of these groups are looking to invest in these manufacturing companies to withdraw huge amounts of dividends, thus dictating the company's strategies. Table 2.8 shows the financial institutions that most acquired Apple shares in 2017.

The company that most acquired Apple shares in 2017 was the gigantic conglomerate Berkshire Hathaway, run by well-known billionaire Warren Buffett. They increased their stake by 23% over the previous year, acquiring 31 million shares and became Apple's fourth-largest institutional investor, holding more than US$ 29 billion in shares. In second place is the Morgan Stanley bank, which increased its positions by 15% and holds more than US$ 7 billion in company shares. The Goldman Sachs Group also acquired more than four million shares, increasing its stake in the company by more than 13%. The three giants BlackRock, Inc., The Vanguard Group, and State Street Corp. also acquired millions of shares, increasing their stake in the company. What does this demonstrate? That increasingly large economic

Table 2.8 Groups that most acquired Apple shares in 2017

Financial institutions	*Purchased shares*	*% of variation (+)*
Berkshire Hathaway	31,241,180	23.30
Morgan Stanley	5,619,361	15.78
BlackRock Inc.	5,112,055	1.63
Goldman Sachs Group Inc.	4,225,958	13.57
The Vanguard Group Inc.	3,879,342	1.13
State Street Corp.	2,291,579	1.11
Invesco Ltd.	1,498,868	3.12
Geode Capital Management, LLC	1,356,879	2.46
T Rowe Price Associates Inc./MD/	973,363	1.36
Bank of New York Mellon Corp.	360,312	0.68

Source: https://www.nasdaq.com/market-activity/stocks/aapl/institutional-holdings

Table 2.9 Groups that most sold Apple shares in 2017

Financial institutions	*Sold shares*	*% of variation (-)*
FMR LLC	23,765,684	16.34
Capital World Investors	10,282,391	27.16
Bank of America Corp/DE/	2,714,395	6.45
Northern Trust Corp.	1,962,144	2.90
Jennison Associates LLC	1,621,737	6.08
JPMorgan Chase & Co	1,140,335	2.16
Legal & General Group PLC	1,030,878	3.91
Wells Fargo & Company/MN	536,277	1.84
Tiaa Cref Investment Management LLC	399,954	1.35
Ameriprise Financial Inc.	211,087	0.79

Source: https://www.nasdaq.com/market-activity/stocks/aapl/institutional-holdings

groups are increasingly participating in the company's shares, controlling huge sums of economic resources and, therefore, significant portions in the power of decision.

2.5 Sale of shares

While the main large groups buy Apple shares, as this has been showing excellent business in the medium and long term, there are those groups that prefer to sell part of what they have in the company. Here we do not have a definitive explanation for this, but apparently, it must have to do with liquidity strategies, as billions of dollars end up tied to these stocks and many of these funds operate preferably in the short term. Table 2.9 shows the main groups that sold Apple shares in 2017.

The companies that most sold Apple shares in 2017 were FMR LLC, a large asset management fund, Capital World Investors and Bank of America Corp /de/. They dropped their stake by between 6% and 27%, but still hold billionaire values in the company. Here we believe that more research must be carried out to better understand what led to these decisions as we do not have further access to the strategic discussions that take place on the boards of directors of these financial institutions. However, the issue of short-termism is a strong hypothesis that we put forward and may help explain why some financial groups sell shares quickly, while others buy shares and keep them for a long period.

2.6 Mergers and acquisitions

One of the current ways to dominate the market in which companies operate is through mergers between companies and acquisitions of competitors or complementary ones. Apple has been conducting this process non-stop and has already acquired 102 companies, from 1988 to 2017 (Crunchbase,

2018). Vertical integration remains a strategy for occupying the market, even though the trend toward "core business" is in effect. In the case of Apple, the companies are in the business of information technology and communication and are related to the company's operations. Table 2.10 shows a list of 26 companies purchased by Apple in thirty years, from 1988 to 2018.

Although many acquired companies do not disclose their purchase values, there are some that present their values, such as NeXT, which had belonged to Steve Jobs, when he was forced out of Apple. The company was acquired in 1996 for US$ 400 million, a small amount compared to Beats Electronics, purchased for US$ 3 billion in 2014. The Siri voice device was also purchased by Apple in 2010 for "more than US$ 200 million", according to Schonfeld (2010).

In short, company acquisitions are a fully functioning phenomenon despite the idea that the era of vertical integration would be over. Vertical integration of companies that are not related to the core business has apparently decreased, at least in the information and communications technology companies. However, in other sectors and countries, such as in Brazil, for

Table 2.10 Apple's acquisitions of companies – 1988-2018

Companies acquired	*Date*	*Value in millions of US$*
Dialog Semiconductor	11/10/2018	600
Shazam Entertainment	11/12/2017	400
Spektral	01/12/2017	30
Vrvana	21/11/2017	30
InVisage Technology	09/11/2017	n/d
PowerbyProxi	24/10/2017	n/d
Regaind	29/09/2017	n/d
SensoMotoric Instruments	26/06/2017	n/d
Lattice	14/05/2017	200
RealFace	19/02/2017	2
Glimpse	22/08/2016	200
Mapsense	15/09/2015	25
Concept.io	28/07/2014	30
Beats Electronics	28/05/2014	3.000
Topsy Labs	02/12/2013	200
HopStop.com	19/07/2013	1.000
Color Labs Inc.	12/11/2012	7
Siri	28/04/2010	200
Lala	05/12/2009	17
PowerSchool	13/03/2001	n/d
NetSelector	07/01/2000	n/d
Xemplar Education	08/01/1999	5
NeXT	20/12/1996	400
Styleware	29/06/1988	n/d
Orion Network Systems	08/06/1988	n/d
Network Innovations	03/03/1988	n/d

Source: https://www.crunchbase.com/organization/apple/acquisitions/acquisitions_list#section-acquisitions
Legend: n/d – non disclosed

example, the phenomenon of vertical integration of non-related companies occurred until recently, when animal protein groups (JBS, which belonged to J&F Holding), for example, meat producers in their core business, acquired slipper and shoe factories, such as Alpargatas. Another example are banks, such as the Original Bank, a result of a merger between JBS Bank and Matone Bank, which occurred in 2011 (The National Provisioner, 2011).

2.7 Origin of Apple's managers

One of our financialization indicators is related to the origin of the companies' managers in the same way that was pointed out by Fligstein (1991). He affirms that the past trajectory of the directors, in addition to their academic training, strongly influences the decisions that are taken by them nowadays. This has to do with the conceptions of control that predominated in the various stages of the development of organizations. Leaders who come from the industrial world may have a mentality that is more linked to production. Managers coming from the world of sales and marketing may tend to think of expanding markets and diversification as the most important factor to weigh in decisions. Furthermore, managers from the world of finance may tend to think more based on financial concepts, allocating assets based on eminently financial considerations. In the last conception of control, that of maximizing the return to the shareholder, this actor gains preponderance and the central concern of the directors would be to meet the shareholders' requirements.

In a master's dissertation on the automotive industry (Carmo, 2017), we noted that nowadays there is a progressive merger between these worlds and managers' decision-making processes. In the assemblers studied, no correlation was found between the origin of the managers and the decisions taken. Whether they were engineers, economists, lawyers, or any other profession that made up the boards of directors of companies, decisions were increasingly channeled to meet shareholders' expectations. At Apple, it seems that the same has been happening. Although the managers listed in Table 2.11 come from a wide range of activities, most come from manufacturing organizations, and the concept of control aimed at maximizing shareholder value has not been questioned or hindered. Starting with CEO Tim Cook, Industrial Engineer, we see that almost all members of the board of directors came from the industrial or manufacturing area. This includes leaders such as Al Gore, who is a politician and was a federal deputy, senator, and vice president of the United States of America. Table 2.11 shows the professional and academic background of the Apple Board members.

As can be seen in Table 2.11, in the case of Apple, the financialized mentality seems to be strong and prevalent, if we take into account the mix of organizations in which these leaders participate or have participated. In the case of Apple, only Sue Wagner passed through the world of finance and still participates in the BlackRock investment fund, one of the well-known members of the Big Three on Wall Street of the North American financial

Table 2.11 Origin of Apple managers

Board of directors	*No. of boards in which they participate*	*Organizations in which they participated or participate*
Timothy D. Cook CEO	5 Robert F. Kennedy Center for Justice & Human Rights. Tsinghua University School of Economics and Management (SEM). Nike; Nebia; Apple.	IBM; Compaq; Apple CEO in 2011; MBA from Duke University; Bachelor of Industrial Engineering from Auburn University.
Al Gore Member of Board	4 Generation Investment Management. Apple. Current Media. The World Economic Forum.	Vice-President of the United States of America. Generation Investment Management. Current TV. Kleiner Perkins Caufield & Byers. Google. The Climate Reality Project. U.S. House of Representatives. U.S. Senate. National Security Council.
Andrea Jung Member of Board	4 Daimler; Avon; GE; Apple.	Avon Products, Inc. Neiman Marcus; I. Magnin. World Federation of Direct Selling Associations. New York Presbyterian Hospital. Graduate at Princeton University.
Aniket Singh Member of Board	1 Apple	Electrical Engineering, ITT Madras, Chennai; Master's degree in Wireless Systems, Polytechnic of Torino, Italy. Intern at University of Southampton, UK and Polytechnic of Lausanne, Switzerland.

Arthur Levinson Chairman of Board	3 Apple; Amyris Biotechnologies; Roche.		Genentech, Inc. Calico; NGM Biopharmaceuticals, Inc. Broad Institute of MIT and Harvard. Google, Inc.; Memorial Sloan-Kettering Cancer Center; California Institute for Quantitative Biomedical Research. Princeton University Department of Molecular Biology; Lewis-Sigler Institute for Integrative Genomics; Bachelor's degree in Sciences, University of Washington; Doctor in Biomedical Sciences, Princeton University.
Howard Green Member of Board	2 Better ATM Services. Apple.		IBM. Sprint. Apple/ISS – Singapore. Apple Business Consortium.
Robert Iger Member of Board	5 The Walt Disney Company. National September 11 Memorial & Museum. Apple. The American Academy of Arts & Sciences. Lincoln Center.		ABC Group. Walt Disney International. U.S.- China Business Council. US President's Export Council. New American Economy. Graduate from Ithaca College.

(Continued)

Board of directors	*No. of boards in which they participate*	*Organizations in which they participated or participate*
James Bell Member of Board	7 The Dow Chemical Company. The Economic Club of Chicago. The Chicago Urban League. CDW Corporation. Apple. Chicago Infrastructure Trust. JPMorgan Chase & Co.	The Boeing Company. Dow Chemical Company. Space Station Electric Power System. Rockwell; Bachelor's degree in Accounting, California State University.
Ronald Sugar Member of Board	15 BeyondTrust; Apple; Air Lease Corporation; Ares Management; Chevron Corporation; Uber. G100 Network. UCLA Anderson; School of Management; Alliance College-Ready Public Schools;	Northrop Grumman Corporation. Litton Industries, Inc. TRW Aerospace. Temasek Americas Advisory Panel. National Academy of Engineering. University of Southern California. Los Angeles Philharmonic Association. Boys and Girls Clubs of America.
Sue Wagner Member of Board	3 Color; Apple; BlackRock	BlackRock

Source: www.crunchbase.com

giants, which also bring together The Vanguard Group and State Street Corp. (Fichtner et al., 2017). Participation in several other boards, which combine several sectors of the economy, such as banking, industry, entertainment, and civil society, establishes an intricate network of relationships between these leaders, spreading and harmonizing decisions in a very homogeneous way. Moreover, its decisions reflect this today, whereby the ideology of maximizing shareholder value prevails and persists.

We believe that there were at least two phases in Apple's management. While Steve Jobs was in charge, the company paid few dividends to shareholders and repurchased few stocks, prioritizing reinvestment and a financial reserve. The "retain and reinvest" strategy (Lazonick & O'Sullivan, 2000) was quite clear, apparently because of its influence. However, after his death in 2011, the values became stratospheric in the following years, as we will see in the indicator that analyzed the dividend payments and stock repurchases. Probably, and we say this because more studies should be conducted to better understand the sudden change in strategy (coincident with its disappearance), its demise must have released the pent-up forces of investors and senior executives who would have liked to have acted differently but did not act due to the physical barrier imposed by the boss, who was still alive. The fact is that after Steve Jobs died, Apple began to comply with this fundamental requirement of the financialization process, which is the regular and ever-increasing payment of dividends and stock repurchases, fully meeting large shareholders' expectations.

Thus, even a board consisting of people from the world of industry, science, and technology has taken decisions in tune with shareholders' wishes, leaving behind the industrial age mentality and strictly following the strategy of periodically "decreasing and distributing" resources to investors (Lazonick & O´Sullivan, 2000, p.13).

2.8 Compensation to CEOs is strong indicators of financialization

Another financialization indicator that has been discussed by several authors, among them Crystal (1992), Barkema and Gomez-Mejia (1998), Bauer and Bertin-Mourot (1999), Lazonick and O´Sullivan (2000), Conyon and Murphy (2000), Conyon and Schwalbach (2000), Bebchuk et al. (2002), Bebchuk and Fried (2004), Erturk et al. (2005), and Bizjak et al. (2008), is the payment of compensation to company executives. For most of these authors, there is no relationship between compensation payments and performance, and the issue of internal power is significant in determining how much to pay executives. In the same way that the increase in dividend payments to shareholders has happened with such speed (we saw in the introduction that more than US$ 400 billion were paid in dividends in four years by only ten companies) the payment of compensation to executives of large companies seems to be going in the same direction.

However, CEO salaries are much lower than the total amounts they receive. There is a fixed salary, around one to two million dollars a year and several options of restricted shares, preferred and common for the directors, who end up accumulating shares, and each time they receive through shares, they help to raise its price, as a large buying movement helps drive the stock price up. In addition, this mechanism of paying hundreds of millions of dollars to executives (the vast majority in shares), also favors the already very wealthy in the sense that only a small salary base is levied on income tax for

Table 2.12 Compensation Payments to Executives. Apple – annual salary in US$

	2013	*2014*	*2015*	*2016*	*2017*
Compensation to top executives	6,885,579	120,979,798	111,433,785	100,069,268	133,637,237
Compensation to all executives	14,800,000	174,350,000	136,490,000	122,880,000	133,640,000
Timothy D. Cook Chief Executive Officer	4,252,727	9,222,638	10,281,327	8,747,719 145,000,000*	12,825,066
Luca Maestri Senior Vice President and Chief Financial Officer	–	14,002,801	25,337,977	22,803,569	24,141,615
Angela Ahrendts Senior Vice President, Retail	–	73,351,124	25,779,229	22,902,892	24,216,072
Johny Srouji Senior Vice President, Hardware Technologies	–	–	–	–	24,162,392
D. Bruce Sewell Former Senior Vice President, General Counsel and Secretary	–	–	25,017,626	22,807,544	24,146,046

Source: https://www.morningstar.com/stocks/xnas/aapl/executive

* Total Compensations to CEO Tim Cook in 2016, according to https://www.bloomberg.com/graphics/2017-ceos-take-home-pay/

the executive. Bonuses and other stock options are not within the calculation of income tax and are charged separately, at even lower rates, decreasing the amount that could be allocated to the State to provide better public services. Table 2.12 shows the highest compensation paid to Apple's managers.

The reader should pay attention when they see the amounts paid to CEO Tim Cook. According to the *morningstar.com* website, he claims to have received just over US$ 8.7 million in 2016, but he actually took home US$ 145 million in total compensation, if we take into account the majority in stock options (vested stocks), whose disclosure we find on the website *bloomberg.com*. This was the highest amount paid to a CEO in the entire ranking of the 500 largest companies listed in the S&P index in 2016 (Meisler et al., 2017). The second-highest amount paid was to Netflix CEO Reed Hastings, who received US$ 106 million, mostly in stock options, the preferred technique to force a rise in the value of shares, one of the main concerns of the current moment in the process of financialization of companies. "Cook has now amassed more than US$ 320 million from vested shares of the 2011 award. His US$ 145 million total take-home pay for fiscal 2016 also includes a US$ 3 million salary, a US$ 5.37 million cash bonus and US$ 377,719 in perks. In a 2015 interview with Fortune magazine, Cook said he plans to donate his fortune to philanthropy" (Meisler et al., 2017).

The total amount paid only to the twenty-five CEOs of the largest companies listed on the S&P 500 in 2016 was US$ 1.650 billion, an average of US$ 66 million per CEO. These executives are part of technology, health, and media companies, thus dominating their main positions (Meisler et al., 2017). All these data were compiled by Bloomberg from Securities and Exchange Commission (SEC) filings and show that increasingly huge sums of money are distributed in the form of compensations to executives, confirming what we are saying and other authors before us, that there is a conscious and intended process to create a layer of millionaire executives (who strongly agree with maximizing shareholder value) while at the base of the pyramid of stakeholders, there are many workers making little money and certainly not reaping the benefits of a fruitful business.

2.9 Dividend payments to shareholders and stock repurchases

The distribution of companies' net income to shareholders and their executives has combined dividend payments to shareholders with stock repurchases. Lazonick (2011) had already shown the numbers of this trend when discussing the compensation given to the executives and the part of which was due to the stock repurchases. According to their data, in 2009, the executives of the 100 largest companies listed on the S&P 500 received an average of US$ 29.6 million in total compensation, of which 44% were through stock options (Lazonick, 2011, p.8). In another paper, he says that from 2001 to 2010, the 459 largest companies listed on the S&P 500 distributed US$ 1.9

trillion in dividends, which meant 40% of their net profit in the period; and US$ 2.6 trillion in stock repurchases, responsible for another 54% of its net profit distributed through this modality (Lazonick, 2012, p.3). That is, an average of 94% of net income was distributed to shareholders and executives, which is a proportion that is only increasing.

At Apple, since 2012, net income has been distributed in increasing proportions both in terms of dividends, and mainly in terms of stock repurchases, as can be seen in Table 2.13.

Since 2012, dividend payments have been growing year by year at Apple, which is when there was little distribution in absolute values, with US$ 2.488 billion distributed as dividends and US$ 665 million in stock repurchases, totaling US$ 3.153 billion. In the following year, this value had already multiplied by ten, increasing to US$ 10.564 billion in dividends and US$ 23.390 billion in stock repurchases. In 2014, the increase continued, this time with the distribution of US$ 11.126 billion in dividends and US$ 45.730 billion in stock repurchases, totaling US$ 56.856 billion in a single year. And so it was in other years, with the distribution of around $11 billion in dividends and around $40 billion in stock repurchases every year. In just six years, from 2012 to 2017, Apple spent US$ 229.4 billion in dividends and stock repurchases.

It should be mentioned that this trend grew after Steve Jobs died, in 2011, as mentioned before, who had another vision of the business. Doing justice to him, *post-mortem*, during his tenure after the launch of the iPhone, there were neither dividend payments on these amounts, nor stock repurchases, but reinvestment and a massive investment of resources in research and development.

In fact, Steve Jobs was isolated in defense of the strategic concept of retaining and reinvesting, because all the main companies listed on the stock exchanges had already been widely practicing dividend payments to shareholders and stock repurchases since 1999, as shown by Mike Shedlock (2018). According to him, the companies listed on the S&P 500 paid around US$ 150 billion per quarter in dividends to shareholders in 1999 and that amount went

Table 2.13 Dividends and Stock Repurchases at Apple – 2012 to 2017

	2012	*2013*	*2014*	*2015*	*2016*	*2017*	*6 years 2012–2017*
Dividend payments Billions of US$	2488	10,564	11,126	11,561	12,150	12,800	60,689
Stock Repurchases Billions of US$	0665	23,390	45,730	35,796	30,217	33,000	168,798
Total Billions de US$	3153	33,954	56,856	47,357	42,367	45,800	229,487

Sources: https://seekingalpha.com/article/4164841-apple-service; https://ycharts.com/companies/AAPL/stock_buyback; https://www.macrotrends.net/stocks/charts/AAPL/apple/total-common-preferred-stock-dividends-paid from US$ 400 billion per quarter in 2017, with only a small gap in 2009, due to the crisis in the American real estate market, which contaminated the entire economy. However, despite this fact, it is a strong, constant, and growing trend in large contemporary companies.

> S&P 500 firms are reportedly on track to give US$ 1 trillion in either dividends or stock repurchases to shareholders this year (2018), based on the lower corporate tax rate, incentives to repatriate overseas cash and strong earnings. Goldman Sachs estimates stock repurchases will jump to US$ 650 billion while JP Morgan predicts they could run as high as US$ 800 billion. Either estimate would far exceed the US$ 530 billion in stock repurchases recorded in 2017.
>
> (Shedlock, 2018)

As we saw in Table 2.13, at Apple there was a jump between 2012 and 2014, going from US$ 665 million in stock repurchases to US$ 45.730 billion, always increasing in the following years, until today. For 2018, there was a forecast to repurchase US$ 47 billion in shares of the company itself, raising its price with this system artificially found to value companies without going through production, something that has become fundamental and a central concern in large companies nowadays.

Stock repurchase mechanisms aim to force the share price upward, with a smaller number of shares held by fewer shareholders, but with a higher price, which means higher market capitalization of the company. At Apple, from six and a half billion shares issued in 2013, more than one and a half billion were repurchased, reaching just over five billion shares in January 2018. It is the classic way to raise the value of stocks artificially, by repurchasing them.

This movement to repurchase stocks at Apple coincides with the movements of large companies, which have been practicing stock repurchases with greater intensity since 1999, leading to a culmination in the third quarter of 2007, when more than US$ 700 billion was spent on stock repurchase in one single quarter. After the fall in 2009, due to the crisis, volumes increased again and already reached around US$ 600 billion per quarter in 2016, reaching US$ 517.7 billion of stock repurchases spent in the last quarter of 2017 (Shedlock, 2018). In short, we can deduce from these data that the various authors' thesis, mainly by William Lazonick, on dividend payments to shareholders, and stock repurchases, are correct, and the theory is strongly supported by the numbers found. In all of Lazonick' s texts, we see the recognition of an intensification of companies in the maximizing shareholder value policy, making an ultra-minority group of stockholders (a group mainly consisting of financial institutions) the beneficiary of almost all gains made by companies, which are made up of more people, and more stakeholders. The alliance between shareholders and super-executives drains net profit for these two business hubs, leaving workers, consumers, and taxpayers in the background, without any substantial benefit brought by the venture (Lazonick, 2011, 2012, 2013).

2.10 Employee salaries

Regarding the financialization indicators, the issue of employee salaries appears to be important as we can see how the results of production are divided among shareholders, executives, and employees. As we have seen throughout this book, the trend in the financialization process of companies is to privilege shareholders, through dividend payments and stock repurchases, and executives, by paying millionaire compensation, between salaries and stock options. It is true that a company´s employee salaries are not included in the analysis of net profit, but in the analysis of gross profit, which is the result between the revenues and costs of that revenue. Salaries fit here, in the cost of revenue. But this is just an accounting distinction we made, without any implications for the economic process we have studied. There could be significant increases in salaries, and this would logically affect the cost of revenue and therefore decrease the net profit to be subsequently distributed among shareholders and executives.

Having taken into account these considerations, we see that Apple's salaries are generally low and below the average salaries of all-American ethnic groups. Remembering here that Apple workers are those in the area of development, projects, research, and stores and not manufacturing workers, which are all outsourced in China, by companies such as Foxconn, Pegatron, and Catcher, which we will see later on, and therefore are not Apple employees.

In Table 2.14, we see that there were salaries of US$ 9 an hour, in 2017, paid to the so-called beginner Mac Specialist, who works in stores. That same

Table 2.14 Hourly and annual salary in US$ at Apple in December 2017

Professional	*Minimum*	*Maximum*	*Wages average*
Specialist	10.00 – hour 20,000 – year	22.00 – hour 44,000 – year	15.28 – hour 30,560 – year
Mac Specialist (Apple Store)	9.00 – hour 18,000 – year	20.00 – hour 40,000 – year	13.34 – hour 26,640 – year
Software Engineer	32.50 – hour 65,000 – year	100.00 – hour 200,000 – year	61.30 – hour 122,608 – year
Mac Genius	13.00 – hour 26,000 – year	30.00 – hour 60,000 – year	20.73 – hour 41,460 – year
Family Room Specialist	11.00 – hour 22,000 – year	20.00 – hour 40,000 – year	15.59 - hour 31,180 – year
Apple Retail Specialist	10.00 – hour 20,000 – year	20.00 – hour 40,000 – year	15.08 – hour 30,160 – year
Technician Specialist	14.00 – hour 28,000 – year	22.00 – hour 44,000 – year	16.38 – hour 32,760 – year
Creative	14.00 – hour 28,000 – year	27.00 – hour 54,000 – year	19.24 – hour 38,480 – year
Manager	21.00 – hour 42,000 – year	100.00 – hour 200,000 – year	41.13 – hour 82,262 – year

Source: https://www.glassdoor.com/Salary/Apple-Salaries-E1138.htm

job earns up to US$ 20 an hour at the most and averages US$ 13.34. This is an average hourly wage below that was being discussed at the US Congress as the minimum amount to be paid across the country, US$ 15 an hour. A claim spearheaded by workers at the McDonald's fast-food chain, who are generally unskilled or low-skilled workers and were not able to earn salaries compared with Apple employees. Table 2.14 shows these data.

The average annual salary paid to all ethnic groups in the United States in 2017 was US$ 61,372 (Fontenot et al., 2018). Except for engineers and some Apple managers, no worker receives this amount annually. A beginner Mac Specialist described in Table 2.14 receives US$ 18,000 a year, three times less than the average annual salary for all-Americans. A Mac Genius receives an average of US$ 41,000 a year, while a Technician Specialist receives only US$ 32,000 a year. An entry-level Creative employee receives US$ 28,000 annually, less than half the average salary for all ethnic groups in the United States in 2017. Even the entry-level manager receives below the US average, US$ 42,000. Certainly, this company is not a dream for those who want to pursue a career or grow financially in the technology area.

As if the low wages compared with the average American wages were not enough, when we then compared the wages of Apple workers with the total earnings of the CEO, we observed a striking difference. Table 2.15 shows these stark differences between employee salaries and total earnings for CEO Tim Cook, who received a total of US$ 145 million in 2016.

There is a ratio that reaches 8,000 times between the lowest salary, a Mac Specialist from the Apple Store and the CEO. Of course, some may argue that different quantities cannot be compared, that the CEO is not an ordinary employee, etc. But the fact is that these numbers demonstrate what has already been discussed among several theorists (Lazonick & O'Sullivan, 2000; Bebchuk et al., 2002; Bebchuk & Fried, 2004; Lazonick, 2011, 2012, 2013; Piketty, 2014; Godechot, 2015; Webber, 2018), i.e., there is a conscious and purposeful tendency to create a layer of millionaire leaders, who are

Table 2.15 Ratio between employee salaries and total CEO earnings – Tim Cook in 2016. US$ 145,000,000.00

Workers X CEO	*Minimum*	*Maximum*	*Wages Average*
Specialist	7250	3295	4744
Mac Specialist (Apple Store)	8055	3625	5442
Software Engineer	2230	725	1182
Mac Genius	4833	2301	3222
Family Room Specialist	6590	3625	4650
Apple Retail Specialist	7250	3625	4807
Technician Specialist	5178	3295	4426
Creative	5178	2685	3768
Manager	3452	725	1762

Source: authors, based on the values of the compensation table paid to the CEO and the workers' salary table.

paid to agree with the dividend payment policy to shareholders and, by their internal power, earn what they want to earn, having nothing to do with their performance gains, while employees have no internal power and are not heard. We just have to look at the level of their remuneration to know that the workers have no influence at Apple, being at the mercy of the wishes of the great shareholders and greedy executives.

According to Piketty (2014) and Godechot (2015), this situation creates a huge inequality between the income brackets worldwide as this policy has been applied worldwide and the trend is increasingly toward wage crunch on one side and expansion in compensation to the executives on the other. Here, this movement can be compared to an alligator's mouth when it opens, where one side goes up while the other goes down. There is no win-win, as some may think, but there is a typical win-lose relationship, where for some to win large amounts, others must lose.

Nothing new on the front? The novelty here is that this process has become more acute as time passes and the concentration of income and capital and the increase in financial assets are growing, posing challenges and questions about the future of this system and the possibility of continuity of a form of capitalist accumulation completely unsustainable for most of the population.

2.11 Employment

The financialization process does not fall on employment in the same way in all companies. In the automotive industry, we saw that in some automakers there was a mass destruction of jobs, as in the case of Ford and GM. At Volkswagen, there have been mass hires in the last few decades. Toyota and Hyundai also hired, but at a slower pace than the German automaker (Carmo, 2017).

What is most striking is that there is a change in the quality of employment and a geographical change. At Volkswagen, for example, more than half of the jobs were created in joint ventures in China, with lower wages than those paid at the German headquarters. In this case, there was no destruction of jobs, but the creation of new jobs in other places, which were cheaper and precarious to the capital-labor relationship.

At Apple, the precariousness is even greater, since the manufacturing work is carried out by third-party companies, which is also the case in China, such as Foxconn, which we will see shortly. The jobs created by Apple in the United States and the rest of the world are mostly concentrated in research and development, design, and stores. The number of employees has grown enormously, as can be seen in Figure 2.3.

In 2005, there were less than 15,000 employees, remaining so until 2007, when the iPhone was launched. After that, the growth was continuous, year by year, reaching 123,000 workers in 2017 (Vailshery, 2021). This growth accompanies the expansion of the company and its main product, and there is nothing new in relation to companies that grow and expand their market share, requiring the hiring of workers in proportion to their growth. We have

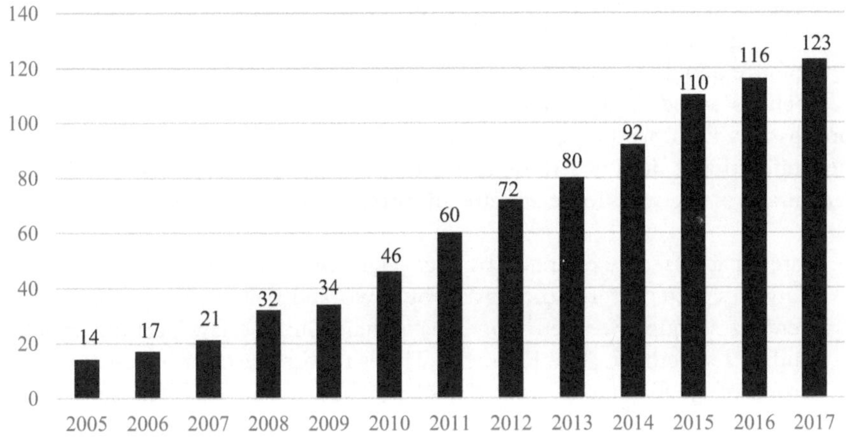

Figure 2.3 Evolution of employment at Apple – 2005 to 2017 – in thousands
Source: https://www.statista.com/statistics/273439/number-of-employees-of-apple-since-2005/

also seen in this work that salaries are low compared to the average ones of all North American ethnic groups, in the previous indicator. Therefore, at Apple, jobs are created that can be considered bad in terms of remuneration, which can position the company in the context of those that earn a large amount of money, sell expensive products and pay their employees relatively little, resulting in a typical situation of financialization in terms of job quality. Production is totally outsourced in China, as we will see now.

2.12 Outsourcing at Apple

The outsourcing process at Apple consists of producing its iPhones and other products through companies outside the United States and which supposedly follow a "standard" established by the "technology giant" company.

2.12.1 Foxconn

The main company hired by Apple is Foxconn, based in Taiwan, and responsible for most of the North American company's smartphone production. Foxconn is the brand name of the Hon Hai Precision Industry, considered the largest electronics manufacturer in the world, under contract, with Apple which is its largest customer. In 2016, around 54% of Foxconn's revenue came from Apple. In 2012, the iPhone 5 was launched and there were more than 1 million workers on Foxconn's production lines, and the dependence on Apple to generate revenue reached 58%. A year later, 300,000 people worked exclusively in the manufacturing of the iPhone 5S, with a daily production of 500,000 units, twenty-four hours a day, seven days a week (Fortune, 2013).

The company was accused of using the work of students, teenagers, on strenuous and illegal hours, which exceeded the working hours allowed by Chinese legislation (Cao & Lanxon, 2017). Foxconn claimed that it needed to use more people to work to handle the production of the iPhone X, which was behind schedule and caused a 39% drop in its revenues in the three months in which production was delayed. The Taiwan-based company further stated that it does not allow teenagers and they represented only a small percentage of the workforce and are admitted to work programs.

> Interns at a factory operated by Hon Hai Precision Industry Co., part of Taiwan's Foxconn Technology Group, worked voluntarily and received benefits, though worked longer days than Chinese law permits, Apple said in a statement. The Financial Times reported earlier Tuesday that a group of 3,000 students from the Zhengzhou Urban Rail Transit School were sent to work at the local facility.
>
> (Cao & Lanxon, 2017)

In 2012, around 150 Foxconn workers threatened to commit suicide protesting against working conditions. There is a history of suicides in the company. In 2010, 14 workers threw themselves off the factory roof and died (The Telegraph, 2012). "The body-catching nets are still there. They look a bit like tarps that have blown off the things they're meant to cover" (Merchant, 2017).

> 'We look at everything at these companies,' Steve Jobs said after news of the suicides broke. 'Foxconn is not a sweatshop. It's a factory – but my gosh, they have restaurants and movie theatres … but it's a factory. But they've had some suicides and attempted suicides – and they have 400,000 people there. The rate is under what the US rate is, but it's still troubling.' Apple CEO, Tim Cook, visited Longhua in 2011 and reportedly met suicide-prevention experts and top management to discuss the epidemic.
>
> (Merchant, 2017)

There are several complaints about abrupt changes from one production line to another, without training, dust, dirt, and other extremely unhealthy working conditions. Foxconn is considered more productive than its competitors, but due to its quasi-military structure, workers are unable to keep up with it. Every month, throughout 2012, 5% of the workforce, that is, 24,000 people, resigned from their factory in Longhua, a gigantic installation with 480,000 workers (The Telegraph, 2012).

Regarding this fact, CNN said:

> Although Foxconn has a reputation in the technology field for its efficiency and low overhead, critics say that workers are treated like low-wage

> machines in an oppressive military-style environment - employees typically eat, sleep and work in the giant complexes.
>
> (CNN, 2012)

Several protests have been taking place around the world against these working conditions, but mainly in Southeast Asia, in countries where it is possible to take a stand against the government, as there is participation by the Chinese Communist Party in controlling employees. There is precarious work and accommodation at Foxconn's factory in Longhua, the largest of the 12 factories the company has in China, with rooms intended for up to eight people to sleep. Dirty and poorly maintained factories, which have already gathered 480,000 workers, twenty-four hours a day, seven days a week, depict a terrible picture of a new type of slavery, perhaps the most developed form of modern slavery.

2.12.2 Catcher and Pegatron

In addition to Foxconn, there are at least ten more Apple suppliers that are in a similar situation of disrespect to the minimum working conditions (China Labor Watch, 2019). Two of them are Catcher Technology Co., based in the industrial city of Suqian, China, and Pegatron, based in Taiwan: they were responsible for producing the iPhone 7.

Catcher has been accused of keeping workers on shifts of more than ten hours a day in a hot and unbearable environment, without personal protective equipment such as glasses and hearing protection, where noisy machines emit noises of more than 80 decibels; the acceptable standard is sixty decibels. Workers are forced to produce almost non-stop, earning an average of US$ 2 dollars an hour (China Labor Watch, 2018). It is even less than the lowest hourly wage at Apple, as we saw earlier, at around US$ 9 an hour. Furthermore, there are no resting places and there are workers sleeping on the cafeteria tables, as denounced by China Labor Watch. The accommodations are also precarious at the company, which keeps its employees practically twenty-four hours a day at the factory. There are dirty and cramped dormitories, without any hygiene or privacy.

Pegatron is another supplier to Apple and has more than 100,000 workers in times of high production. The company has been accused by China Labor Watch of forcing employees to work harder than Chinese law allows. According to the Chinese watchdog of working conditions, in March 2016, most workers had a workday of more than eighty hours per week, in which 62% worked around 100 hours per week. China Labor Watch, based in New York, USA, concludes that "Apple consistently suppresses labor costs by shifting production to cheaper manufacturers" (China Labor Watch, 2015, p.2). This is what we have seen in recent years, as was pointed out by Froud et al. (2014), that "Apple's partnership with Foxconn, the largest supplier, and other companies, helped to greatly reduce smartphone production costs and increased profitability" (Froud et al., 2014, p.46).

For more than twenty years, China Labor Watch has observed the working conditions and has already trained workers specially to spy on the actual circumstances.

> Dubbed Apple's 'iPhone City', Zhengzhou Foxconn is the largest iPhone factory in the world. Spanning 1.4 million square meters, it is here that workers toil daily to produce half of the iPhones sold worldwide. The working conditions have remained relatively the same over the years the investigators were employed at the factory. The base wage remained at 2100 RMB (US$ 295), insufficient to sustain the livelihood for a family living in Zhengzhou city.
>
> (China labor Watch, 2019, p.3)

This is one of the cruelest aspects of financialization: working like machines, earning very little, to produce wealth that will be fully distributed to top executives and shareholders, who, as we have seen, are a minority of rich and powerful groups of institutional investors, banks, and other financial organizations, which currently dominate these companies.

An apparently contradictory aspect of financialization in terms of employment is that there are two distinct movements. As we saw in the case of car manufacturers (Carmo et al., 2021) at Ford and GM, there were drastic job cuts. GM had almost 800,000 workers in the late 1980s and today, more than thirty years later, it has around 200,000. At Ford, a similar process took place. At Volkswagen, however, there was a reverse movement: from 300,000 workers in 2000 to over 600,000 today, most of them in joint ventures in China. Even if employment increases in China and India, for example, it is still in a financialized way, that is, cutting more expensive jobs in central countries in order to create thousands of cheaper jobs in countries considered "in development".

Apple simply ignored this strategy of establishing joint ventures and has already gone directly to outsourcing, using ultra-cheap labor in China with labor relations that are analogous to slavery and highly critical to the health and dignity of the human person. According to China Labor Watch (2015, p.3) the "labor costs estimated to be 18% of Apple profits, 4% of revenues". In other words, we can safely say that Apple is having great success at the expense of hungry workers who have no life outside of work and factories, and this business model seems neither modern nor fair. China is going through its industrial revolution, two centuries later than western countries, and presenting the very same problems of the nineteenth century, related to exploitation, bad wages and housing, harsh working conditions, and suicides. The sad news is that Apple, unfortunately, is part of this.

References

Apple *Annual Report*, 2014. Available at: https://www.annualreports.com/HostedData/AnnualReportArchive/a/NASDAQ_AAPL_2014.pdf

Apple *Annual Report*, 2017. Available at: https://www.annualreports.com/HostedData/AnnualReportArchive/a/NASDAQ_AAPL_2017.pdf

Apple *Annual Report*, 2020. Available at: https://annualreport.stocklight.com/NASDAQ/AAPL/201273977.pdf

Barkema, H.G. and Gomez-Mejia, L.R. 1998. Managerial compensation and firm performance: a general research framework. *Academy of Management Review*, 41(2), 135–146.

Bauer, M. and Bertin-Mourot, B. 1999. National models for making and legitimating elites: a comparative analysis of the 200 top executives in France, Germany and Great Britain. *European Societies*, 1(1), 9–31.

Bebchuk, L.A., Fried, J.M., and Walker, D.I. 2002. Managerial power and rent extraction in the design of executive compensation. *University of Chicago Law Review*, 69(3), 751–847.

Bebchuk, L.A. and Fried, J.M. 2004. Pay without performance, the unfulfilled promise of executive compensation, part II: power and pay, draft of the book *Pay without Performance, the Unfulfilled Promise of Executive Compensation.*

Bergvall-Käreborn, B. and Howcroft, D. 2013. The Apple business model: crowdsourcing mobile applications. *Accounting Forum*, 37, 280–289.

Bizjak, J., Lemmon, M.L., and Naveen, L. 2008. Does the use of peer groups contribute to higher pay and less efficient compensation? *Journal of Financial Economics*, 90(2), 152–168.

Cao, J. and Lanxon, N., 2017. Apple finds Foxconn interns worked illegal overtime on iPhone X. Available at: https://www.bloomberg.com/news/articles/2017-11-21/apple-s-iphone-x-built-with-illegal-overtime-teen-labor-ft-says. Accessed 07/05/2018.

Carmo, M.J., 2017. Análise do processo de financeirização do setor automotivo. *Dissertação de Mestrado apresentada ao programa de Pós-Graduação em Engenharia de Produção da Universidade Federal de São Carlos-* UFSCar, 135 f. Available at: https://repositorio.ufscar.br/handle/ufscar/8917

Carmo, M.J., Sacomano Neto, M., and Donadone, J.C. 2021. *Financialization in the Automotive Industry: Capital and Labour in Contemporary Society*. London: Routledge. Available at: https://www.routledge.com/Financialisation-in-the-Automotive-Industry-Capital-and-Labour-in-Contemporary/Carmo-Neto-Donadone/p/book/9780367751395

China Labor Watch, 2015. Analyzing labor conditions of Pegatron and Foxconn: Apple's low-cost reality. Available at: https://3on4k646b3jq16ewqw1ikcel-wpengine.netdna-ssl.com/wp-content/uploads/2021/04/Analyzing-Labor-Conditions-of-Pegatron-and-Foxconn_vF.pdf. Accessed 04/13/2017.

China Labor Watch, 2019. iPhone 11 illegally produced in China. Apple allows supplier factory Foxconn to violate labor laws. Available at: https://3on4k646b-3jq16ewqw1ikcel-wpengine.netdna-ssl.com/wp-content/uploads/2021/06/Zhengzhou-Foxconn-English-09.06.pdf. Accessed 11/15/2020.

CNN. (8 June 2012). Report: Foxconn factory workers riot in China. By Madison Park. Available at: https://edition.cnn.com/2012/06/07/world/asia/foxconn-workers-riot/index.html

Conyon, M.J. and Murphy, K.J. 2000. The prince and the pauper? CEO pay in the United States and United Kingdom. *Economic Journal*, 110, 640–671.

Conyon, M.J. and Schwalbach, J. 2000. Executive compensation: evidence from the UK and Germany. *Long Range Planning*, 33(4), 504–526.

Crunchbase, 2018. Apple acquisitions. Available at: https://www.crunchbase.com/organization/apple/acquisitions/acquisitions_list#section-acquisitions. Accessed 11/20/2018.

Crystal, G.S. 1992. *In Search of Excess: The Overcompensation of American Executives.* New York: Norton.

Erturk, I., Froud, J., Johal, S., and Williams, K. 2005. Pay for corporate performance or pay as social division: re-thinking the problem of top management pay in giant corporations. *Competition and Change*, 9(1), 49–74.

Fichtner, J., Heemskerk, E.M., and Garcia-Bernardo, J. 2017. Hidden power of the Big Three? Passive index funds, re-concentration of corporate ownership, and new financial risk. *Business and Politics*, 19(2), 298–326.

Fligstein, N. 1991. The structural transformation of American industry: an institutional account of the causes of diversification in the largest firms, 1919–1979. *The New Institutionalism in Organizational Analysis.* Paul J. DiMaggio and Walter W. Powell (eds.), 311–336. Chicago, IL: University of Chicago Press.

Fontenot, K., Semega, J., and Kollar, M., 2018. Income and poverty in the United States 2017. Available at: https://www.census.gov/content/dam/Census/library/publications/2018/demo/p60-263.pdf. Accessed 10/06/2019.

Fortune, 2013. By the numbers: how Foxconn churns out Apple's iPhone 5S. Available at: http://fortune.com/2013/11/27/by-the-numbers-how-foxconn-churns-out-apples-iphone-5s/. Accessed 05/10/2018.

Froud, J., Johal, S., Leaver, A., and Williams, K. 2014. Financialization across the Pacific: manufacturing cost ratios, supply chains and power. *Critical Perspectives on Accounting*, 25, 46–57.

Garvin, D.A. 1984. What does "product quality" really mean? *MIT Sloan Review.* Available at: https://sloanreview.mit.edu/article/what-does-product-quality-really-mean/

Godechot, O. 2015. Financialization is marketization! A study on the respective impact of various dimensions of financialization on the increase in global inequality. *MaxPo Discussion Paper,* 15(3), 1–20. https://www.econstor.eu/bitstream/10419/125777/1/845026364.pdf

Haslam, C., Tsitsianis, N., Andersson, T., and Yin, Y.P. 2013. Apple's financial success: the precariousness of power exercised in global value chains. *Accounting Forum*, 37, 268–279.

Heracleous, L. 2013. Quantum strategy at Apple Inc. *Organizational Dynamics*, 42, 92–99.

Lazonick, W. and O'Sullivan, M. 2000. Maximizing shareholder value: a new ideology for corporate governance. *Economy and Society*, 29(1), 13–35.

Lazonick, W. 2011. How 'maximizing value' for shareholders robs workers and taxpayers. *Huffpost Business.* Available at: https://www.huffpost.com/entry/how-maximizing-value-for-_b_892396

Lazonick, W. 2012. How American corporations transformed from producers to predators. *Huffpost Business.* Available at: https://www.huffpost.com/entry/how-american-corporations_b_1399500

Lazonick, W. 2013. Robots don't destroy jobs: rapacious corporate executives do. *Huffpost Business.* Available at: https://www.huffpost.com/entry/robots-dont-destroy-jobs-_b_2396465

Lazonick, W., Mazzucato, M., and Tulum, Ö. 2013. Apple's changing business model: what should the world's richest company do with all those profits? *Accounting Forum*, 37, 249–267.

Lehman, G. and Haslam, C. 2013. Accounting for the Apple Inc. business model: corporate value capture and dysfunctional economic and social consequences. *Accounting Forum*, 37, 245–248.

Lo, C.P. 2011. Global outsourcing or foreign direct investment: why Apple chose outsourcing for the iPod. *Japan and the World Economy*, 23, 163–169.

Mazzucato, M. 2014. *O Estado empreendedor. Desmascarando o mito do setor público vs. setor privado*. Editora Schwarcz S.A, São Paulo, Brasil.

Meisler, L., Ritcey, A., and Zhao, J., 2017. Apple's Cook reaped $145 million last year, most of S&P 500 CEOs. Available at: https://www.bloomberg.com/graphics/2017-ceos-take-home-pay/. Accessed 12/03/2017.

Merchant, B., 2017. Life and death in Apple's forbidden city. Available at: https://www.theguardian.com/technology/2017/jun/18/foxconn-life-death-forbidden-city-longhua-suicide-apple-iphone-brian-merchant-one-device-extract. Accessed 12/03/2017.

Montgomerie, J. and Roscoe, S. 2013. Owning the consumer: getting to the core of the Apple business model. *Accounting Forum*, 37, 290–299.

Nasdaq, 2018. Apple institutional holdings. Available at: https://www.nasdaq.com/market-activity/stocks/aapl/institutional-holdings. Accessed 04/18/2018.

Piketty, T. 2014. *O Capital no século XXI*. Editora Intrínseca: Rio de Janeiro, Brasil.

Richter, F. 2016. Apple is the odd one out in China's smartphone market. Available at: https://www.statista.com/chart/4376/top-5-smartphone-vendors-in-china/. Accessed 05/21/2017.

Schonfeld, E. 2010. Silicon Valley Buzz: Apple paid more than $200 million for Siri to get into mobile search. Techcrunch. Available at: https://techcrunch.com/2010/04/28/apple-siri-200-million/. Accessed 08/14/2018.

Shedlock, M. (11 Mar 2018). Record Buybacks at worst possible time. Available at: https://www.investing.com/analysis/record-buybacks-at-worst-possible-time-200297051. Accessed 02/15/2022.

The National Provisioner, 2011. JBS holding company buys Brazilian bank. Available at: https://www.provisioneronline.com/articles/95559-jbs-holding-company-buys-brazilian-bank. Accessed 03/21/2020.

The Telegraph. (11 Jan 2012). Mass suicide protest at Apple manufacturer Foxconn factory. By Malcolm Moore. Available at: https://www.telegraph.co.uk/news/worldnews/asia/china/9006988/Mass-suicide-protest-at-Apple-manufacturer-Foxconn-factory.html

Vailshery, L.S., 2021. Apple's number of employees in the fiscal years 2005 to 2020*(in 1,000s)*. Available at: https://www.statista.com/statistics/273439/number-of-employees-of-apple-since-2005/. Accessed 04/30/2021.

Veblen, T. 1899. *The Theory of Leisure Class: An Economic Study in the Evolution of Institutions*. US: Macmillan. Available at: http://moglen.law.columbia.edu/LCS/theoryleisureclass.pdf. Accessed 10/01/2021.

Webber, D.H. 2018. *The Rise of the Working-Class Shareholder: Labor's Last Best Weapon*. Cambridge, MA: Harvard University Press.

Yang, S.H., Nam, C., and Kim, S. 2018. The effects of M&A's within the mobile ecosystem on the rival's shareholder value: the case of Google and Apple. *Telecommunications Policy*, 42, 15–23.

3 Google

Google was founded on September 4, 1998, in Menlo Park, California, USA, thanks to the development of the World Wide Web. Google is a company that fosters innovation and entrepreneurship, which are at the "heart and soul of the company's success" (Finkle, 2012, p.866). Google belongs to the Internet content and information industry, having moved from the technology sector to the communication services sector. It is part of the Alphabet Inc. group, based in the state of Delaware, USA, which owns dozens of companies. Google is the largest and most important of them all.

According to the company:

> The goal of our advertising business is to deliver relevant ads at just the right time and to give people useful commercial information, regardless of the device they're using. We also provide advertisers with tools that help them better attribute and measure their advertising campaigns across screens. Our advertising solutions help millions of companies grow their businesses, and we offer a wide range of products across screens and formats. We generate revenues primarily by delivering both performance advertising and brand advertising.
>
> (Alphabet, 2017, p.4)

Google has been a representative of what is called *Platform Capitalism* by Nick Srnicek. The author states that "at the most general level, platforms are digital infrastructures that enable two or more groups to interact. Therefore, they position themselves as intermediaries that bring together different users: customers, advertisers, service providers, producers, suppliers and even physical objects" (Srnicek, 2016, p.25).

Its oligopolistic nature, which provides about 90% of searches in most countries in Europe and above 80% on average in the rest of the world (Burguet et al., 2015, p.44), has enabled Google to achieve incredible growth for a company in its twenties, which manages to produce billionaire revenues, and is one of the main financialization indicators. "Oligopoly is a market structure in which only a few sellers offer similar or identical products" (Mankiw, 2009, p.349). In the case of Google, this basic concept in

DOI: 10.4324/9781003309536-3

economics, introduced by Professor Gregory Mankiw, fits like a glove. The company exists in a typical environment where oligopolistic forces operate and is able to dictate prices and make a large profit. The Internet search engine market is extremely small, where literally half a dozen companies hold almost the entire market. The following figures show how the Internet search engine market is divided: Google, 91.9%; Bing, 2.88%; Yahoo!, 1.51%; Yandex, 1.27%; Baidu, 1.16%; DuckDuckGo, 0.69%. The six companies represent 99.41% of the search engine market in the world (StatCounter, 2022). One of the explanations for Google's success all this time is precisely its oligopoly status, far ahead of the runner-up, and for this very reason, it can absorb 90% of the revenues generated in this sector of the economy.

We will now analyze the sources of profitability at Google.

3.1 Comparison between the sources of profitability

Google's revenues have been growing at an accelerated rate, having doubled its revenue in just four years, from 2013 to 2017. In 2013, it had revenues of US$ 55.5 billion, rising to US$ 66 billion in 2014, US$ 74 billion in 2015, US$ 90 billion in 2016, and US$ 110.8 billion in 2017. Its net profit, however, does not have a linear growth that accompanies the growth of revenues, but it is variable and unpredictable. It was US$ 12.7 billion in 2013, increased to US$ 14.1 billion in 2014, US$ 16.3 billion in 2015, US$ 19.4 billion in 2016, and fell to US$ 12.6 billion in 2017. Table 3.1 presents these data.

The most interesting aspect when analyzing their revenue is the high profitability, which is around 25% return on revenue, in terms of operating profit. Net income is always around 20% of the revenue, which is quite substantial compared to manufacturing companies. Google is certainly not just any manufacturer, as it mixes communication platform structures (productive activity) and services, marketing, among other activities, which provides the possibility of high returns to the business. This is much higher than the automotive industry, for example, whose rates of return on revenue rarely exceed 10% (Carmo, 2017; Carmo et al., 2021a). Figure 3.1 shows the evolution of

Table 3.1 Google's revenues

	2013	*2014*	*2015*	*2016*	*2017*
Revenues in billions of US$	55,519	66,001	74,989	90,272	110,855
Operating profit in billions of US$	15,403	16,496	19,360	23,716	26,146
% Return on revenue	27,74	24,99	25,81	26,27	23,58
Net operating profit	13,160	13,620	16,348	19,478	12,662
Net income or (loss) from discontinued operations	(427)	516	0	0	0
Net profit in billions of US$	12,733	14,136	16,348	19,478	12,662

Source: Alphabet *Annual Report*, 2017, p.25. Available at: https://abc.xyz/investor/pdf/20171231_alphabet_10K.pdf. Average 25.67% return on revenue, from 2013 to 2017

Google's revenues since 2002, and in those fifteen years, it has grown every year and consistently. From 2002 to 2003, its revenue tripled and then doubled until it showed a significant growth of 25% to 50% per year.

In terms of segments, Google does not have a productive sector and a financial sector to compare, as demonstrated in the case of financialization of the automotive industry (Carmo, 2017, Carmo et al., 2021a). It does not have a separate service sector, as in Apple's case, but features Google Property Segment Revenue, Google Network Member Property Revenue, Other Revenue, Other Bets Revenue, and most recently introduced Google Cloud as a segment, and these figures can be found in their annual reports, which we present in Table 3.2.

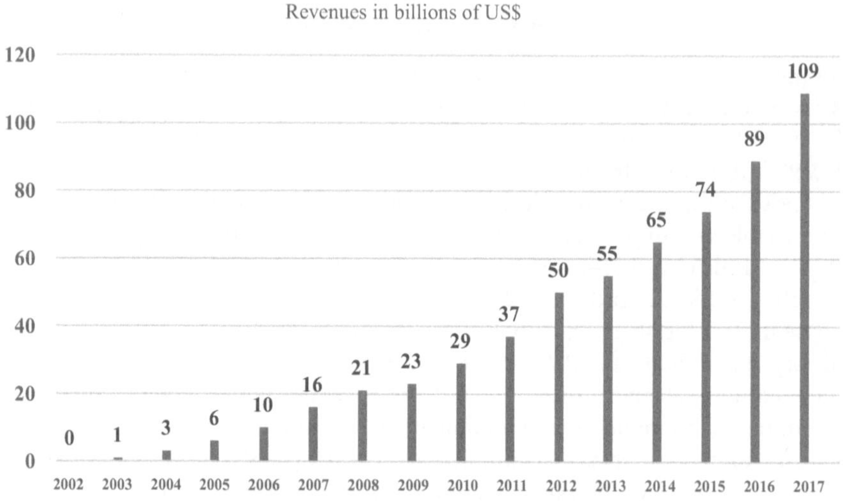

Figure 3.1 Google's revenues

Table 3.2 Revenues by segment

Segment revenues	*2015*	*2016*	*2017*	*2018*	*2019*	*2020*
Google properties	52,357	63,785	77,961	96,451	113,264	123,834
Google network members´ properties	15,033	15,598	17,616	20,010	21,547	23,090
Other revenues	7154	10,080	14,277	14,063	17,014	21,711
Google Cloud	n/a	n/a	4056	5838	8918	13,059
Revenue from Other bets	445	809	1203	595	659	657
Total revenue in billions of US$	74,989	90,272	110,855	136,819	161,857	182,527

Source: Alphabet *Annual Reports*, 2017, p.28; 2019, p.29 and 2020, p.33

Revenues from Google properties comprises Advertising, Android, Chrome, Commerce, Google Cloud, Google Maps, Google Play, Hardware, Search, and YouTube. Google generates revenue primarily from advertising, app sales, in-app purchases, hardware and digital content products, licensing and service fees, including fees received for Google Cloud offerings. Other bets are a combination of multiple operating segments that are not individually material. They include businesses, such as Access, Calico, CapitalG, GV, Nest, Verily, Waymo, and X. Revenues from Other Bets are derived primarily from sales from Internet and TV services through Fiber, sales of Nest products and services, and services from licensing and R&D through Verily.

Here, the exponential growth of the Google Cloud segment in the business, as a whole, stands out. As of 2017, data from this segment began to be presented in annual reports, in the section on selected financial data. The Cloud segment generated revenue of US$ 4 billion in 2017, rose to US$ 5.8 billion in 2018, advanced to US$ 8.9 billion in 2019, reaching US$ 13 billion in 2020, as shown by the data in Table 3.2. That is, from 2017 to 2020, revenues from the Cloud segment more than tripled, emphasizing a trend of these technology and communication companies, that is to explore more technology-intensive segments, where specific knowledge can bring more added value and greater profits. The Cloud segment has been increasing its share of revenues and this comes from the power to impose prices, as an oligopoly. That is, in addition to the monetization metrics, whose increases in the amounts paid per click are borne by the company, which practically charges whatever it wants, as we will see in the next session.

3.2 Monetization metrics

According to Google,

> When assessing our advertising revenues performance, we present information regarding the percentage change in the number of paid clicks and cost-per-click for our Google properties and Google Network Members' properties. Management views these as important metrics for understanding our business.
>
> (Alphabet, 2017, p.28)

The annual report continues:

> Paid clicks for our Google properties represent engagement by users and include clicks on advertisements by end-users related to searches on Google.com, clicks related to advertisements on other owned and operated properties including Gmail, Google Maps, and Google Play, and viewed YouTube engagement ads. Paid clicks for our Google Network Members' properties include clicks by end-users related to advertisements served on Google Network Members' properties participating in

> AdMob, AdSense for Content, and AdSense for Search. In some cases, such as programmatic and reservation based advertising buying, we primarily charge advertisers by impression; while growing, this represents a small part of our consolidated revenues base.
>
> Cost-per-click is defined as click-driven revenues divided by our total number of paid clicks and represents the average amount we charge advertisers for each engagement by users. We periodically review, refine and update our methodologies for monitoring, gathering, and counting the number of paid clicks and for identifying the revenues generated by click activity.
>
> (Alphabet, 2017, p.28)

Note that the activity of counting clicks and monetizing them is what has been growing enormously at Google. In 2015, Google's property revenues were US$ 52 billion and in 2017, that amount rose to US$ 77 billion, that is, a 50% increase in just two years. In this regard, the company stated that

> in the first quarter of 2017, we refined our methodology for paid clicks and cost-per-click to include additional categories of TrueView engagement ads and exclude non-engagement based trial ad formats. This change resulted in a modest increase in growth of paid clicks and a modest decrease in growth of cost-per-click.
>
> (Alphabet, 2017, p.29)

In fact, judging by the revenues from this click-counting segment, it does not look like the growth was modest, as the company's statement indicates. From 2017 to 2020, revenues, which had already grown by more than 50% from 2015 to 2017, they grew even more, from US$ 77 billion in 2017 to US$ 123 billion in 2020 in this segment. A growth of more than 60% in just over two years, as can be seen in Table 3.2.

In other words, financialization at Google, concerning the indicator that compares the sources of profitability, can be considered as an increasingly greater extraction of value from users, either by increasing the price charged per click or by increasing users, and what the company sees as a modest increase in the growth of paid clicks represented a 130% increase in revenue in five years. It is more money for the company's coffers in an almost monopolistic market that guarantees very advantageous deals, and Google is there to take advantage of it.

3.3 Shareholding composition

At Google, the same shareholder movement occurs at Apple, where the largest shareholders are large financial institutions that hold millions of shares and billions of dollars in market capitalization. Having a unit share worth US$ 1167.14 on July 10, 2018, 299 million shares were outstanding. Google had

Table 3.3 Google's largest shareholders on March 31, 2018

Financial groups	*Shares held*	*Value in thousands of US$*	*% of institutional shares*
Vanguard Group Inc.	21,608,472	25,223,137	9.12
BlackRock Inc.	18,733,196	21,866,885	7.91
Fidelity management resources LLC	15,531,664	18,129,801	6.56
State Street Corp.	11,055,024	12,904,308	4.67
Price T Rowe Associates Inc./MD/	6,298,213	7,351,778	2.66
Capital Research Global Investors	5,060,436	5,906,946	2.13
Capital World Investors	4,018,348	4,690,537	1.69
Wellington Management Group LLP	3,670,331	4,284,304	1.55
Northern Trust Corp	3,649,150	4,259,580	1.54
Invesco LTD	3,537,832	4,129,641	1.49
Norges Bank	3,504,538	4,090,777	1.48
Geode Capital Management, LLC	3,451,869	4,029,298	1.45
JPMorgan Chase & Co.	3,275,299	3,823,191	1.38
Bank of New York Mellon Corp.	3,225,646	3,765,232	1.36
Massachusetts Financial Services CO/ MA/	2,627,529	3,067,062	1.10
Total (15 biggest)	109,247,547	127,522,477	46,09

Source: https://www.nasdaq.com/symbol/googl/institutional-holdings

2,423 institutional investors in that year, who represented 79.26% of its shareholding control and held 236,714,868 shares (Nasdaq, 2018). Table 3.3 shows the fifteen largest shareholders, which is practically the same as Apple. All of them are large investment funds, banks, and other financial institutions.

As can be seen in Table 3.3, the fifteen largest shareholders owned 109.2 million shares, which, in a universe of 236 million shares, represented 46.09% of the total shares in the hands of institutional investors and more than 36% of all outstanding shares. Once more, in the case of Google, there is an enormous concentration of many shares in the hands of a few groups. The Vanguard Group, for example, which owns 21.6 million shares, has almost 9% of the shares alone. If we join its two large investment fund colleagues, BlackRock and State Street Corp, 51.3 million shares are held by the so-called Big Three of investment funds (Fitchner et al, 2017).

In summary, in this regard, there is no difference from the case of Apple, where the same large financial groups also operate and concentrate huge portions of shares, money, and decision-making power.

3.4 Shareholding acquisitions

Moreover, at Google, the groups that acquired the most shares were those of a financial type. Capital Research Global Investors, who bought the most shares in early 2018, acquired nearly 800,000 shares and increased its stake in Google by 18.2%. Next, Norges Bank, which is the Central

Table 3.4 Groups that most bought Google shares on March 31, 2018

Financial Groups	*Acquired shares*	*% change (+)*
Bank of Montreal/CAN/	419,180	35.27
Capital Research Global Investors	779,091	18.20
Norges Bank	485,637	16.09
Ameriprise Financial Inc	166,016	8.29
UBS Asset Management Americas Inc	88,899	6.68
Deutsche Bank AG/	75,744	5.20
Geode Capital Management, LLC	166,177	5.06
UBS Group AG	47,752	3.09
JPMorgan Chase & Co	86,817	2.72
Vanguard Group Inc.	377,947	1.78
BlackRock Inc.	269,848	1.46
American Century Companies Inc.	23,524	1.05
Invesco LTD	8206	0.23
Canada Pension Plan Investment Board	2684	0.17

Source: https://www.nasdaq.com/symbol/googl/institutional-holdings/increased

Bank of Norway, acquired more than 485,000 shares, increasing its stake by 16% in Google shares. The third-largest buyer of shares in early 2018 was the Bank of Montreal, acquiring 419,000 shares, and increasing its stake by 35% compared to what it previously had at Google (Nasdaq, 2018) (Table 3.4).

These shareholdings in the Google shares confirm the theses on financialization that more and more large financial groups are taking control of contemporary companies, investing heavily in them, and taking huge resources from them, determining the trajectory and business strategies. Although Google has not been paying dividends to shareholders, as we will see later, the company has been practicing stock repurchases with increasing values, indicating that it has been adhering to these artificial practices of stock appreciation on the stock exchanges, as it sees fit; in other words, from these same shareholders.

3.5 Stock sales

Among the biggest stock sellers are also large financial groups. The largest seller in early 2018 was Fidelity Management Resources (FMR LLC), a large investment fund that sold 1.1 million Google shares and decreased its stake in the business by 6.72%. State Street Corp sold 568,000 shares and decreased its stake by 4.89%, followed by the Bank of New York Mellon Corp, which sold 233,000 shares and decreased its stake in Google's shares by 6.74%. Jennison Associates LLC sold 139,000 shares and decreased its shares in Google by more than 8%. Table 3.5 shows the fifteen largest sellers of shares in Google as of March 31, 2018.

Table 3.5 Groups that most sold Google shares on March 31, 2018

Financial groups	*Shares sold*	*% change (−)*
Fidelity Management Resources LLC	1,117,982	6.72
State Street Corp	568,520	4.89
Price T Rowe Associates Inc./MD	82,807	1.30
Wellington Management Group LLP	1093	0.03
Northern Trust Corp.	107,030	2.85
Bank of New York Mellon Corp.	233,186	6.74
Massachusetts Financial Services CO/MA	2616	0.10
Morgan Stanley	25,677	0.99
Goldman Sachs Group Inc.	109,667	4.32
Primecap Management CO/CA	54,354	2.34
Bank of America Corp/DE	13,136	0.59
Wells Fargo & Company/MN	66,885	3.35
Tiaa Cref Investment Management LLC	62,180	3.65
Jennison Associates LLC	139,740	8.12
Alecta Pensionsforsakring, Omsesidig	53,000	3.74

Source: https://www.nasdaq.com/symbol/googl/institutional-holdings/decreased

Among the groups are banks, for instance, Morgan Stanley, Goldman Sachs, Bank of America, investment funds, such as Price T. Rowe, Wells Fargo, Tiaa Cref, among other well-known names in American business. The sale of shares is linked to a short-term policy, which is part of the strategy of all groups. Although they are long-term investors and claim in their reports to defend the long-term as a way of earning money and developing business, in practice, selling for short-term billing or at least losing less when there is a decrease in stock prices is widely used by financial institutions.

3.6 Mergers and acquisitions

As Yang et al. (2018, p.15) pointed out, "Google and Apple are the keystones of the mobile ecosystem and have been quite active in acquiring firms over the past years". If in a previous moment, the vertical integration of companies not related to the core business predominated, it currently seems that the vertical integration occurs in companies related to the central mission of the parent company. Google has acquired 233 companies since its founding in 1998 (Crunchbase, 2019). Table 3.6 lists twenty-seven companies acquired by Google, from 2003 to 2019.

The acquisition that most stands out is that of Motorola Mobility, purchased in 2012 for US$ 12.5 billion, a clear willingness to enter the competition in the area of cellular phones. If we go back in time, we can see: the acquisition of YouTube, in 2006, for US$ 1.65 billion; DoubleClick, in 2008 for US$ 3.2 billion; Waze, for US$ 1.1 billion in 2013; and Nest Labs, in 2014, for US$ 3.2 billion. The Android operating system, developed by Linux, was acquired in 2012 for just US$ 50 million.

Table 3.6 Google's acquisitions of companies. From 2003 to 2017

Company acquired	*Purchase date*	*Value in millions of US$*
Fitbit	2019	2,100
Part of HTC mobile division and Licenses	2017	1100
Apigee	2016	625
Bebop	2015	380
Nest Labs	2014	3200
DeepMind	2014	500
Skybox Imaging	2014	500
Divide	2014	120
Waze	2013	1,100
Channel Intelligence	2013	125
Android	2012	50
Meebo	2012	100
Wildfire	2012	350
ITA Software	2012	700
Motorola Mobility	2012	12,500
Admeld	2011	391
Zagat	2011	151
Slide	2010	182
Widevine Technologies	2010	160
Invite Media	2010	80
Global IP Solutions	2010	68
AdMob	2009	750
DoubleClick	2008	3200
Postini	2007	625
FeedBurner	2007	100
dMarc Broadcasting	2006	102
YouTube	2006	1650
Applied Semantics	2003	102
Total in billions of US$		30,011

Sources: https://www.statista.com/statistics/192300/price-of-selected-acquisitions-by-google/; https://www.crunchbase.com/organization/google/acquisitions/acquisitions_list#section-acquisitions

According to Yang et al. (2018), it would not be possible to assess whether these acquisitions positively influenced the increase in wealth production for shareholders, but glancing at the volume spent on acquiring only these twenty-seven companies listed in Table 3.6, US$ 30 billion were paid and that certainly meant an advantage for the company, which only grew its revenues and market share, in addition to the ever-increasing importance it acquired in market capitalization and in the "mobile ecosystem" (Yang et al., 2018).

This advantage can be measured by the reserves that Google had in 2016, valued at US$ 73.1 billion, of which US$ 42.9 billion or 58.7% were kept outside the USA (Srnicek, 2016, p.17), in a clear and profitable antitax maneuver. Finally, based on these numbers, it can be said that Google's acquisitions contributed to increasing its market cap and, therefore, the wealth of its shareholders.

3.7 Origin of managers

Our reference for the construction of this financialization indicator is Fligstein (1991), who considers that the academic background and professional trajectory of company executives speaks volumes about the decisions they take today.

The members of the Google Board of Directors, in a similar way to those of Apple, have no experience in financial institutions, as can be seen in Table 3.7. They come from industrial organizations, have a degree in Engineering, Mathematics, Computer Science, Arts, among other professions far from the stock and financial market in general.

They also participate in several other boards, generally from related companies, in the area of information technology and universities. Unlike the automotive sector, for example, they did not participate in banks, pension funds, investment funds, and other financial institutions before joining the organization.

At Google, however, concerning the available data, dividends have not been paid to shareholders, a classic indicator of financialization, and the official reasons for this are the position of its leaders that the company would be truly different from the others, and would retain its profits for reinvestment in R&D, human resource training, etc. Table 3.7 shows the Board Members in 2018.

Most of the Board members are executives who have not worked in the world of finance, having limited their activities to universities and research centers in science and technology or technology companies. At Google, the founders played an important role in the company's decisions, mainly because of their innovative and entrepreneurial character. Risky investments, often against shareholders, as we will see soon in Larry Page and Sergey Brin's joint statement about not paying dividends, were and are commonplace in the company.

Perhaps because of this context of innovation and the quest to expand markets, to improve the Cloud segment and other issues, concerns about immediate shareholder returns have not been essential until now. However, as we have said before and we will see soon, even not paying dividends to shareholders, the company has been practicing stock repurchases, which is an indication that, at least in part, the demands of shareholders will be met by the company. The fact is that, at Google, the speech seems to be in harmony with the practice in terms of meeting shareholders' expectations, with no reason to believe that the company has gone through a process of greater indoctrination for implementing measures considered financialized, but, of course, more analysis is needed, together with the combination of all indicators to have a more complete view of the financialization process that occurs at Google.

Table 3.7 Google—Board of Directors—2018

Members	*No. of boards in which it operates*	*Organizations in which they participate or participated*
Ann Mather Board member since 2010 Netflix Executive	8 Alphabet Arista Shutterfly MGG Dodge & Cox	Glu Mobile Inc. MGM Holdings Inc. Solazyme, Inc. Shutterfly, Inc. Dodge & Cox Funds. Pixar. Village Roadshow Pictures. Master of Arts na Cambridge University.
Dianne Greene Senior Vice President Google Cloud Board member since 2015	2 Alphabet Google	Google Cloud Platform Intuit Inc. VMware, Inc. EMC Corporation. Silicon Graphics Inc. VXtreme, Inc. The MIT Corporation. Master of Science in Computer Science from the University of California, Berkeley. Master of Science in Naval Architecture from the Massachusetts Institute of Technology Bachelor of Arts in Mechanical Engineering from the University of Vermont.
Eric Schmidt Alphabet's Executive President since 2015	12 Alphabet Otoy Google Princeton University	Novell, Inc. Sun Microsystems, Inc. Sun Technology Enterprises. Apple Inc. PhD and Master of Science in Computer Science from the University of California, Berkeley. Bachelor of Science in Electrical Engineering from Princeton University.

John Doerr Partner of Kleiner Perkins Caufield & Byers	29 Alphabet Shyp MyFitnessPal Zynga Erly	Intel. Amyris, Bloom Energy, Coursera, Essence Healthcare, Flipboard, FloDesign Wind Turbines, Google, iControl, mCube, Quantumscape, Renmatix, Upthere; NewSchools.org, TechNet.org, the Climate Reality Project and ONE.org. American Academy of Arts and Sciences, U.S. President Barack Obama's Council on Jobs and Competitiveness. Bachelor of Science and Master of Science in Electrical Engineering from Rice University and a M.B.A. from the Harvard Business School.
John Hennessy Board member since 2015 Stanford University President since 2000	5 Google Cisco Gordon and Betty Moore Foundation	Atheros Communications Inc. Dean of Stanford University. PhD and Master of Science in Computer Science from the State University of New York, Stony Brook, and Bachelor of Science in Electrical Engineering from Villanova University.
Larry Page CEO and Founder	3 Alphabet Google XPRIZE	Alphabet. Google. Master of Science in Computer Science from Stanford University and Bachelor of Science in Engineering, majoring in Computer Engineering from the University of Michigan.
Paul Otellini Board member since 2014	2 Alphabet Google	Intel Corporation. Bachelor of Economics from the University of San Francisco; MBA from the University of California, Berkeley. President's Council on Jobs and Competitiveness.
Sergey Brin Alphabet President and Founder	2 Alphabet Google	Alphabet. Google. Master of Science in Computer Science from Stanford University and Bachelor of Science with honors in Mathematics and Computer Science from the University of Maryland at College Park.

Source: https://www.crunchbase.com/organization/alphabet/advisors/current_advisors_image_list#section-board-members-and-advisors

3.8 Compensation to executives

In the indicator that analyzes compensation payment to executives, the finding of financialization appears in full force. The growth trend of payments in the form of stock options and other bonuses is also seen at Google.

In fact, it was the largest compensation paid to an executive in the entire year of 2016. Table 3.8 shows the total compensation to the main executives, broken down into total cash, shares, and others. The interesting thing to note is that cash wages per year are insignificant compared to what the executive earns at the end of the year.

This reinforces the idea that relatively small wages serve two functions: paying less income tax, which only applies to wages in cash, and earning the bulk of the amount in shares, a move that helps to artificially increase their price. Table 3.8 shows the data.

Table 3.8 Compensation payments to executives. Alphabet/Google—annual salary in US$—2016

Compensations to executives	*Cash*	*Stock options*	*Others*	*Total compensations*
Sundar Pichai CEO—Google	650,000.00	198,695,790.00	372,410.00	199,718,200.00
Ruth M. Porat Senior Vice President and Chief Financial Officer, Alphabet and Google	650,000.00	38,313,173.00	110.956,00	39,074,129.00
Eric E. Schmidt Executive Chairman, Alphabet	1,250,000.00	0	629,106.00	1,879,106.00
David C. Drummond Senior Vice President, Corporate Development, Chief Legal Officer, and Secretary, Alphabet	650,000.00	0	14,387.00	664,387.00
Sergey Brin President, Alphabet, and Co-Founder	1.00	0	0	1.00
Larry Page CEO, Alphabet, and Co-Founder	1.00	0	0	1.00

Source: https://www1.salary.com/ALPHABET-INC-Executive-Salaries.html. And https://www.salary.com/tools/executive-compensation-calculator/alphabet-inc-executive-salaries?year=2016&view=table#bd

Note that CEO Sundar Pichai received only US$ 650,000 in cash and US$ 198.6 million in stock options. He became an executive and shareholder at the same time. At Google, there is another difference, which is the lack of remuneration to the founders, Sergey Brin and Larry Page, who has set a salary of US$ 1.00. In our point of view, this is merely symbolic data as the other executives received millionaire compensation, consistent with the current trend of paying compensation to executives, who created a layer of millionaire leaders, increasing the difference between the income brackets, corporate income, and economic inequality within society as a whole, and Google is reinforcing this trend.

3.9 Dividend payment

Although in its annual report, net income is made available to all shareholders, at the amount of US$ 15.826 billion in 2015, US$ 19.478 billion in 2016, and US$ 12.662 billion in 2017 (Alphabet, 2017, p.49), the fact is that Google has not been paying dividends to shareholders despite mounting investor pressure. According to Moses (2019), the fact is due to the declaration of principles:

> as Sergey and I wrote in the original founders' letter 11 years ago, 'Google is not a conventional company. We don't intend to become one'. As part of that, we also said that you could expect us to make 'smaller bets in areas that might seem very speculative or even strange when compared to our current businesses'. From the start, we´ve always strived to do more, and to do important and meaningful things with the resources we have.
>
> (Moses, 2019)

Table 3.9 shows the amount of stock repurchases at Google from 2015 to 2020.

According to Moses, "some argue that, rather than pay dividends, the company could always reinvest its profits to fund more such projects" (Moses, 2019). Others argue that investors should avoid buying Google shares until it pays dividends (Healy, 2018), but the most widespread idea is that if Google

Table 3.9 Dividend payments and stock repurchases at Google

	2015	*2016*	*2017*	*2018*	*2019*	*2020*
Dividend payments in billions of US$	0	0	0	0	0	0
Stock repurchases in billions of US$	1.780	3.693	4.846	9.075	18.396	31.149
Totals in billions of US$	1.780	3.693	4.846	9.075	18.396	31.149

Source: https://abc.xyz/investor/pdf/20171231_alphabet_10K.pdf, pp.21, 22 and 49

starts paying dividends, it may create a mandatory obligation that in the future it will compromise company acquisitions, which is very important for the business (Burns, 2017). Google is the first large company that has not paid dividends to shareholders, which is a total exception in our studies on financialization.

However, we may see in Table 3.9 that the amounts spent on stock repurchases are increasing and growing exponentially. In 2015, only US$ 1.7 billion was used to repurchase stocks, US$ 3.6 billion in 2016, US$ 4.8 billion in 2017, US$ 9 billion in 2018, US$ 18 billion in 2019, and US$ 31 billion in 2020. As we said earlier, the practice of stock repurchases aims to artificially increase the price of shares on the stock exchanges, through a purchase movement made by the company's treasury, through which it withdraws shares from the market and thus causes an increase in the share price, in addition to allocating billions of dollars to investors, who do not receive dividends, but periodically receive money from the company. This is also a way to partially meet shareholders' demands, without them having to leave the company, but patiently understanding that the investor prioritization process is also underway at Google, but with different characteristics and at different paces when compared to other companies and sectors, such as the automotive industry and Apple, for example.

3.10 Employee salaries

Google employee salaries are similar to those of Apple. Table 3.10 shows the data.

There are several salaries below the average paid to all North American ethnic groups, an average already cited in this study, which was US$ 61,372 annually in 2017 (Fontenot et al., 2018, p.1). But there is a great disparity between the starting and maximum wages, in each profession. A customer service representative starts out earning US$ 18,000 and can reach US$ 39,000, with an average of US$ 28,000 annually, less than half the average American salary. Computer technicians, content analysts, field service technicians, event coordinators, compliance analysts, facilities technicians, hardware engineers; all these professions pay starting salaries below the average of all North American salaries. As at Apple, wages cannot be considered good wages; although at Google, there is no predominance of outsourcing and wages start to rise more than at Apple over time.

In summary, Google can be considered as a company that does not pay large salaries to most of its employees, but only to a minority, as can be seen in Table 3.10, and this fact confirms yet another indicator of financialization, which is valuing the workforce to a lower standard than their wealth production could allow.

When we compare employee salaries to the earnings of CEO Sundar Pichai, who in 2016 earned US$ 199.7 million in total compensation, we have a situation that shows enormous inequality, which can reach 11,000 times the ratio between their earnings and that of the Consumer Services

Representative, for example. When compared to the salary of a Hardware Engineer at the end of his/her career, the difference between the CEO and the engineer can reach 1158 times. Table 3.11 shows these salary ratios.

In short, the comparison between the total CEO earnings with the rest of the workers confirms our salary indicator, that we are facing huge inequalities

Table 3.10 Google employee salaries—annual salary in US$—2017

Professional	*Minimum*	*Maximum*	*Average salary*
Customer Service Representative	18,074	39,717	28,885
Nanny	22,461	60,083	41,272
Computer Technician	25,836	60,083	42,959
Content Analyst	26,912	55,287	41,099
Field Service Technician	29,204	67,583	48,393
Events Coordinator	35,217	79,736	57,476
Compliance Analyst	35,560	86,083	60,821
Installation Technician	35,962	76,367	56,164
Hardware Engineer	36,418	172,428	104,423
Graphic designer	38,208	86,443	62,325
IT Specialist	38,843	138,342	88,592
Executive Assistant	39,558	93,152	66,355
Human Resource Specialist	41,241	89,004	65,122
Implementation Consultant	43,315	100,047	71,681
Java Software Developer	44,578	107,738	76,158
Computer Programmer	45,277	134,357	89,817

Source: https://www.payscale.com/research/US/Employer=Google%2c_Inc./Salary/by_Job

Table 3.11 Ratio between employee salaries and total CEO earnings—Sundar Pichai in 2016. US$ 199,718,200.00

Employees X CEO	*Minimum*	*Maximum*	*Average*
Customer Service Representative	11050	5028	6914
Nanny	8891	3324	4839
Computer Technician	7730	3324	4649
Content Analyst	7421	3612	4859
Field Service Technician	6838	2955	4127
Events Coordinator	5671	2504	3474
Compliance Analyst	5616	2320	3283
Installation Technician	5553	2615	3555
Hardware Engineer	5484	1158	1912
Graphic Designer	5227	2310	3204
IT Specialist	5141	1443	2254
Executive Assistant	5048	2144	3009
Human Resource Specialist	4842	2243	3066
Implementation Consultant	4610	1996	2786
Java Software Developer	4480	1853	2622
Computer Programmer	4411	1486	2223

Source: author, based on the values of the compensation table paid to the CEO and the workers' salary table

in the income brackets, creating a layer of millionaire leaders, while the workers' salaries are on average below the overall average of all North American ethnic groups. Moreover, Google is the company that has presented, up until then, the biggest discrepancy between the salary ranges found by us.

3.11 Employment

Our last financialization indicator shows the level of employment. It is important to portray the performance of companies in the market, and in the case of Google and Apple, we find only expansion in the number of vacancies. Remember that this is an indicator that shows huge differences in results in other sectors, such as the automotive one (Carmo, 2017, Carmo et al., 2021a). While companies are hiring, as was the case with Volkswagen and Hyundai and, to a lesser extent with Toyota, at Ford, and GM, there was great job destruction around the world (Figure 3.2).

At Google, there was a 525% increase in the number of employees in just a decade, from 16,805 in 2007 to 88,110 in 2017. The financialization process is not aimed at destroying or increasing the level of employment, because it is not a fully conscious process, but it can be developed using two tools: cutting vacancies and increasing vacancies. This is a contradictory feature of the financialization process in terms of employment, which makes it even more interesting and worthy of further studies.

The question of employment and employability in current times always refers to discussions between neoclassical economists, on the one hand, and Keynesians or Marxists on the other. Societies always face the trade-off between

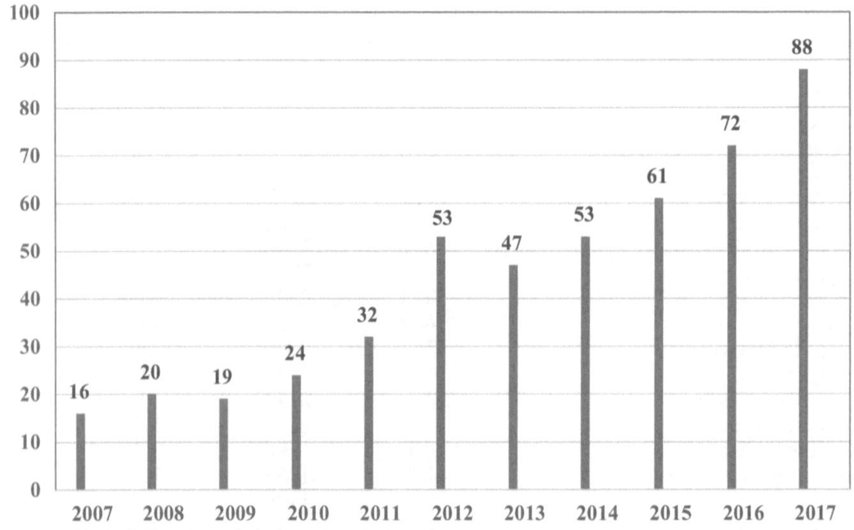

Figure 3.2 Evolution of employment at Google – 2007 to 2017

unemployment and inflation. More people employed, more economic activity, more consumption, and more inflation. A little unemployment will not hurt; it is even welcome to keep inflation low, remembering that inflation is negative for society as a whole. Keynesians think that full employment is necessary, and the issue of product supply can be solved with more production. That is, there is no disjunctive between employment and inflation, but if there is more employment and more consumption, more money will be issued and therefore a new equilibrium should appear. "In one of his first economic works entitled *Unemployment: A Problem of Industry* in 1909, Beveridge argued that unemployment was 'largely a problem of industrial organization' and advocated measures for full employment" (Carmo et al., 2021b, p.174).

Whether for full employment or at the mercy of the laws of the market, which impose trade-offs between unemployment and inflation, the fact is that, in reality, capitalism as a whole, systemically, has not yet solved the problem of employment in society. There are millions of people, worldwide, who suffer from the problem of unemployment, underemployment, precariousness, low wages, and among other ills that should have been purged from our time.

Platform Capitalism, although providing intermediation between people, through communication technologies, allows thousands of people to use their devices, set up companies, and finally be able to work. However, from the point of view of absorbing millions of unemployed people, this Platform Capitalism is not going to solve most people's problems. Only a reformulation of world economic policy, slowing down the financialization process, and re-industrializing developed societies and industrialization of developing societies, investing heavily in infrastructure, and all that remains to be done will create conditions for resumption of employment with better wages and working conditions for everyone.

References

Alphabet, 2017. Alphabet *Annual Report*, 2017. Available at: https://abc.xyz/investor/pdf/20171231_alphabet_10K.pdf. Accessed 10/20/2018.

Alphabet, 2019. Alphabet *Annual Report*, 2019. Available at: https://abc.xyz/investor/static/pdf/20200204_alphabet_10K.pdf?cache=cdd6dbf. Accessed 05/13/2020.

Alphabet, 2020. Alphabet *Annual Report*, 2020. Available at: https://abc.xyz/investor/static/pdf/20210203_alphabet_10K.pdf?cache=b44182d. Accessed 03/17/2021.

Burguet, R., Caminal, R., and Ellman, M. 2015. In Google we trust? *International Journal of Industrial Organization*, 39(C), 44–55. Available at: https://econpapers.repec.org/article/eeeindorg/v_3a39_3ay_3a2015_3ai_3ac_3ap_3a44-55.htm. Accessed 01/21/2017.

Burns, S. (21 June 2017). Why Google does not pay a dividend. Available at: http://www.newtraderu.com/2017/06/21/google-pay-dividend/. Accessed 10/20/2018.

Carmo, M.J. 2017. Análise do processo de financeirização do setor automotivo. *Dissertação de Mestrado apresentada ao programa de Pós-Graduação em Engenharia de Produção da Universidade Federal de São Carlos*- UFSCar, 135 f. Available at: https://repositorio.ufscar.br/handle/ufscar/8917

Carmo, M.J., Sacomano Neto, M., and Donadone, J.C. 2021a. *Financialisation in the Automotive Industry: Capital and Labour in Contemporary Society*. London: Routledge. Available at: https://www.routledge.com/Financialisation-in-the-Automotive-Industry-Capital-and-Labour-in-Contemporary/Carmo-Neto-Donadone/p/book/9780367751395

Carmo, M.J., Sacomano Neto, M., and Donadone, J.C. 2021b. The financialization process at a crossroads: searching the industrial welfare. *Progress in Economics Research* v. 47, 1ª ed. Albert Tavidze. (Org.). New York: Nova Science Publishers, Inc, 149–196. Available at: https://novapublishers.com/shop/progress-in-economics-research-volume-47/

Crunchbase, 2019. Google companies´ acquisitions. Available at: https://www.crunchbase.com/organization/google/acquisitions/acquisitions_list#section-acquisitions. Accessed 02/10/2020.

Finkle, T.A. 2012. Corporate entrepreneurship and innovation in Silicon Valley: the case of Google, Inc. *Entrepreneurship, Theory and Practice*, 36(4), 863–887. Available at: https://doi.org/10.1111/j.1540-6520.2010.00434.x

Fontenot, K., Semega, J., and Kollar, M. 2018. Income and poverty in the United States 2017. Available at: https://www.census.gov/content/dam/Census/library/publications/2018/demo/p60-263.pdf. Accessed 10/06/2019.

Healy, W. (21 Sept 2018). Investors should avoid alphabet until it starts doing one thing: time for alphabet to pay a dividend on GOOG stock. *InvestorPlace*, Available at: https://investorplace.com/2018/09/investors-avoid-goog-stock-starts-thing/. Accessed 09/29/2018.

Mankiw, N.G. 2009. *Introdução à Economia*. São Paulo: Cengage Learning.

Moses, P. (31 Jan 2019). Should Google Pay a dividend to stockholders? Available at: https://www.investopedia.com/financial-edge/0712/should-google-pay-a-dividend.aspx. Accessed 01/31/2019.

Nasdaq, 2018. Google institutional holdings. Available at: https://www.nasdaq.com/symbol/googl/institutional-holdings. Accessed 11/20/2021.

Srnicek, N. 2016. *Platform Capitalism*. Cambridge: Polity Press. Available at: https://www.wiley.com/en-au/Platform+Capitalism-p-9781509504862

Yang, S.H., Nam, C., and Kim, S. 2018. The effects of M&A's within the mobile ecosystem on the rival's shareholder value: the case of Google and Apple. *Telecommunications Policy*, 42, 15–23.

4 Microsoft Corporation

Founded on April 4, 1975, by Bill Gates and Paul Allen, Microsoft Corporation "develops and supports software, services, devices and solutions that deliver new value for customers and help people and businesses realize their full potential". According to the company's annual report,

> our products include operating systems; cross-device productivity applications; server applications; business solution applications; desktop and server management tools; software development tools; and video games. We also design, manufacture, and sell devices, including PCs, tablets, gaming and entertainment consoles, other intelligent devices, and related accessories.
>
> (Microsoft *Annual Report*, 2018, p.3)

The annual report continues: "we offer an array of services, including cloud-based solutions that provide customers with software, services, platforms, and content, and we provide solution support and consulting services. We also deliver relevant online advertising to a global audience" (Microsoft *Annual Report*, 2018, p.3). According to Microsoft, "to achieve our vision, our research and development efforts focus on three interconnected ambitions: Reinvent productivity and business processes; Build the intelligent cloud platform; Create more personal computing" (Microsoft *Annual Report*, 2018, p.4).

The company

> operates the business and reports financial performance using three segments: Productivity and Business Processes, Intelligent Cloud, and More Personal Computing. The segments provide management with a comprehensive financial view of key businesses. The segments enable the alignment of strategies and objectives across the development, sales, marketing, and services organizations, and they provide a framework for timely and rational allocation of resources within businesses.
>
> (Microsoft *Annual Report*, 2018, p.6)

DOI: 10.4324/9781003309536-4

Microsoft is typically an oligopolistic company, operating in a market where just six companies hold more than 90% of the share of operating systems. This advantage came from its longevity compared to the others. Windows practically existed on its own for a long time, having obtained its first patent in 1985. Apple's macOS operating system, for example, was only released in 2001 and, even having constantly grown, occupies a distant and tiny second place, far behind Microsoft Windows. As of April 2013, Windows held 91.28% of the operating system market and nine out of ten computers used it worldwide; macOS represented 7.47%, Linux 1.05%, and ChromeOS 0.02%, with other brands no more than 0.18% of the market share. In December 2017, Windows dropped to 82.68% of the market, macOS grew to 13.06%, Linux to 1.54%, ChromeOS to 0.91%, and the rest to 1.81% of the operating system market. In December 2021, Windows fell slightly to 73.72% of the market, macOS rose slightly to 15.33%, Linux increased to 2.09% of the market, ChromeOS also went up to 2.18%, and the other brands, mostly unknown to the general public, rose to 6.68% participation (Statista, 2022).

This oligopolistic position in a market with few supplier companies is what explains the company's growing revenue, benefiting from the exclusivity that still gives it three quarters of the market. Although its share is falling, the gap to second place is still huge, representing five times more than the second place, that is, macOS. Although its market share fell, its revenues are constantly on the rise, probably because of services, notably cloud services, which have greatly contributed to the success of the business, as we will see later.

After this brief presentation of the company, its mission, and its position on the market, we will proceed to the comparison between the sources of profitability, our specific objective in this work and the first indicator of financialization.

4.1 Comparison between the sources of profitability

Our first indicator of financialization is the comparison between the profitability sources, because, as already stated by all this work, it is from this comparison that we can analyze the participation of each segment in the business as a whole and its subsequent comparison with the valuation of company shares in the financial and stock market, which is a relationship that is central to our goals.

Table 4.1 shows Microsoft's total revenues over the six-year period, from 2013 to 2018. The table shows the revenues, gross margin, operating profit, net profit, percentage of return on revenue, earnings per share, and cash dividends per share.

Microsoft is a rapidly expanding revenue company, rising from US$ 77.8 billion in 2013 to US$ 110.3 billion in 2018, almost a 40% increase in six years. It can be observed that 40% revenue growth corresponds to an average of 6.5% revenue growth per year. However, the percentage of profit on total revenue is quite high for a company that is also a manufacturer. In these six years, the average return on revenue was 29.35%, having reached a 34.37% return on revenue in 2013.

By segment, Productivity and Business Processes revenue was the most profitable, having achieved a 50.22% return on revenue in 2015. Intelligent Cloud was also profitable, with a 41% return on revenue, 33% in the same year. Finally, the More Personal Computing segment was responsible for 11.73% return on revenues. Table 4.2 shows these data.

Over the years, the Productivity and Business Processes segment dropped as a percentage of return on revenue, to 45.58% in 2016, 38.12% in 2017, and 36.03% in 2018, but still with the average return on revenue of 42.48%

Table 4.1 Microsoft's revenues

	2013	*2014*	*2015*	*2016*	*2017*	*2018*
Revenues in billions of US$	77,849	86,833	93,580	91,154	96,571	110,360
Gross Margin	57,464	59,755	60,542	58,374	62,310	72,007
Operating profit	26,764	27,759	18,161	26,078	29,025	35,058
% return on revenue	34.37	31.96	19.40	28.60	30.05	31.76
Net profit in billions of US$	21,863	22,074	12,193	20,539	25,489	16,571*
EPS (earnings per share) – US$	2,58	2,63	1,48	2,56	3,25	2,13
Cash dividends per share – US$	0,93	1,12	1,24	1,44	1,56	1,68

Source: https://www.sec.gov/Archives/edgar/data/789019/000156459018019062/msft-10k_20180630.htm, p.31

* This includes a net expense of US$ 13.7 billion related to the Tax Cut and Employment Act, which reduced net income and diluted earnings per share by $ 13.7 billion and $ 1.75, respectively. Average of 29.35% return on revenue in six years, from 2013 to 2018

Table 4.2 Revenues by segment

	2015	*2016*	*2017*	*2018*
Revenues in billions of US$	93,580	91,154	96,571	110,360
Revenues by segment				
Productivity and business processes	26,430	25,792	29,870	35,865
Operating profit	13,274	11,756	11,389	12,924
% return on revenue	50.22	45.58	38.12	36.03
Intelligent cloud	23,715	24,952	27,407	32,219
Operating profit	9803	9249	9127	11,524
% return on revenue	41.33	37.06	33.30	35.76
More personal computing	43,435	40,410	39,294	42,276
Operating profit	5095	6183	8815	10,610
% return on revenue	11.73	15.30	22.43	25.09
Operating profit	18,161	26,078	29,025	35,058
Net profit in billions of US$	12,193	20,539	25,489	16,571

Sources: https://www.sec.gov/Archives/edgar/data/789019/000156459018019062/msft-10k_20180630.htm, p.35

in four years. Intelligent Cloud also dropped from 41.33% in 2015 to 37.06% in 2016, 33.30% in 2017 and rose to 35.76% in 2018, showing a return on revenue of 36.86% on average for the four years between 2015 and 2018. The More Personal Computing segment rose from 11.73% return on revenue to 15.30% in 2016, 22.43% in 2017 and 25.09% in 2018, resulting in a return on revenue of 18.63% on average between 2015 and 2018. It was the least profitable segment of the company, although the most representative in total revenue, reaching US$ 42.2 billion in a total revenue of US$ 110, 3 billion.

This reinforces the idea that the company's manufacturing part is less profitable than its part of services, licenses, cloud, business processes, among other intangible products, confirming the trend toward financialization in this regard as well. When we look at the appreciation of Microsoft shares, it occurs more strongly than the financial markets and stock exchanges, as shown in Table 4.3.

Microsoft shares appreciated more than the group of the 500 largest companies listed on the stock exchange in the Standard and Poor's index (S&P 500) and Nasdaq Computer. Whereas in the S&P 500, there was a 97.92% appreciation from 2012 to 2017 and in the Nasdaq Computer an appreciation of 123.98% over five years; Microsoft's shares appreciated 158.45% in the same period, representing an average of 31.69% per year. In fact, from 2012 to 2016, there was an appreciation of the order of 20% per year and in 2016 the US$ 100 reached US$ 187.22, rising to US$ 258.45 in 2017, an increase of 40% in a single year.

These data on the valuation of Microsoft's shares are not far removed from the figures presented by the performance of revenues, which, as we saw earlier, is very high in the case of a manufacturing company, different from Google, which obtains profit mainly by counting clicks and Apple, which profits from outsourced manufacturing through cheap labor. Moreover, the appreciation of its shares is far removed from the performance of its revenues. It is yet another variant of financialization, which presents different dynamics depending on the characteristics of each company and each sector of the economy. However, in the case of companies related to communication, digital technology, the Internet and platforms, there are also different dynamics in the financialization process when the indicator is the comparison between the sources of profitability.

Table 4.3 Valuation of US$ 100 invested on 6/30/2012

	06/2012	*06/2013*	*06/2014*	*06/2015*	*06/2016*	*06/2017*
Microsoft Corporation	100.00	116.38	144.62	157.17	187.22	258.45
S&P 500	100.00	120.60	150.27	161.43	167.87	197.92
Nasdaq Computer	100.00	98.40	140.53	157.83	162.37	223.98

Source: https://www.microsoft.com/investor/reports/ar17/index.html, p.9

4.2 Shareholding composition

In the shareholding indicator, Microsoft is the same as Apple and Google. The largest shareholders are the large North American investment funds, although there are also foreign banks, such as the Bank of Norway, for example, which holds more than 72 million Microsoft shares.

Having launched 7.6 billion shares on the market, the company had 2,888 institutional investors, with 5.6 billion shares, or 73.81%. Each share was worth US$ 112.43 on August 30, 2018 (Nasdaq, 2018). As in the other two companies analyzed previously, there is a large concentration of shares in a few hands. The Vanguard Group alone had 569 million shares, exactly 10% of the shares held by institutional investors, with a market cap of more than US$ 63 billion, an amount almost equal to that of BlackRock Inc., which owned 506 million shares, or US$ 56 billion, i.e., 9% of the shares held by institutional investors. State Street Corp, the third of the so-called Big Three of investment funds (Fichtner, 2017), accounted for more than 289 million shares, bringing together more than US$ 32 billion in Microsoft shares, or 5% of the shares held by institutional investors. Table 4.4 shows the fifteen largest shareholders of Microsoft on June 30, 2018.

The three major investors hold more than 1350 billion shares in Microsoft, bringing together more than US$ 150 billion. Around 24% of all shares held by institutional investors are accounted for by only 3 institutional investors. When we add the top fifteen, they hold 2.8 billion shares, exactly 50.59% of the 5.6 billion shares that are distributed among almost 3000 institutional

Table 4.4 Microsoft's largest shareholders on 6/30/2018

Financial groups	*Shares held*	*Value in thousands of US$*	*% of institutional shares*
Vanguard Group Inc.	569,057,510	63,745,822	10.16
BlackRock Inc.	506,636,253	56,753,393	9.04
State Street Corp.	289,618,867	32,443,105	5.17
Capital World Investors	252,142,526	28,245,006	4.50
FMR LLC	231,776,134	25,963,563	4.13
Price T Rowe Associates INC/MD	202,863,755	22,724,798	3.62
Capital Research Global Investors	103,326,554	11,574,641	1.84
Northern Trust Corp	93,907,688	10,519,539	1.67
Geode Capital Management LLC	91,550,157	10,255,449	1.63
Bank of New York Mellon Corp.	90,744,168	10,165,162	1.62
Wellington Management Group LLP	87,073,852	9,754,013	1.55
JPMorgan Chase & Co.	86,514,270	9,691,329	1.54
Invesco LTD	85,376,773	9,563,906	1.52
Bank of America Corp/DE/	73,364,889	8,218,335	1.31
Norges Bank	72,426,175	8,113,180	1.29
Totals (15 biggest)	2,836,379,571	317,731,241	50.59

Source: https://www.nasdaq.com/symbol/msft/institutional-holdings

Table 4.5 Groups that most acquired Microsoft shares in 2018

Financial groups	*Shares acquired*	*% of change (+)*
BlackRock Inc.	6,786,483	1.36
FMR LLC	5,367,919	2.37
Price T Rowe Associates Inc./MD	2,746,285	1.37
Capital Research Global Investors	2,713,274	2.70
Northern Trust Corp.	768,875	0.83
Geode Capital Management LLC	1,435,077	1.59
JPMorgan Chase & Co.	2,885,045	3.45
Invesco LTD	3,120,607	3.79
Bank of America Corp/DE	469,671	0.64
Norges Bank	36,376	0.05
Morgan Stanley	2,007,248	3.58

Source: https://www.nasdaq.com/symbol/msft/institutional-holdings/increased

investors. That is, 0.5% of institutional investors hold 50% of the shares and the corresponding dollar value, which reaches US$ 317 billion only in the sum of these fifteen largest institutional investors.

4.3 Shareholding acquisitions

Following the same trend as the shareholding structure, the share acquisitions were also in charge of the largest groups of financial institutions. BlackRock Inc., which bought more than 6 million shares, increased its stake in the company by 1.36% in 2018. FMR LLC also bought more than 5 million shares, increasing its stake by 2.37%. Table 4.5 shows the groups that most acquired Microsoft shares in 2018.

Banks also participated in the biggest purchases. JPMorgan Chase & Co. acquired 2.8 million shares, increasing its shares by 3.45%, while Morgan Stanley bought 2 million shares and increased its stake in Microsoft by 3.58%. The largest purchase proportional to the participation was that of the Invesco Ltd fund, which, by acquiring 3.1 million shares, increased its participation by 3.79%.

These numbers reinforce the thesis that more and more large groups of investors and financial institutions participate in the day-to-day activities of manufacturing companies, regardless of the sector to which they belong, making the strategies and the entire destiny of the company be defined by exclusively financial considerations, a fact that is a clear and a positive indicator of financialization in a large and well-known contemporary company.

4.4 Share sales

Similar to Apple and Google, Microsoft's major shareholder movements were carried out by financial groups. The Vanguard Group sold 17 million shares,

Table 4.6 Groups that most sold Microsoft shares in 2018

Financial groups	*Shares sold*	*% of change (−)*
Vanguard Group Inc.	17,033,234	2.91
State Street Corp	1,169,084	0.4
Capital World Investors	5,690,844	2.21
Bank of New York Mellon Corp.	2,985,995	3.19
Wellington Management Group LLP	4,321,703	4.73
Wells Fargo & Company/MN	3,548,271	5.67
Tiaa Cref Investment Management LLC	925,322	1.92
Goldman Sachs Group Inc.	7,564,225	14.1
Franklin Resources Inc.	8,954,571	17.01
Primecap Management Co/CA/	737,000	1.76

Source: https://www.nasdaq.com/symbol/msft/institutional-holdings/decreased

reducing its stake by 2.91% in the company's shares. Table 4.6 shows these data.

Even more striking was Franklin Resources Inc., which reduced its stake in Microsoft shares by 17.01%, by selling more than 8 million shares; followed by Goldman Sachs Group, which sold 7.5 million shares and fell 14.1% in the company's shares.

The issue of the sale of shares has already been analyzed by us in other cases and reflects a short-term positioning in investments. Although groups that have sold Microsoft shares have participated in it for many years, they are always divesting in one company and investing in others, to make a quicker profit. This has already been discussed by Lazonick (2011) and is one of the bases of financialization, which is the concern to return to the investor as much as possible in the shortest possible time. As always, it was profitable for those who sold the shares in the high period, and for those who bought them in the low period, as they will benefit later on when the share price is at a higher level than it is today.

In short, the buying and selling share movements have their own dynamics, very independent from company revenues and very different from the narratives that seek to give a more rational character to this phenomenon. The policy of maximizing shareholder value is in full force, hence the investment/divestment in the shares of companies carried out by these large financial institutions.

4.5 Mergers and acquisitions

Having a list of 214 companies acquired since 1987, Microsoft is one of the companies with the highest number of acquisitions among which we are analyzing. From 1999 to 2018, just thirty companies acquired by Microsoft consumed more than US$ 50 billion, but Microsoft spent much more than

Table 4.7 Microsoft's acquisitions of companies – 1999 to 2018

Purchased company	*Date of purchase*	*Value in millions of US$*
GitHub	June 3, 2018	7,500
Cloudyn	June 28, 2017	60
Hexadite	May 24, 2017	100
LinkedIn	June 13, 2016	26,200
SwiftKey	Feb 2, 2016	250
Secure Islands Technology	Feb 2, 2016	77
VoloMetrix	Sept 3, 2015	250
Adallom	July 19, 2015	320
Sunrise	Feb 4, 2015	100
Acompli	Dec 1, 2014	200
Aorato	Nov 13, 2014	200
Equivio	Oct 8, 2014	200
Mojang	Sept 15, 2014	2,500
Parature	Jan 6, 2014	100
Yammer	June 25, 2012	1,200
VideoSurf	Nov 23, 2011	100
Greenfield Online	Aug 29, 2008	486
Powerset	July 1, 2008	100
Farecast	Apr 9, 2008	115
Danger	Feb 11, 2008	500
Musiwave	Nov 15, 2007	46
Jellyfish	Oct 3, 2007	50
aQuantive	May 18, 2007	6400
Tellme Network	Mar 14, 2007	800
Whale Communications	May 18, 2006	75
Massive	May 1, 2006	200
Vicinity Corporation	Oct 22, 2002	96
Rare, Inc.	Sept 24, 2002	337
Navision	May 7, 2002	1,500
Intrinsa	July 28, 1999	58
Total in billions of US$		50,120

Source: https://www.crunchbase.com/organization/microsoft/acquisitions/acquisitions_list#section-acquisitions

that since we do not have data from the other 184 companies purchased since 1987. Table 4.7 shows only those whose sales prices were disclosed by the website crunchbase.com.

The most expensive company acquired by Microsoft was LinkedIn, US$ 26.2 billion in 2016. "LinkedIn's revenue increased from US$ 3.0 billion to US$ 5.3 billion and consisted mainly of Talent Solutions revenue" (Microsoft *Annual Report*, 2018, p.36).

Looking back on the biggest purchases, companies such as GitHub, for example, cost US$ 7.5 billion in 2018; Mojang US$ 2.5 billion in 2014; Yammer US$ 1.2 billion in 2012; aQuantive US$ 6.4 billion in 2007, and Navision US$ 1.5 billion in 2002 (Crunchbase, 2019).

These acquisitions are a frequent part of the economic process of financialization, and although companies, except Google, pay heavy dividends and stock repurchases to shareholders, they make huge profits, which allow them to buy dozens of other companies. An example of financialization is that the huge revenues generated by companies do not mean new investments, but the concentration of what already exists, with a small growth in fixed capital. Instead, these companies tend to do three things: (1) save their money and evade taxes: Microsoft had reserves in March 2016 in the order of US$ 102.6 billion, of which US$ 96.3 billion was kept offshore abroad, which accounts for 93.9% of its reserves abroad; (2) use large resources for mergers and acquisitions, which is a process capable of centralizing competencies rather than building new competencies; and (3) channel resources to start-ups, many of them from advertising platforms, becoming their largest shareholders (Srnicek, 2016, pp.16–17, 32).

Nevertheless, we can infer from this acquisition process that it is recurrent in companies with higher market capitalization, especially those that are part of the new platform capitalism, the new economy, as is the case with technology and communication companies.

4.6 Origin of managers

Microsoft's top executives, except Satya Nadella, the current CEO, who joined Microsoft in 1992, have moved on or remain in several private organizations, including banks, investment funds, and credit card companies. Board members such as Charles Noski have already participated in the Bank of America, Northrop Grumman Corporation, AT&T, among other giant corporations. Charles Scharf, director since 2014, has participated in Visa Inc., One Equity Partners, JPMorgan Chase & Co., Bank One Corporation, and Salomon Smith Barney. Mason Morfit was from Credit Suisse; Helmut Panke, director since 2003, was at BMW, while John Thompson participated at Symantec Corp and IBM. Other directors have worked at Johnson & Johnson, Motorola, Bayer, among other companies, which are also manufacturers, in addition to their bank and fund colleagues. Table 4.8 presents Microsoft Managers that comprised the Board of Directors in 2016.

The passage through financial institutions is very present in the Board of Directors of Microsoft, similar to the boards of the Ford and GM automakers (Carmo, 2017, Carmo et al., 2021) and others that we will see later. That is, at Microsoft, the financialized mentality is older, and its network of relationships is long-standing with members from the world of finance. This allows shareholder value maximization to be taken into consideration whenever decisions must be made. The next financialization indicators, such as compensation paid to executives and the dividend payments to shareholders, in addition to the stock repurchase, will demonstrate how the financialization process is typical at Microsoft, bringing together all the indicators that a company could joint together.

Table 4.8 Microsoft Managers – Board of Directors

Executives	*Organizations in which they participated*
William H. Gates III Co-President of the Bill & Melinda Gates Foundation. On the Microsoft Board since 1981	Microsoft founder; Berkshire Hathaway Board Member.
Charles H. Noski Former Vice President Director since 2003	Bank of America; Northrop Grumman Corporation; AT&T; Hughes Electronics Corporation; Financial Accounting Foundation.
Charles W. Scharf Director since 2014	Visa Inc.; One Equity Partners; JPMorgan Chase & Co; Bank One Corporation; Salomon Smith Barney.
Helmut Panke Director since 2003	Former Chairman of the Board of BMW; Former CEO of BMW.
John W. Stanton Director since 2014	Trilogy International Partners, Inc.; Trilogy Equity Partners; First Avenue Entertainment LLLP; Western Wireless Corporation.
John W. Thompson Director since 2012	Virtual Instruments; Symantec Corp; IBM.
G. Mason Morfit Director since 2014	ValueAct Capital; Credit Suisse First Boston; B.A pela Princeton University.
Padmasree Warrior Director since 2015	NextEV; Cisco Systems, Inc.; Motorola, Inc.; B.S. in Chemical Engineering from Indian Institute of Technology, New Delhi; M.S. in Chemical Engineering from Cornell University.
Sandra E. Peterson Director since 2015	Johnson & Johnson; Bayer CropScience AG; Medco Health Solutions, Inc. Merck-Medco Managed Care LLC.
Satya Nadella CEO Director since 2014	Joined Microsoft in 1992.
Teri L. List-Stoll Director since 2014	DICK'S Sporting Goods, Inc; Kraft Foods Group; Procter & Gamble.

Source: https://iiwisdom.com/msft-2016/board-of-directors/

4.7 Compensation paid to executives

The compensation paid to Microsoft executives was lower than that of Apple and Google (Apple paid US$ 145 million and Google paid US$ 199 million to their CEOs in 2016 and 2017). Microsoft CEO Satya Nadella received US$ 25.8 million in total compensation in 2018, divided into US$ 8.9 million in cash earnings, US$ 16.8 million in stock options, and US$ 111,000 in other income. Executive Vice President, Amy Hood, received a total of US$ 14.9 million, distributed in US$ 4.5 million in cash earnings, US$ 10.2 million in stock options, and US$ 98,000 in other earnings. Bradford Smith, on the other hand, earned a total of US$ 13.5 million, divided into US$ 4.3 million in cash earnings, US$ 9 million in shares, and US$ 111 thousand in other earnings not specified in our reference source (Salary.com, 2019). Table 4.9 shows data referring to compensations to main executives.

Two other top executives, Jean-Philippe Courtois, received a total of US$ 11 million in total compensation and Margareth Johnson received a sum of US$ 8.7 million in total compensation, with cash wages in the range of US$ 2.9 million to US$ 3.9 million.

These cash salaries, which ranged between US$ 3 million and US$ 9 million, are far less than the total earnings that executives receive each year. This is for two reasons, at least. The first is to pay less income tax on wages, since a lower rate is charged at a lower rate, and the tax on earnings in shares is lower than on wage income. And the second is that, when paying their executives on stock options, a large stock purchase raises their price on the stock exchanges, as more shares will have to leave the company's treasury into

Table 4.9 Compensation payments to executives. Microsoft – annual salary in US$ – 2018

Compensations to executives	*Total in cash*	*Stock options*	*Others*	*Total compensations*
Satya Nadella CEO Director since 2014	8.925,000	16.807,208	111,055	25.843,263
Amy E. Hood Executive Vice President and Chief Financial Officer	4.593,750	10.232,265	98,442	14.924,457
Bradford L. Smith President and Chief Legal Officer	4.366,700	9.033,868	111,055	13.511,623
Jean-Philippe Courtois Executive Vice President, President, Global Sales, Marketing and Operations	3.925,513	7.149,549	51,187	11.126,249
Margaret L. Johnson Executive Vice President, Business Development	2.967,236	5.702,554	88,225	8.758,015

Source: https://www1.salary.com/MICROSOFT-CORP-Executive-Salaries.html

private hands, but this time the executives, equivalent to a purchase process. This methodology of stock repurchases and paying compensation to executives through stock options is an artificial tactic to raise the price of shares in the markets, already widely denounced by Lazonick (2011, 2012, 2013), among others.

4.8 Payment of dividends to shareholders and stock repurchases

Microsoft has been paying dividends to shareholders in the billions of dollars for several years. From 2015 to 2018, it paid more than US$ 46 billion in dividends, of which US$ 10 billion were in 2015, US$ 11,3 billion in 2016, US$ 12 billion in 2017, and US$ 12,9 billion in 2018.

Added to the dividends, in September 2013, the company launched a stock repurchase plan, in the amount of US$ 40 billion for the next five years. In four years, it nearly used up the entire sum, disbursing around US$ 38 billion to buy back its shares. Table 4.10 shows these numbers.

It should be mentioned that Microsoft paid more dividends and stock repurchases than its announced net income in 2015, 2016, and 2018. This is because the company has reserves and its stock repurchases program was designed to use existing resources. In 2015, it had a net profit of US$ 12.1 billion, but paid a total of US$ 20.8 billion between dividends and stock repurchases, as shown in Table 4.10. In 2016, the profit was US$ 20 billion, and disbursements were US$ 23 billion, and in 2018, for a net profit of US$ 16.5 billion, there was an expense of US$ 20.6 billion between dividends and stock repurchases.

This shows that dividend payments and stock repurchase are not directly related to their annual revenue but are a result of the establishment of programs in each period. The same is true for earnings per share and money spent per share, which are independent of each year's earnings. Apparently, they have their own dynamics. Table 4.11 shows the data related to earnings per share and cash dividend per share.

Table 4.10 Dividend payments and stock repurchases at Microsoft

Act	*2015*	*2016*	*2017*	*2018*
Net profit in billions of US$	12,193	20,539	25,489	16,571
Dividend payment in billions of US$	10,063	11,329	12,040	12,917
Stock repurchases in billions of US$	10,744	12,283	8,798	7699
Totals in billions of US$	20,807	23,612	20,838	20,616

Source: https://www.nasdaq.com/symbol/msft/financials and Microsoft annual report, 2018, p.55 and 2017, p.53

Table 4.11 Earnings per share and cash dividend per share regarding revenue

	2015	*2016*	*2017*	*2018*
Revenue	93,580	91,154	96,571	110,360
Totals in billions of US$				
EPS (earnings per share) – US$	1.48	2.56	3.25	2.13
Cash dividends per share – US$	1.24	1.44	1.56	1.68

Source: https://www.sec.gov/Archives/edgar/data/789019/000156459018019062/msft-10k_20180630.htm, p.31

Table 4.11 illustrates that while 2015 earnings were US$ 93.5 billion, earnings per share were US$ 1.48 and cash dividends paid per share were US$ 1.24. The following year, with a drop in earnings to US$ 91.1 billion, instead of a drop in earnings per share, the opposite happened, a rise in earnings per share to US$ 2.56 and the following year, US$ 3.25. In 2018, with revenues rising to US$ 110.3 billion, earnings per share fell to US$ 2.13 while cash dividends reached US$ 1.68, compared to US$ 1.56 in 2017 and US$ 1.44 in 2016, always higher than in previous years.

That is, the dividend payments to shareholders and stock repurchases depend more on decisions by shareholders' meetings than on the actual performance of the company's revenues. It is clear that if the company starts to make losses or the level of revenue and profits drops, adjustments will have to be made in the level of dividend payments and stock repurchases, but the data of our work show that the power to decide, in the final analysis, is stronger than the explanations based on the absolute belief in the dictates of economic rationality suppose.

4.9 Employee salaries

The indicator that discusses Microsoft employee salaries shows that the company is at a level of salary payment compatible with Apple and Google. It is true that several starting salaries are low and are below the average level of all North American ethnic groups, already widely discussed here, which was about US$ 61,000 in 2017 (Fontenot et al., 2018). However, the average salary is higher than at Apple and Google, for jobs considered to be lower and less qualified. Table 4.12 lists ten professions and their respective minimum, maximum wages and their average.

We can see that at least the first six professions listed above begin their duties with annual salaries ranging from US$ 19,000 for a Sales Associate to US$ 25,000 for a Computer Technician. Only for positions of Engineers upward do we see starting salaries around the average salary of all North American ethnic groups, US$ 61,000 in 2017. A Field Engineer starts his/her career at Microsoft earning US$ 57,264.00 and an Electrical Engineer starts with US$ 59,263.00.

Table 4.12 Microsoft. Annual salary in US$ – 2018

Professions	*Minimum*	*Maximum*	*Average*
Sales associate	19,354	65,973	42,663
Data Technician	19,618	35,824	27,721
Nanny	20,033	45,161	32,597
Sales consultant	20,441	66,796	43,618
Consumer Services Consultant	21,992	47,035	34,513
Computer Technician	25,686	73,603	49,644
Field Engineer	57,264	130,379	93,821
Electric Engineer	59,263	148,342	103,802
Engineering Director	115,575	270,613	193,094
Communications Director	142,264	312,535	227,399

Source: https://www.payscale.com/research/US/Employer=Microsoft_Corp/Salary/by_Job

When we talk about the average, the first six professions in Table 4.12 receive between US$ 27,000 and US$ 49,000; in general, not unlike those of Apple and Google. This wage issue has been affecting homogeneously large companies all over the world, since the trend is that there is no longer that type of work that prevailed in the period after World War II, in most of the world, with "job security and increasing remuneration, guaranteed pensions, robust health benefits and much more" (Wartzman, 2017). In his book, Rick Wartzman analyzes the situation of workers at General Motors, General Electric, Coca-Cola, and Kodak. According to him, the golden age of the worker's wages has come to an end. Its results are very similar to the data found here.

Regarding the relationship between the total CEO earnings and the salaries of other employees, at Microsoft, the difference is smaller than at Apple and Google, not because of salaries, but because the compensation to the CEO was much smaller at Microsoft, which paid US$ 25 million to Satya Nadella in 2018, while Apple paid US$ 145 million to Tim Cook in 2016, and Google paid US$ 199 million to Sundar Pichai in 2017. Hence, the differences between income brackets at Microsoft were much smaller than at Apple and Google, as can be seen in Table 4.13.

Even so, there is a huge difference between the total CEO earnings and that of the Sales Associate at the beginning of his/her career, for example, reaching 1335 times the gain of one over the other. The smallest difference we found was between the earnings of the CEO and the Director of Communications in their maximum remuneration, reaching "only" eighty-two times the earnings of one over the other.

These data reveal a situation of persistent and encouraging wage differentiation between income brackets in companies, which is characteristic of financialization, and which results in a progressive increase in economic inequality in the company and in society.

Table 4.13. Ratio between employee salaries and total CEO earnings Satya Nadella in 2018 – US$ 25,843,263.00

Employees X CEO	*Minimum*	*Maximum*	*Average*
Sales associate	1335	391	605
Data Technician	1317	721	932
Nanny	1290	572	792
Sales consultant	1264	386	592
Consumer Services Consultant	1175	549	748
Computer Technician	1006	351	520
Field Engineer	451	198	275
Electric Engineer	436	174	248
Engineering Director	223	95	133
Communications Director	181	82	113

Source: author, based on the values of the compensation table paid to the CEO and the workers' salary table.

4.10 Employment

Concerning the employment issue, Microsoft states in its annual report:

> As of June 30, 2018, we employed approximately 131,000 people on a full-time basis, 78,000 in the U.S. and 53,000 internationally. Of the total employed people, 42,000 were in operations, including manufacturing, distribution, product support, and consulting services; 42,000 were in product research and development; 36,000 were in sales and marketing; and 11,000 were in general and administration. Certain of our employees are subject to collective bargaining agreements.
>
> (Microsoft *Annual Report*, 2018, p.16)

Figure 4.1 shows the evolution of employment at Microsoft, from 2005 to 2018.

As we can see in Figure 4.1, the level of employment has been growing continuously since 2005, having grown 50% between 2005 and 2008 and 116% between 2005 and 2018. The year of greatest growth was 2014, when it rose to 128,000 workers, having surpassed 99,000 in 2013, a 28% growth in just one year. Here, the trajectory of Apple and Google is repeated, with the creation of many job vacancies, characterizing financialization as not having had a negative influence on employment, as it happened with the automakers Ford and GM, for example (Carmo, 2017; Carmo et al., 2021).

From the employment data at Microsoft, whose results are similar to those of Google and Apple, with regard to job creation, we see that the process of financialization of production does not necessarily destroy jobs, but as we saw in the case of Apple, it often shifts employment, notably from developed countries in Europe and the United States to developing countries, such as Asia, Eastern Europe, and Latin America, presenting a different

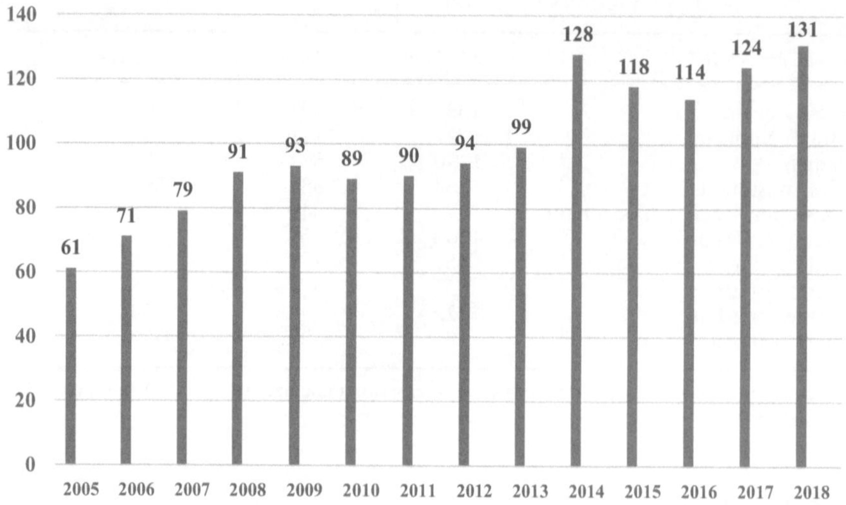

Figure 4.1 Evolution of employment at Microsoft – 2005 to 2018

dynamic in each company when this indicator is used. The heterogeneity of the occurrences of each indicator shows that financialization is a complex and specific process. In the same way that dividend payments and the stock repurchases also presented different dynamics in each company studied, employment is also affected in different ways. In this work, which studies ten contemporary companies, employment grew in nine of them, as we will see until the end of the book, and only decreased in one, Exxon Mobil, demonstrating that the sectors to which the companies belong, mainly information and communications technology, in addition to banks, manage to create jobs while dedicating themselves to paying dividends, buying back shares, paying millionaire compensation to executives and relatively low salaries to the rest of the workers, that is, they do not need to destroy job vacancies to practice financialization. This heterogeneity is one of the findings of our work and challenges a vision of watertight financialization, where all companies must comply with the same script to be considered a financialized company. In the following chapters, we will see several cases where heterogeneity applies, mainly in the case of dividend payments and stock repurchases.

References

Carmo, M.J. 2017. Análise do processo de financeirização do setor automotivo. *Dissertação de Mestrado apresentada ao programa de Pós-Graduação em Engenharia de Produção da Universidade Federal de São Carlos*- UFSCar, 135 f. Available at: https://repositorio.ufscar.br/handle/ufscar/8917

Carmo, M.J., Sacomano Neto, M., and Donadone, J.C. 2021. *Financialisation in the Automotive Industry: Capital and Labour in Contemporary Society*. London: Routledge. Available at: https://www.routledge.com/Financialisation-in-the-Automotive-Industry-Capital-and-Labour-in-Contemporary/Carmo-Neto-Donadone/p/book/9780367751395

Crunchbase. 2019. Microsoft acquisitions. Available at: https://www.crunchbase.com/organization/microsoft/acquisitions/acquisitions_list#section-acquisitions. Accessed 05/03/2019.

Fichtner, J., Heemskerk, E.M., and Garcia-Bernardo, J. 2017. Hidden power of the Big Three? Passive index funds, re-concentration of corporate ownership, and new financial risk. *Business and Politics*, 19(2), 298–326. Available at: https://www.cambridge.org/core/journals/business-and-politics/article/hidden-power-of-the-big-three-passive-index-funds-reconcentration-of-corporate-ownership-and-new-financial-risk/30AD689509AAD62F5B677E916C28C4B6#

Fontenot, K., Semega, J., and Kollar, M. 2018. Income and poverty in the United States 2017. Available at: https://www.census.gov/content/dam/Census/library/publications/2018/demo/p60-263.pdf. Accessed 10/06/2019.

Lazonick, W. (7 July 2011). How 'Maximizing value' for shareholders robs workers and taxpayers. *Huffpost Business*. Available at: https://www.huffpost.com/entry/how-maximizing-value-for-_b_892396. Accessed 08/10/2017.

Lazonick, W. (4 Mar 2012). How American corporations transformed from producers to predators. *Huffpost Business*. Available at: https://www.huffpost.com/entry/how-american-corporations_b_1399500. Accessed 08/10/2017.

Lazonick, W. (1 Feb 2013). Robots don't destroy jobs; rapacious corporate executives do. *Huffpost Business*. Available at: https://www.huffpost.com/entry/robots-dont-destroy-jobs-_b_2396465. Accessed 08/10/2017.

Salary.com. 2019. Microsoft executive salaries. Available at: https://www1.salary.com/MICROSOFT-CORP-Executive-Salaries.html. Accessed 01/09/2019.

Srnicek, N. 2016. *Platform Capitalism*. Cambridge: Polity Press. Available at: https://www.wiley.com/en-us/Platform+Capitalism-p-9781509504862

Statista, 2022. Global market share of windows. Available at: https://www.statista.com/statistics/218089/global-market-share-of-windows-7/#:~:text=Operating%20systems%20market%20share%20of%20desktop%20PCs%202013%2D2021%2C%20by%20month&text=Microsoft%20Windows%20is%20the%20dominating, of%20just%20under%2074%20percent. Accessed 02/19/2022.

Wartzman, R. 2017. *The End of Loyalty: The Rise and Fall of Good Jobs in America*. New York: Public Affairs. Available at: https://www.publicaffairsbooks.com/titles/rick-wartzman/the-end-of-loyalty/9781586489144/

5 Amazon.com Inc.

Amazon.com, Inc. was incorporated in 1994 in the state of Washington and reincorporated in 1996 in the state of Delaware, United States. Its main corporate offices are in Seattle, Washington. The company completed its initial public offering in May 1997 and its common shares are listed on the Nasdaq Global Select Market under the symbol "AMZN". Amazon.com opened its virtual doors on the World Wide Web in July 1995 (Amazon *Annual Report*, 2017, p.3).

According to the company's annual report,

> We seek to be Earth's most customer-centric company. We are guided by four principles: customer obsession rather than competitor focus, passion for invention, commitment to operational excellence, and long-term thinking. In each of our segments, we serve our primary customer sets, consisting of consumers, sellers, developers, enterprises, and content creators. In addition, we provide services, such as advertising services and co-branded credit card agreements
>
> (Amazon *Annual Report*, 2017, p.3)

The annual report continues: "We have organized our operations into three segments: North America, International, and Amazon Web Services ("AWS"). These segments reflect the way the Company evaluates its business performance and manages its operations" (Amazon *Annual Report*, 2017, p.3). Amazon is one of the biggest technology and communication companies belonging to the platform strategy, as defined by Nick Srnicek in his book *Platform Capitalism* (2016). It invests in advertising platforms, cloud platforms, and products platforms, and is one of the largest participants in the global retail trade through electronic means.

It has become a giant in terms of market capitalization, almost reaching half a trillion dollars in just over twenty years of existence; it has growing revenues, it is constantly creating jobs, and is increasingly present in the retail market. It is also a major investor in its cloud infrastructure, which it increasingly rents, and is a major competitor of Google in this regard.

DOI: 10.4324/9781003309536-5

Although it states in its mission, presented in the annual reports, that it focuses on customer obsession rather than competitor focus, in practice, it seeks to cover various services on the Internet and also makes use of all the instruments that are intertwined in the platforms, in addition to services such as credit cards, etc. This demonstrates the desire to increase its power in the market and supplant its competitors, extracting profits from wherever they may come from, which reinforces the thesis that platform capitalism aims to work with data extraction, processing, analysis, and subsequent sale to the customer, seeking to make investments profitable that conventional manufacturing and commercial activity cannot achieve.

Next, we will start by analyzing Amazon comparing its sources of profitability.

5.1 Comparison between the sources of profitability

Amazon's revenues have been growing year by year and the numbers are increasingly robust, as can be seen now. Net revenues went from US$ 74.4 billion in 2013 to US$ 386 billion in 2020, 500% growth in eight years. Although operating and net profit have increased, they are still small for total revenues. In 2017, for a net revenue of US$ 177 billion, net profit was just over US$ 3 billion, only 1.69% return on revenue, which is very low for a technology company. Table 5.1 shows Amazon's revenues and other data.

Table 5.1 Amazon's revenues

	2013	*2014*	*2015*	*2016*	*2017*	*2018*	*2019*	*2020*
Net revenues in billions of US$	74,452	88,988	107,006	135,987	177,866	232,887	280,522	386,064
Operating income	0745	0178	2233	4186	4106	12,421	14,541	22,899
Net income	0274	-0241	0596	2371	3.033	10,073	11,588	21,331
EPS (earnings per share) in US$	0.60	-0.52	1.28	5.01	6.32	20.68	23.46	42.64
Total assets in billions of US$	39,528	53,618	64,747	83,402	131,310	162,648	225,248	321,195
Cash generation from operating activities in billions of US$	5553	6848	12,039	17,272	18,434	30,723	38,514	66,064

Source: Amazon *Annual Reports*, 2017, p.18; 2018, p.17; 2019, p.18; 2020, p.18

However, these numbers increased significantly in the following years, reaching a net profit of US$10 billion in 2018, US$ 11 billion in 2019, and US$ 21 billion in 2020. For a revenue of US$ 386 billion in 2020, the profit net accounted for only 5.44% of revenue. It can be observed that Amazon's profit margins are strongly influenced by the retail and e-commerce segment, and its Internet service division, although growing strongly, as we will see later when analyzing the revenues by segment with higher returns, has not yet represented a very significant share of the business as a whole.

Total assets have grown significantly from US$ 39 billion in 2013 to US$ 321 billion in 2020, a growth of more than 800% over eight years. Earnings per share also grew exponentially, from US$ 0.60 per share in 2013 to US$ 42.64 in 2020, more than a 7,000% increase in earnings per share. The same occurred with the cash flow generated by operating activities, which increased drastically from US$ 5.5 billion in 2013 to US$ 66 billion in 2020, more than eleven times the growth.

It turns out that these figures alone do not show the breakdown by business segment, which is the demonstration of the contribution that each sector gives to the company. When we see revenues by segment, it confirms our initial suspicions also for the case of Amazon, that is, the service sector is by far the most profitable in the business, although a minority in absolute numbers. Table 5.2 shows these data.

Amazon.com Inc. is divided into three segments. North America is largely responsible for the volume of revenues, which went from US$ 63 billion in 2015 to US$ 236 billion in 2020. However, the return on revenues is small, fluctuating around 3.4% per year. The International segment has been

Table 5.2 Revenue by segment – in billions of US$

Amazon.com Inc.	*2015*	*2016*	*2017*	*2018*	*2019*	*2020*
North America	63,708	79.785	106,110	141,366	170,773	236,282
Operating income	1425	2361	2837	7267	7033	8651
% return on revenue	**2.23**	**2.95**	**2.67**	**5.14**	**4.11**	**3.66**
International	35,418	43,983	54,297	65,866	74,723	104,412
Operating income	−699	−1283	−3062	−2142	−1693	717
% return on revenue	**−1.97**	**−2.91**	**−5.63**	**−3.25**	**−2.26**	**0.68**
AWS (Amazon Web Services)	7,880	12,219	17,459	25,655	35,026	45,370
Operating income	1507	3108	4331	7296	9201	13,531
% return on revenue	**19.12**	**25.43**	**24.80**	**28.43**	**26.26**	**29.82**
Y/Y Percentage Growth						
North America	25%	25%	33%	33%	21%	38%
International	6%	24%	23%	21%	13%	40%
AWS (Amazon Web Services)	70%	55%	43%	47%	37%	30%

Source: Amazon *Annual Reports*, 2017, pp.25 and 69; 2018, p.23 and 66; 2019, pp.24 and 67; 2020, pp.25 and 65

in deficit for the past five years, with losses of US$ 699 million in 2015, US$ 1283 billion in 2016, and US$ 3062 billion in 2017. Only in 2020 was this segment profitable but with return on revenue of just 0.68%. Even with an increase in revenues, which surpassed US$ 34 billion in 2015 to US$ 104 billion in 2020, this segment is the least profitable in the company.

Saving profitability is Amazon Web Services (AWS), which had revenues of US$ 7.8 billion in 2015, US$ 12.2 billion in 2016, US$ 17.4 billion in 2017, and reached US$ 45 billion in 2020, with percentage returns on revenues of 19.12% in 2015, 25.43% in 2016, 24.8% in 2017, and 29.82% in terms of return on revenue. It was the sector that was most profitable at Amazon, which has invested heavily in developing cloud platforms and constructing infrastructure for data storage, to rent them to other companies, earning great profits in terms of data exploration and treatment, as previously discussed by Srnicek (2016).

A fact that draws attention is that even with profits that we can consider small compared to those of Apple, Google, and Microsoft, Amazon has one of the shares that has most appreciated recently. Those who invested US$ 100 at the end of 2012 reached a significant US$ 466 at the end of 2017, an appreciation of 466% in the share price. The most appreciated stock exchange index was the S&P 500 Retailing Index, which went from US$ 100 in 2012 to US$ 280 in 2017, an appreciation of 180%; the S&P 500 went from US$ 100 in 2012 to US$ 208 in 2017 and the Morgan Stanley Technology Index went from US$ 100 in 2012 to US$ 247 in late 2017, totaling a 147% appreciation in just five years. Table 5.3 presents the share price performance.

The fact that Amazon's shares have appreciated by more than 466% in five years is an interesting phenomenon, as it shows a tendency for investors to believe in converting the company to the web services segment, especially constructing the cloud infrastructure, which is very profitable as we have seen. This means that its participation in the retail segment through shopping sites and operations outside North America, through the International segment, which has been causing losses, may be revised and even discontinued if things do not change in this segment.

This trajectory toward data exploration, storage, and servitization is in full agreement with the financialization process, which aims to find more profitable niches to produce more value, always in the interest of investors, whether in the short or long term.

Table 5.3 Share price performance. US$ 100 invested in 2012

	2012	*2013*	*2014*	*2015*	*2016*	*2017*
Amazon.com Inc.	100.00	159.00	124.00	269.00	299.00	466.00
Morgan Stanley Technology Index	100.00	132.00	148.00	158.00	177.00	247.00
S&P 500	100.00	132.00	151.00	153.00	171.00	208.00
S&P 500 Retailing Index	100.00	146.00	162.00	203.00	215.00	280.00

Source: Amazon *Annual Report*, 2017, p.79

5.2 Shareholding composition

Having issued 488 million shares, Amazon had one of the most valuable shares in the global financial market. On July 27, 2018, each share was at US$ 1814.81. It has almost ten times the value of Apple's shares, which are around US$ 200. Institutional investors held 58.27% of the shares, bringing together 284.2 million units. This does not include Amazon founder Jeff Bezos, who holds 16% of the common shares of the company he founded in 1994. He is not an institutional investor but an individual.

Table 5.4 shows who the fifteen largest institutional shareholders of Amazon are, in the number of shares held, percentage, and their corresponding dollar value.

The fifteen largest shareholders are all large investment funds and banks, which are practically the same participants in the ten companies we are analyzing here. Once more, the Big Three of North American investment funds (Vanguard, State Street, and BlackRock) have a relevant stake in Amazon's shares. Together, they held nearly 70 million shares in 2018 for nearly US$ 120 billion, almost 20% of all shares. The fifteen largest shareholders bring together 155 million shares and a value of US$ 282 billion and represent 54.58% of the shares and values. These fifteen largest shareholders represented 0.62% of the 2,414 institutional investors (Nasdaq, 2018).

We are trying not to make the analysis repetitive, but also in the case of Amazon, very few investors have massive amounts of economic resources and, of course, a great deal of decision-making power in a company with few large shareholders and thousands of small, isolated investors who have almost

Table 5.4 Amazon's largest shareholders on 3/31/2018

Financial groups	*Shares held*	*Value in thousands of US$*	*% of institutional shares*
Vanguard Group Inc.	28,527,398	51,841,985	10.03
BlackRock Inc.	25,207,255	45,808,388	8.86
FMR LLC	17,123,825	31,118,613	6.02
Price T Rowe Associates INC/MD	15,248,641	27,710,898	5.36
State Street Corp.	15,142,670	27,518,320	5.32
Capital World Investors	9,826,349	17,857,129	3.45
Capital Research Global Investors	8,131,258	14,776,691	2.86
Baillie Gifford & Co.	5,427,762	9,863,709	1.90
Invesco LTD	5,138,869	9,338,712	1.80
Northern Trust Corp.	4,625,889	8,406,489	1.62
Morgan Stanley	4,556,630	8,280,627	1.60
Geode Capital Management LLC	4,466,859	8,117,489	1.57
Norges Bank	4,046,883	7,354,279	1.42
Bank of New York Mellon Corp.	4,004,446	7,277,160	1.40
JPMorgan Chase & Co.	3,918,786	7,121,492	1.37
Totals (15 biggest)	155,393,520	282,391,981	**54.58%**

Source: https://www.nasdaq.com/symbol/amzn/institutional-holdings

Table 5.5 Groups that most acquired Amazon shares in 2018 on 9/30/18

Financial groups	*Acquired shares*	*% of changes (+)*
Vanguard Group Inc.	516,913	1.78
BlackRock Inc.	144,135	0.57
FMR LLC	330,516	1.92
State Street Corp.	621,421	4.08
Invesco LTD	17,603	0.33
Geode Capital Management LLC	137,681	2.98
Morgan Stanley	113,503	2.45
Capital International Investors	4,120,783	976.63
JPMorgan Chase & Co.	29,227	0.74
Bank of New York Mellon Corp.	13,616	0.34

Source: https://www.nasdaq.com/symbol/amzn/institutional-holdings/increased

no decision-making power. Having the presence of an "owner" such as Jeff Bezos, who holds 16% of the shares, is a differential from the other companies we studied. Although Microsoft also has the Bill Gates family as having a large share in the company, and Facebook, through Mark Zuckerberg, what counts for our analysis is the composition of most shares, which are owned by institutional investors. The fact that the leader/founder participates actively in the company's shares apparently does not change the tendency to work with the objective of maximizing shareholder value, because he himself is an interested shareholder, and increasing the shares prices is one of his duties.

5.3 Share acquisitions

The stock acquisitions in Amazon had the same behavior as the companies previously analyzed. Investment funds and banks were the main stock buyers on September 30, 2018. Table 5.5 shows the fifteen groups that most acquired Amazon shares.

Having acquired more than 4 million shares, the Capital International Investors fund increased its stake by almost 1000% in Amazon shares. The Vanguard Group bought more than 500,000 shares, the State Street Corp more than 600,000 shares, Fidelity Management & Research more than 300,000 shares, which altogether increased participation in Amazon.

5.4 Share sales

In a slightly different way from the other companies analyzed in this work, those who most sold Amazon shares were not the largest investment funds or traditionally known banks but less well-known financial groups. Table 5.6 shows the groups.

Except for Capital World Investors, which sold more than 4 million shares, reducing its stake in Amazon's shares by 47.58%; Baillie Gifford & Co., which reduced its amount in the company by 16.44% and Capital Research Global

Table 5.6 Groups that most sold Amazon shares on 9/30/2018

Financial groups	*Sold shares*	*% of change (-)*
Capital World Investors	4,631,661	47.58
Baillie Gifford & Co.	892,059	16.44
Capital Research Global Investors	795,005	11.63
UBS Asset Management Americas Inc.	83,427	4.32
Tiaa Cref Investment Management LLC	99,008	3.65
Ameriprise Financial Inc.	65,511	2.93
Price T Rowe Associates INC/MD	451,744	2.83
Janus Henderson Group PLC	49,779	2.61
Jennison Associates LLC	49,822	1.84
Northern Trust Corp	365	0.01

Source: https://www.nasdaq.com/symbol/amzn/institutional-holdings/decreased

Investors, which reduced its shares in Amazon by 11.63%, the other largest stock sellers slightly reduced their positions in the company with sales that represented a decrease of 2% to 4%.

Buying shares in a company such as Amazon is a good deal, as can be seen in Table 5.3 that demonstrated the history of stock price performance, which went from US$ 100 in 2012 to US$ 466 in 2017. This may be obvious for those who have resources to invest. But, what about these sales? How do we qualify them?

We previously analyzed that stock sales greatly influence the short-term practiced in the financial market. "We have already earned a lot, we are going to sell a little to make some money and invest elsewhere" some small or medium investors might say, and this seems to have happened on Amazon. No major investor has sold so many shares in the company recently. Why?

We have already pointed out that the segment that has been yielding more profits proportionally to Amazon is the web services, represented by AWS (Amazon Web Services) and it indicates a trend of investment in cloud platforms and infrastructure (cloud platform) that has a promising future ahead, as it is very profitable and is still only at the beginning. Along with this trend is the International segment, which has a deficit and should be reformulated.

Thus, the bet of large investors seems to be linked to this trend of revenue growth in the AWS segment, making sense to stay in the business to see it be successful and reap increasing profits from this company, today, as it has happened, and later on.

5.5 Mergers and acquisitions

Amazon.com has acquired eighty-two companies since 1998. Since 1999, more than US$ 20 billion have been spent on acquiring at least twenty companies, among others whose figures have not been disclosed. Table 5.7 shows these twenty companies and their respective purchase values.

Table 5.7 Amazon's acquisitions of companies

Acquired company	*Date*	*Value in millions of US$*
CloudEndure	Jan 8, 2019	200
PillPack	June 28, 2018	1000
Ring	Feb 27, 2018	1000
GameSparks	July 8, 2017	10
Whole Foods Market	June 16, 2017	13,700
Souq	Mar 27, 2017	580
harvest.ai	Jan 9, 2017	20
Elemental Technologies	Sept 3, 2015	500
Annapurna Labs	Jan 22, 2015	370
Twitch	Aug 25, 2014	970
Evi	Apr 17, 2013	26
Kiva Systems	Mar 19, 2012	775
Quidsi	Nov 8, 2010	545
BuyVIP	Oct 7, 2010	80
Zappos	July 22, 2009	1,200
LOVEFiLM	Feb 4, 2008	260
Joyo.com	Aug 19, 2004	75
Convergence Corporation	Oct 4, 1999	23
Accept.Com	June 11, 1999	101
Alexa.com	May 23, 1999	250
Totals in billion US$		21,685

Source: https://www.crunchbase.com/organization/amazon/acquisitions/acquisitions_list#section-acquisitions

The company that acquired the most value was Whole Foods Market, purchased on June 16, 2017, for US$ 13.7 billion. Several other companies were also acquired in the cloud sector, such as CloudEndure, purchased on January 8, 2019, for US$ 200 million. PillPack and Ring were acquired in January and February 2018, respectively, for US$ 1 billion each.

Acquisitions of companies are fully in line with maximizing shareholder value because it aims to gather in a single corporation the assets previously dispersed and that will help to produce greater wealth, on larger scales.

Regarding industry 4.0, attention is drawn to the recent decision by Amazon to enter a strategic partnership with Volkswagen to create an "industry cloud", whose function would be to harmonize the different software systems used by the German automaker, increasing its productivity. Today Volkswagen works with several independent programs and this creates confusion and little synergy. This strategic partnership would also aim to connect the thousands of suppliers and data set generated to automaker's plants to receive orders and work with greater uniformity (Minkoff, 2019).

However, both acquisitions, mergers and strategic partnerships, still have a direct influence on the search for greater productivity and, therefore, greater profitability for the business and fulfill the willingness to create more value for the shareholder.

5.6 Origin of managers

The trajectory of the directors from the Amazon Board of Directors is linked to industry and education, mainly to the technology and communication industry. Most of them are on more than one Board and have a solid academic background, having studied at important North American universities. CEO and founder Jeff Bezos is on 4 boards and graduated from Princeton University.

Table 5.8 shows the trajectory of the directors, their academic background (of those who had published data) and their path through companies, boards, and universities.

Virtually none of the nine directors (out of the ten members of the Board of Directors), analyzed here, have worked in financial institutions. On the

Table 5.8 Amazon Managers – Board of Directors

Board of Directors	*No. of Boards*	*Organizations in which they participated*
Jeffrey P. Bezos Founder, President Chairman of the Board – 1994 Chief Executive Officer – 1996	4 Amazon, A9, Basecamp, Kosmix	D. E. Shaw & Co., Graduated from Princeton University B.Sc. in Electrical Engineering and Computer Science, 1986
Tom A. Alberg Director – 1996	8 Amazon, vLinx, SNUPI Technologies, ShopIgniter, Technet	Madrona Venture Group, LLC; LIN Broadcasting Corporation; McCaw Cellular Communications, Inc., AT&T Wireless Services, Perkins Coie
John Seely Brown Director Independent Co – Chairman – Deloitte's Center for the Edge	8 Deloitte, Amazon, CBRITE, MacArthur Foundation	Xerox Corporation, Palo Alto Research Center, Institute for Research on Learning, American Academy of Arts and Sciences, National Academy of Education. London Business School, Honorary Doctor of Science in Economics
Jamie S. Gorelick Director – 2012	2 VeriSign, Amazon	Wilmer Cutler Pickering Hale and Dorr LLP, Deputy Attorney General of the United States, General Counsel of the Department of Defense, Assistant to the Secretary of Energy, VeriSign, Inc. United Technologies Corporation

Daniel P. Huttenlocher Director – 2016	3 Cornell Tech, Amazon, Corning Incorporated	Dean and Vice Provost, Cornell Tech at Cornell University, Corning Incorporated, Xerox Palo Alto Research Center Ph.D. in Computer Science, M.Sc. in Electrical Engineering – MIT, B.A. in Computer Science and Psychology - University of Michigan
Jonathan J. Rubinstein Director – 2010	2 Qualcomm, Amazon	Bridgewater Associates, LP, Hewlett-Packard Company ("HP"), Senior Vice President at Apple Inc., National Academy of Engineering, B.Sc. and M. Eng. in Electrical Engineering from Cornell University and an M.Sc. in Computer Science from Colorado State University
Thomas O. Ryder Director – 2002	5 Amazon, Quad/Graphics, RPX Corporation, Starwood Hotels & Resorts	Reader's Digest Association, Inc., American Express, Interval Leisure Group, Inc., RPX Corporation, Quad/Graphics, Inc., Starwood Hotels & Resorts Worldwide, Inc., Virgin Mobile USA, Inc.
Patricia Q. Stonesifer Director – 1997	1 Amazon	Martha's Table, Board of Regents of the Smithsonian Institution, Bill and Melinda Gates Foundation, Microsoft Corporation
Wendell P. Weeks Director – 2016	5 Merck & Co., Inc., Corning Incorporated, Corning Museum of Glass, Corning Foundation, Amazon	Corning Incorporated, Merck & Co., Inc., Graduate of Lehigh University and Master of Business Administration from Harvard University as a Baker Scholar.

Source: Amazon annual report, 2017, p.5 and www.crunchbase.com

contrary, the trend was to have followed academic education in the field of exact sciences at reputable universities, such as Harvard, Princeton, MIT, Cornell, and the London Business School, and to have participated in manufacturing companies, such as AT&T, Merck & Co. Inc., and Hewlett-Packard, among others.

This fact reinforces the idea that currently the worlds of industry, universities, and finance have been merging more and more, producing a financialized mentality in all participants. At Amazon, the intertwining of its executives, directors, and leaders with the world of finance is apparently small, although its largest investors are major financial institutions, as we saw earlier. However, in management, the appearance is that scientists, engineers, developers, and other employees have a degree of influence that they appear not to have in other companies.

5.7 Compensation paid to executives

Amazon had a policy of paying compensation to executives up to 2017 that was quite different from the other three technology companies previously studied, such as Apple, Google, and Microsoft. In that year, compensation paid to the executives in the millions (CEOs received US$ 145 million at Apple in 2016, US$ 199 million at Google in 2016, US$ 25 million at Microsoft in 2018), but at Amazon, the amounts were much lower, at least until 2017. The month of December 2017 was the time cut that we used to freeze most of the data that appear in this research work. Other data have been stretched to 2020 or even 2021 in a few cases. Our intention is to discuss in the appendix what the situation of these ten companies is in 2022 almost five years after the 2017 data. The data in Table 5.9 show the compensation paid to Amazon executives in 2017 and give the impression that the compensation at this company is much lower than at the other companies analyzed here. In 2017, they were much lower, but from 2018 and in the following years of 2019 and 2020, the amounts paid to executives grew enormously, characterizing Amazon as a company that pays millionaire compensation to its executives, as almost all the other companies described in this book. Even though founder Jeff Bezos continues to earn US$1.6 million a year (Salary.com, 2017b). Table 5.9 shows the data on compensations to executives at Amazon in 2017.

Earning very modest salaries compared to the companies studied in this work, CEO Jeff Bezos received US$ 81,840.00 in cash, US$ 0 in shares, US$ 1.6 million in other compensations, for a total of US$ 1,681,840.00. Other executives received higher salaries in cash, from US$ 160,000 to US$ 175,000, but without gains in shares and very little in other remunerations, which were from US$ 3200 to US$ 19,447, having received total compensation which was US$163,200 for Brian Olsavsky, US$ 178,500 for Jeffrey Blackburn, US$ 184,700 for Jeffrey Wilke, and US$ 194,400 for Andrew Jassy (Salary.com, 2017a). However, from 2018 onward, Amazon significantly increased executives' earnings, reaching the same levels as other companies, although still below Apple and Google.

In 2018, Andrew Jassy earned US$ 19.7 million in total compensation, Jeffrey Wilke also earned US$ 19.7 million, and Jeffrey Blackburn earned US$ 10.3 million (Salary.com, 2018). In 2019, Jeffrey Blackburn received

Table 5.9 Compensation payments to executives. Amazon – annual salary in US$ – 2017.

Compensation to executives	*Total in cash*	*Stock options*	*Others*	*Total compensations*
Jeffrey P. Bezos Chief Executive Officer, Director	81,840	0	1,600,000	1,681,840
Andrew R. Jassy CEO Amazon Web Services	175,000	0	19,447	194,447
Jeffrey A. Wilke CEO Worldwide Consumer	175,000	0	9781	184,781
Brian T. Olsavsky SVP and Chief Financial Officer	160,000	0	3200	163,200
Jeffrey M. Blackburn SVP, Business Development	175,000	0	3500	178,500

Source: https://www1.salary.com/AMAZON-COM-INC-Executive-Salaries.html

US$ 57.7 million, of which US$ 57.5 million was in stock options (Salary.com, 2019). In 2020, executive Andrew Jassy earned US$35.8 million, of which US$ 35.6 million was through stock options; David Clark received US$ 46.2 million in total compensation, of which US$ 46.1 million was in stock options; Brian Olsavsky and David Zapolsky both received US$17.1 million, of which US$ 17 million was in stock options (Salary.com, 2020a, 2020b and 2020c). That is, even though CEO and founder Jeff Bezos continues to receive a mere US$ 1.6 million annually, his main executives have been receiving millionaire values, equating these gains with those of the other executives of the ten largest companies in market capitalization analyzed here, with rare exceptions in this financialization indicator.

5.8 Dividend payments to shareholders and stock repurchases

Similar to Google, Amazon has not been paying dividends to shareholders. The company has also not repurchased shares since 2012, when it spent US$ 960 million and repurchased 5.3 million shares (Kilgore, 2019). In the first quarter of 2018, the company announced that it would not repurchase shares for twenty-four quarters, that is, six years (Kilgore, 2019). Table 5.10 shows that Amazon does not pay dividends neither stock repurchases.

Amazon's conduct in this indicator is different from the main companies we studied. Google also operates similarly in terms of not paying dividends, as we have seen. Furthermore, we will see that Berkshire Hathaway and Facebook are two other companies that have also not been paying dividends to shareholders, although Facebook authorizes stock repurchases. The other six companies pay dividends, as we will see in the next chapters.

Table 5.10 Dividend payments to Amazon's shareholders and stock repurchases

	2014	*2015*	*2016*	*2017*	*2018*
Dividend payments in billions of US$	0	0	0	0	0
Stock Repurchases in billions of US$	0	0	0	0	0
Total in billions of US$	0	0	0	0	0

Sources: https://www.nasdaq.com/symbol/amzn/financials?query=income-statement; https://www.dividend.com/dividend-stocks/services/department-stores/amzn-amazoncom-inc/ and Kilgore (2019)

This is an important aspect of the discussion of financialization indicators. This is because one of the theses is that financialization would basically be the predominance of maximizing shareholder value and it would materialize through dividend payments to shareholders and stock repurchases, which would force an artificial increase in share prices. And when there is absolutely no such thing being practiced by the company, would we say that it is not a financialized company?

There is already one indicator that Amazon does not fit in, which is dividend payments and stock repurchases that do not exist, at least for now. In addition to the fact that its directors have not passed through the world of finance, until now, we could say that Amazon.com, Inc. is one of the least financialized companies when analyzed by the indicators we used.

5.9 Employee salaries

In this financialization indicator, Amazon does not differ much from its counterparts Apple, Google, Microsoft, and others that we will see later. Several jobs have lower wages than the average of all North American wages, as previously mentioned in this work, which was around US$ 61,000 per year in 2017 (Fontenot et al., 2018). Table 5.11 shows a list of eleven professions, their starting salaries, at the end of their careers and on average.

We can say that most professions have an average salary below the average of all-American salaries. Starting with a cashier, who has a starting salary of US$ 15,825 and on average earns US$ 22,109 per year. This category also includes computer technicians, fashion stylist assistants, associate auditors, and even call center managers, who all earn less than the average salary for all North American ethnic groups. Amazon wages were considered low by US congressmen, such as Senator Bernie Sanders from the "Democratic Party", who introduced a bill called the "Stop Bezos Act" and which aims to tax companies that are wealthy and have government aid, as a way to compensate for the low wages they pay their employees. The act was dubbed "BEZOS",

Table 5.11 Amazon. Annual salary in US$ – 2018

Professional	*Minimum*	*Maximum*	*Average*
Cashier	15,825	28,393	22,109
Computer Technician	20,439	50,640	35,539
Ambassador	21,512	49,131	35,321
Fashion Stylist Assistant	23,941	55,346	39,643
Assistant Customer Service Manager	25,301	66,810	46,055
Associate Auditor	26,927	49,024	37,975
Call Center Manager	30,278	84,813	57,545
Business Analyst	31,627	123,291	77,459
Data Engineer	90,522	162,708	126,615
Operations Development Engineer	97,715	182,732	140,223
Chief Operating Officer – (COO)	157,318	455,310	306,314

Source: https://www.payscale.com/research/US/Employer=Amazon.com_Inc/Salary/by_Job

the CEO of Amazon, standing for his initials that means "Bad Employers by Zeroing Out Subsidies", a provocation made by the Vermont senator and former Democratic party precandidate in the 2016 and 2020 presidential elections (Bhattarai, 2018).

In fact, wages are not good, but if we analyze the retail segment, Amazon pays US$ 15 an hour as a minimum amount for its employees, while its direct competitors pay even less, such as Target, which pays US$ 13 an hour, Walmart US$ 11 an hour, and Costco US$ 14 an hour (Taylor, 2019). They are low wages compared to a dishwasher in any pizzeria or American restaurant, without the slightest qualification, who can earn from US$ 8 to US$ 9 per hour.

When we compare workers' wages to the total CEO earnings, we see a different situation at Amazon. Not so much because salaries are higher than at other companies, but because CEO Jeff Bezos received very little total compensation, just over US$ 1.6 million, which greatly narrowed the gap between the CEO earnings and employee salaries, as shown in Table 5.12.

The difference between the CEO's earnings and a cashier's salary, for example, was "only" 106 times compared to each other. Compared to the Call Center Manager, the average difference was 29 times, and compared to the Chief Operating Officer (COO), the average difference was only 5 times the earnings of the CEO and the other executive.

At Amazon, this indicator showed that the differences between salary ranges are much smaller than at other companies, such as Apple and Google, which showed distances between 8 and 11,000 times between the CEO's earnings and the salaries of some employees. This is not so much because the salaries are good, but because of the low compensation that was paid to the CEO and shareholder Jeff Bezos, as we saw earlier. However, if we take the compensation paid to other executives (not Bezos) in 2018, 2019, and 2020, we would see many more differences in the ratio between executives and the rest or employees' gains.

Table 5.12 Ratio between employee salaries and total CEO earnings – Jeffrey P. Bezos in 2017 – US$ 1,681,840.00

Employees X CEO	*Minimum*	*Maximum*	*Average*
Cashier	106	59	76
Computer Technician	82	33	47
Ambassador	78	34	47
Fashion Stylist Assistant	70	30	42
Assistant Customer Service Manager	66	25	36
Associate Auditor	62	34	44
Call Center Manager	55	19	29
Business Analyst	53	13	21
Data Engineer	18	10	13
Operations Development Engineer	17	9	12
Chief Operating Officer – (COO)	10	4	5

Source: Authors, based on the values of the compensation table paid to the CEO and the workers' salary table

5.10 Employment

Amazon has been the fastest-growing company in terms of number of employees in the past decade. Particularly from 2014 to 2015, when it more than doubled its number of employees, going from 154,000 to more than 230,000. In just a decade, the company went from 17,000 workers in 2007 to 566,000 in 2017, a growth of 3,300%, which is the largest of all companies studied by us in this work. Figure 5.1 shows the level of employment at Amazon.

Most of the employees are temporary or seasonal, as demonstrated by the hiring of thousands of seasonal delivery drivers in 2018 to save costs (Betz, 2018b). In 2018, around 100,000 seasonal workers were hired, which was 20,000 less than expected as "robots are more efficient" and are gradually replacing workers in simple functions such as picking up products, for example, among others (Betz, 2018a).

Despite this precarious movement of work being in full force, there is also the hiring of more qualified personnel but on a smaller scale. Since the end of 2018, the East Coast Hub, located in Nashville, Tennessee, USA, has been expanded with the hiring of 5,000 new workers (Aycock, 2018). In April 2019, 800 workers were hired in Austin, Texas, in an expansion program for their technology hub, which has opened vacancies for software and hardware engineers, scientific research and cloud computing, their current favorite projects (Betz, 2019).

In summary, we can see that the expansion of employment at Amazon is twofold. On one hand, thousands of unskilled, seasonal, low-cost, low-paid workers, and on the other, a minority of skilled, better-paid workers related to cloud infrastructure areas, which are more profitable for the company.

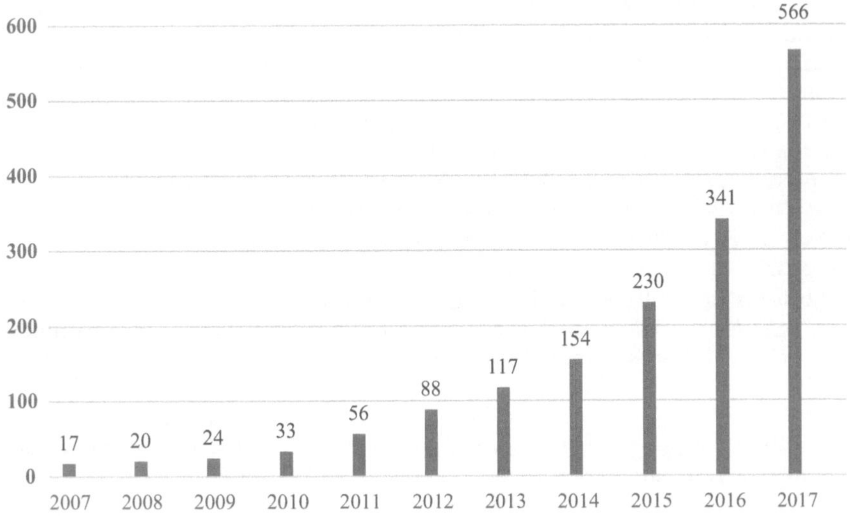

Figure 5.1 Evolution of employment at Amazon – 2007 to 2017

By participating in Platform Capitalism, Amazon tries in every way to extract value from its business, which is obvious as its mission is to create value for investors, regardless of whether through cloud platform experts or seasonal drivers who will spend their holidays making deliveries to the giant that is the second-largest private employer in the United States, second only to Walmart (Schlosser, 2018).

From the point of view of the financialization process, there is no contradiction between employing a lot and practicing the policy of maximizing shareholder value as the bulk of contracts, as we have seen, are based on a policy of maximum cost savings and precarious work, essential aspects for the occurrence of this economic process. Volkswagen, for example, more than doubled its hiring in a short period of time (Carmo, 2017), in a very similar way to Amazon, but the jobs generated were not of quality, substantial remuneration, labor rights, etc. On the contrary, jobs were created outside Germany or developed countries, mainly in China, in joint ventures that pay low wages, maintain harsh working conditions, and thus, crown the policy of maximizing the shareholder value and financialization.

References

Amazon.com Inc. 2017. *Annual Report* 2017. Available at: https://www.annualreports.com/Company/amazoncom-inc and https://www.sec.gov/Archives/edgar/data/1018724/000101872418000005/amzn-20171231x10k.htm

Amazon.com Inc. 2018. *Annual Report* 2018. Available at: https://www.annualreports.com/Company/amazoncom-inc and https://www.sec.gov/Archives/edgar/data/1018724/000101872419000004/amzn-20181231x10k.htm

Amazon.com Inc. 2019. *Annual Report* 2019. Available at: https://www.annualreports.com/Company/amazoncom-inc and https://www.sec.gov/Archives/edgar/data/1018724/000101872420000004/amzn-20191231x10k.htm

Amazon.com Inc. 2020. *Annual Report* 2020. Available at: https://www.annualreports.com/Company/amazoncom-inc; https://www.sec.gov/Archives/edgar/data/1018724/000101872421000004/amzn-20201231.htm

Aycock, J. (13 Nov 2018). Amazon to set operations hub in Nashville, with 5,000 jobs. Available at: https://seekingalpha.com/news/3408966-amazon-set-operations-hub-nashville-5000-jobs?dr=1#email_link. Accessed 11/13/2018.

Betz, B. (2 Nov 2018a). Citi: Amazon hiring fewer holiday workers for first time. Available at: https://seekingalpha.com/news/3404882-citi-amazon-hiring-fewer-holiday-workers-first-time?dr=1#email_link. Accessed 11/03/2018.

Betz, B. (5 Nov 2018b). Amazon hiring thousands of holiday delivery drivers. Available at: https://seekingalpha.com/news/3405470-amazon-hiring-thousands-holiday-delivery-drivers?dr=1#email_link. Accessed 11/05/2018.

Betz, B. (28 Mar 2019). Amazon adding 800 jobs in Austin. Available at: https://seekingalpha.com/news/3446483-amazon-adding-800-jobs-austin?dr=1#email_link. Accessed 03/28/2019.

Bhattarai, A. (5 Sept 2018). Bernie Sanders takes aim at wealthy companies that don´t pay workers a living wage. Available at: https://www.pressherald.com/2018/09/05/bernie-sanders-takes-aim-at-wealthy-companies-that-dont-pay-workers-a-living-wage/. Accessed 03/30/2019.

Carmo, M.J. 2017. Análise do processo de financeirização do setor automotivo. *Dissertação de Mestrado apresentada ao programa de Pós-Graduação em Engenharia de Produção da Universidade Federal de São Carlos*- UFSCar, 135 f., Disponível em: https://repositorio.ufscar.br/handle/ufscar/8917

Fontenot, K., Semega, J., and Kollar, M., 2018. Income and poverty in the United States 2017. Available at: https://www.census.gov/content/dam/Census/library/publications/2018/demo/p60-263.pdf. Accessed 10/06/2019.

Kilgore, T. (1 Feb 2019). Amazon buys back zero shares again, and stock keeps outperforming. Available at: https://www.marketwatch.com/story/amazon-buys-back-zero-shares-again-and-stock-keeps-outperforming-2019-02-01. Accessed 04/30/2019.

Minkoff, Y. (27 Mar 2019). Amazon, Volkswagen partnership for 'industry cloud'. Available at: https://seekingalpha.com/news/3445942-amazon-volkswagen-partnership-industry-cloud?dr=1#email_link. Accessed 03/27/2019.

Nasdaq. 2018. Amazon institutional holdings. Available at: https://www.nasdaq.com/symbol/amzn/institutional-holdings. Accessed 07/28/2018.

Salary.com. 2017a. Amazon executive salaries. Available at: https://www1.salary.com/AMAZON-COM-INC-Executive-Salaries.html. Accessed 01/12/2019.

Salary.com. 2017b. Amazon executive salaries. Jeffrey P. Bezos. Available at: https://www.salary.com/tools/executive-compensation-calculator/jeffrey-p-bezos-salary-bonus-stock-options-for-amazon-com-inc. Accessed 11/23/2019.

Salary.com. 2018. Amazon executive salaries. Available at: https://www1.salary.com/AMAZON-COM-INC-Executive-Salaries.html. Accessed 12/08/2019.

Salary.com. 2019. Amazon executive salaries. Available at: https://www.salary.com/tools/executive-compensation-calculator/amazon-com-inc-executive-salaries?-year=2019. Accessed 09/10/2020.

Salary.com. 2020a. Amazon executive salaries. Available at: https://www.salary.com/tools/executive-compensation-calculator/andrew-r-jassy-salary-bonus-stock-options-for-amazon-com-inc?year=2020. Accessed 02/22/2022.

Salary.com. 2020b. Amazon executive salaries. Available at: https://www.salary.com/tools/executive-compensation-calculator/david-h-clark-salary-bonus-stock-options-for-amazon-com-inc?year=2020. Accessed 02/22/2022.

Salary.com. 2020c. Amazon executive salaries. Available at: https://www.salary.com/tools/executive-compensation-calculator/brian-t-olsavsky-salary-bonus-stock-options-for-amazon-com-inc?year=2020. Accessed 02/22/2022.

Schlosser, K. (1 Feb 2018). Amazon now employs 566,000 people worldwide - a 66 percent jump from a year ago. Available at: https://www.geekwire.com/2018/amazon-now-employs-566000-people-worldwide-66-percent-jump-year-ago/. Accessed 07/29/2018.

Srnicek, N. 2016. *Platform Capitalism*. Cambridge: Polity Press. Available at: https://www.wiley.com/en-au/Platform+Capitalism-p-9781509504862

Taylor, K. (11 Apr 2019). Jeff Bezos called for Amazon's competitors to raise their minimum wage. Here's how retail rivals like Walmart, Target, and Costco stack up on worker pay. Available at: https://www.businessinsider.com/amazon-costco-walmart-target-compare-minimum-wage-2019-4. Accessed 05/12/2020.

6 Berkshire Hathaway

Berkshire Hathaway was established as a result of a series of mergers over the last century. Mergers began in 1923 between a textile company, Valley Falls in Rhode Island, founded in 1839, with the Berkshire Cotton Company in Adams, Massachusetts, which was founded in 1889. This merger resulted in the Berkshire Fine Spinning Associates. In 1955, the Berkshire Fine Spinning Associates merged with the Hathaway Manufacturing Company, which was founded in 1888 in New Bedford, Massachusetts (Warren Buffett Archive, 2022). From then onward, the Berkshire Hathaway we know today was established.

Berkshire Hathaway Inc. is a holding company that has subsidiaries involved in many business activities.

> The most important of these are insurance businesses conducted on both a primary basis and a reinsurance basis, a freight rail transportation business and a group of utility and energy generation and distribution businesses. Berkshire also owns and operates a large number of other businesses engaged in a variety of activities, as identified herein. Berkshire is domiciled in the state of Delaware, and its corporate headquarters are located in Omaha, Nebraska.
>
> (Berkshire Hathaway *Annual Report*, 2017, p.33)

According to the Annual Report,

> Berkshire's operating businesses are managed on an unusually decentralized basis. There are essentially no centralized or integrated business functions (such as sales, marketing, purchasing, legal or human resources) and there is minimal involvement by Berkshire's corporate headquarters in the day-to-day business activities of the operating businesses. Berkshire's corporate senior management team participates in and is ultimately responsible for significant capital allocation decisions, investment activities and the selection of the Chief Executive to head each of the operating businesses. It also is responsible for establishing and monitoring Berkshire's corporate governance practices, including, but not

DOI: 10.4324/9781003309536-6

limited to, communicating the appropriate "tone at the top" messages to its employees and associates, monitoring governance efforts, including those at the operating businesses, and participating in the resolution of governance-related issues as needed.

(Berkshire Hathaway *Annual Report* 2017, p.33)

Berkshire Hathaway was the fifth company with the highest market capitalization on December 31, 2017, valued at more than US$ 400 billion. It invests 43.08% of its capital, 27.11% in technology, 14.34% in noncyclical consumption, and 7% in industry in the financial sector. At the end of 2018, it invested in forty-nine companies, such as Apple, Coca Cola, American Express, Bank of America, General Motors, Visa, among other very important companies in the US and global economy (Nasdaq, 2019a).

Although it owns equity held by Warren Buffet, known as the "Oracle of Omaha", one of the richest men in the world, known for his forecasts and famous for his good investments, the Holding is, in turn, a product of combined capital, among others, for the "Big Three" of investment funds, which are Vanguard Group, BlackRock, and State Street Corp, as we will see later (Fichtner et al., 2017).

We will discuss financialization indicators at Berkshire Hathaway later on.

6.1 Comparison between the sources of profitability

The holding company Berkshire Hathaway operates insurance, financial services, rail and energy, investments, derivatives, etc. Table 6.1 shows the company's revenues in billions of dollars, from 2013 to 2017 and divided by segment. It presents the total revenues and revenues by segment, in addition to the percentage that each segment represents of return on revenues. We reached this percentage by dividing the revenues of each segment by the total revenues, which can be seen in Table 6.1.

Before any analysis, we have to remember that

the net earnings in 2017 included approximately $29.1 billion attributable to a one-time net benefit from the enactment of the Tax Cuts and Jobs Act ("TCJA") on December 22, 2017 (…) this benefit included approximately US$ 29.6 billion related to a one-time non-cash reduction of our net deferred income tax liabilities that arose from the reduction in the statutory U.S. corporate income tax rate from 35% to 21%.

(Berkshire Hathaway *Annual Report* 2017, p.K-32)

This law enacted by Donald Trump greatly benefitted the Berkshire coffers, as it reduced income tax obligations from 35% to 21%, saving billions of dollars, resulting in a higher profit. Here we can recall, incidentally, the thesis of Fligstein (2001), that markets are social institutions, and that they are strongly influenced by government forces that can create, maintain, stabilize, or destabilize,

Table 6.1 Berkshire Hathaway's revenue by segment

	2013	*2014*	*2015*	*2016*	*2017*
Revenue in billions of US$ by segment	182,412	194,699	210,943	223,604	242,137
Premium insurance	36,684	41,253	41,294	45,881	60,597
% return on revenue	20.11	21.18	19.57	20.51	25.02
Service sales and revenue	92,993	97,097	107,001	119,489	125,963
% return on revenue	50.97	49.87	50.72	53.43	52.02
Railways and energy	34,757	40,690	40,004	37,542	39,943
% return on revenue	19.05	20.89	18.96	16.78	16.49
Interest, dividends, and other investment income	5196	5052	5357	4725	5144
% return on revenue	2.84	2.59	2.53	2.11	2.12
Finance and financial products sales and service revenues and interest and dividend income	6109	6526	6940	7663	8362
% return on revenue	3.34	3.35	3.28	3.42	3.45
Investments and derivatives	6673	4081	10,347	8,304	2128
% return on revenue	3.65	2.09	4.9	3.71	0.87

Source: Berkshire Hathaway *Annual Reports*, 2014, p.46; 2015, p.38; 2016, p.32; 2017, p.K-31 (63)

and even close a business through institutional decisions, regulation, control, prohibition, etc. In this case, by means of a legislative procedure (initiated by the executive), there was a positive influence on the profitability of the business, because the tax expenses were lower, a result directly created by the state and not an increase in revenues through more sales, higher prices, etc., strictly through the market. Here, a legal decision was needed to rearrange the profits of many of the giants of American capitalism upward.

Returning to the analysis of the sources of profitability, as expected in this financialized economic environment, the item on sales and service revenues reached more than 50% of revenues in all the years analyzed. Premium insurance represents 20% to 25% of total revenues. Railroad and energy revenues represent around 20% of total revenues and gains from dividends and interest, investments, derivatives, etc., range from 2% to 4% of total revenues, having reached 10.7% in 2015.

That is, financial services, the sale of all types of insurance, are increasingly profitable for the holding while rents from railroads, utilities, and energy are stagnating at less than 20%, as in 2013, 2015, 2016, and 2017. This advantage of financial activities in the business is one of the characteristics of financialization, although here we are dealing with a holding with an eminently financial character. There would be no contradiction in a financial company obtaining more than half of its revenues from financial activities, but as Erturk (2016) observed even in banks and financial companies, the financialization process is a developing movement. Erturk clarifies that the services charged by banks, such as restrictions on withdrawals and extracts, which are charged separately, among other "products" that are not part of the core

Table 6.2 Share price performance. US$ 100 invested in 2012

	2012	*2013*	*2014*	*2015*	*2016*	*2017*
Berkshire Hathaway Inc.	100.00	132.00	168.00	147.00	182.00	221.00
S&P 500 Property & Casualty Insurance Index	100.00	138.00	160.00	175.00	203.00	248.00
S&P 500	100.00	132.00	151.00	153.00	171.00	208.00

Source: Berkshire Hathaway *Annual Report* 2017, p.K-30 (62)

business (funding and loans) are in full expansion and increasingly occupy an important position contribution to the business as a whole.

We see in the case of Berkshire Hathaway that its financial investments, sales, services, and insurance are much more profitable than its profits from productive activities, such as railroads, utilities, and electricity. This is a very prominent financialization indicator when we analyze these financial services holdings.

Another aspect of financialization at Berkshire is its appreciation on the stock exchanges. The holding's shares appreciated very well over a five-year period, from 2012 to 2017. For every US$ 100.00 invested in December 2012, its shares rose 121%, resulting in a value of US$ 221.00 in 2017. The S&P index 500 went from US$ 100.00 to US$ 208.00, an increase of 108% in five years. The S&P 500 Property & Casualty Insurance index went from US$ 100.00 in 2012 to US$ 248.00 in 2017, up 148%. Table 6.2 shows these numbers.

That is, the valuation of Berkshire´s shares on the stock exchanges averaged 24% per year or more, while Berkshire's revenues had less than 10% growth year by year. In 2013, total revenues went from US$ 182.412 billion to US$ 242.137 billion in 2017, a 33% increase in five years, while the performance of the share price was 121% in appreciation, well above the growth in revenues. This is also an aspect of financialization, the relative autonomy that financial capital acquires in relation to productive capital, much less profitable than stock exchanges and financial activities, such as services, insurance, investments, derivatives, and other financial products that appreciate very quickly.

6.2 Shareholding composition

As in the other companies analyzed in this work, Berkshire Hathaway's shareholding structure is similar and presents the same large investors in its shareholder group. The highlight goes to "the Big Three" of North American investment funds, the Vanguard Group, BlackRock Inc., and State Street Corp, which held more than 300 million shares at a value of more than US$ 60 billion. Table 6.3 shows the fifteen largest shareholders of Berkshire Hathaway on 2018 (Nasdaq, 2019a).

Having a total of 2,278 institutional shareholders, comprising 891,441,745 shares, or 65.41% of more than 1.3 billion type B shares issued (the shares

Table 6.3 Berkshire Hathaway's largest shareholders as of September 30, 2018

Financial groups	*Shares held*	*Value in thousands of US$*	*% of institutional shares*
Vanguard Group Inc.	132,051,625	26,505,402	14.81
BlackRock Inc.	104,141,871	20,903,356	11.68
State Street Corp.	81,330,866	16,324,731	9.12
Bill & Melinda Gates Foundation Trust	62,078,974	12,460,492	6.96
Geode Capital Management LLC	21,790,965	4,373,882	2.44
Northern Trust Corp.	19,839,001	3,982,084	2.22
Bank of New York Mellon Corp.	16,212,788	3,254,231	1.81
FMR LLC	16,174,656	3,246,577	1.81
Eagle Capital Management LLC	9,468,066	1,900,430	1.06
Morgan Stanley	9,372,004	1,881,149	1.05
Bank of America Corp/DE	8,850,307	1,776,434	0.99
AllianceBernstein L.P.	8,149,773	1,635,822	0.91
Dimensional Fund Advisors LP	8,140,690	1,633,999	0.91
Goldman Sachs Group Inc.	8,135,592	1,632,976	0.91
Boston Partners	8,074,034	1,620,620	0.90
Total (15 biggest shareholders)	513,811,212	103,132,185	57.63%

Source: https://www.nasdaq.com/symbol/brk.b/institutional-holdings

we are analyzing here), Berkshire also has a large concentration of shares. The fifteen largest shareholders held more than 513 million shares in 2018, 57.63% of the shares that are in the hands of institutional investors. The first three hold more than 300 million shares, more than 35% of the shares of institutional investors. These figures show a greater concentration than in the other companies analyzed. The Vanguard Group alone, for example, held 132 million shares in September 2018, representing 10% of all shares issued and almost 15% of the shares in the hands of institutional investors.

These data reveal an inescapable reality of today; that of the enormous concentration and reconcentration (Davis, 2008) of the shares in gigantic investment funds, which congregate the bulk of the resources and decision-making power in these organizations, confirming what has already been widely demonstrated throughout this work.

6.3 Shareholding acquisitions

The groups that most acquired Berkshire Hathaway shares were the same banks and investment funds that are present in their shareholding structure. One of those that acquired more shares was the Alliance Bernstein L.P fund, which bought more than 2.3 million shares, increasing its participation by 41.59%. The Bill and Melinda Gates Foundation Trust acquired the largest absolute number of shares, 8.5 million, increasing their shares in the company by 15.88%. Vanguard Group bought 3 million shares and State Street Corp 2.4 million shares, as shown in Table 6.4 (Nasdaq, 2019b).

Table 6.4 Groups that most acquired Berkshire Hathaway shares on September 30, 2018

Financial groups	*Acquired shares*	*% of change (+)*
Vanguard Group Inc.	3,037,951	2.36
BlackRock Inc.	488,864	0.47
State Street Corp.	2,496,472	3.17
Bill & Melinda Gates Foundation Trust	8,509,002	15.88
Geode Capital Management LLC	395,933	1.85
Bank of New York Mellon Corp	49,917	0.31
FMR LLC	1,182,812	7.89
AllianceBernstein L.P.	2,394,031	41.59
Dimensional Fund Advisors LP	429,745	5.57
Schwab Charles Investment Management Inc.	269,932	3.64

Source: https://www.nasdaq.com/symbol/brk.b/institutional-holdings/increased

Table 6.5 Groups that sold the most shares in Berkshire Hathaway on September 30, 2018

Financial groups	*Sold shares*	*% of change (−)*
Northern Trust Corp.	90,148	0.45
Eagle Capital Management LLC	115,297	1.2
Morgan Stanley	904,161	8.8
Bank of America Corp/DE	70,744	0.79
Goldman Sachs Group Inc.	197,062	2.37
Boston Partners	143,099	1.74
Capital Research Global Investors	2,850,817	26.53
Ameriprise Financial Inc.	129,834	2.1
Tiaa Cref Investment Management LLC	181,356	2.97
New York State Common Retirement Fund	54,629	1

Source: https://www.nasdaq.com/symbol/brk.b/institutional-holdings/decreased

This is another typical case that demonstrates the financialization process, which is the growing participation of financial organizations in the shareholding structure of companies, buying, and selling shares, participating in their daily lives and strongly influencing the strategies of companies, also in Berkshire Hathaway.

6.4 Share sales

In the case of stock sales, there is nothing new concerning the other companies analyzed by us in this work, although the volume sold was lower than that purchased in the same period closed on 30/09/2018. Capital Research Global Investors sold the most shares, which sold 2.8 million shares and reduced its participation by 26.53%. Afterward, Morgan Stanley sold 904 thousand shares, decreasing its amount in the company's shares by 8.8%, as shown in Table 6.5 (Nasdaq, 2019c).

It is interesting to note that only these two large shareholders mentioned above sold shares in a significant volume in the period closed on September 30, 2018, and the rest of the ten largest sellers of shares reduced their positions very little, from 0.5% to 3%, which was not very substantial. The New York State Common Retirement Fund pension fund sold just 54,000 shares, with its stake in Berkshire Hathaway holding back just 1%. This fact also demonstrates financialization, in the sense of the short-termism that we have already discussed and that coexists perfectly well with the other long-term strategies, practiced by most investors.

6.5 Mergers and acquisitions

Berkshire Hathaway has in the acquisitions of companies one of its most outstanding characteristics, which is a very old business strategy. For the company

> there are four pillars that add value to Berkshire: (1) considerable autonomous acquisitions; (2) acquisitions that adjust to companies that we already own; (3) growth in domestic sales and margin improvement in our many and varied businesses; and (4) investment gains from our huge portfolio of stocks and bonds.

The 2017 annual report continues:

> In our search for new stand-alone businesses, the key qualities we seek are durable competitive strengths; able and high-grade management; good returns on the net tangible assets required to operate the business; opportunities for internal growth at attractive returns; and, finally, a sensible purchase price.
>
> (Berkshire Hathaway *Annual Report*, 2017, p.4)

Table 6.6 shows some of the acquisitions made by Berkshire over time (Crunchbase, 2018), totaling more than US$ 45 billion in just thirteen companies acquired and whose values have been disclosed. The total amount is certainly much higher.

As already mentioned in its annual report, Berkshire Hathaway seeks to buy solid companies in various sectors of the economy, including various manufacturing companies, unrelated to the insurance and financial businesses conducted decades ago by Warren Buffett, Howard Buffett, and Charles Munger.

Participation in traditional companies is commonplace, such as Coca-Cola, for example, where Berkshire holds 9.4% of the company; Apple, with a 3.3% stake; Delta Airlines, with a 7.4% stake, Southwest Airlines Co., with

Table 6.6 Berkshire Hathaway's acquisitions

Acquired company	*Date of purchase*	*Value in millions of US$*
Pilot Flying J	Oct 3, 2017	n/d
HomeServices of America	Jan 18, 2017	n/d
Medical Liability mutual insurance co	July 18, 2016	n/d
Precision Castparts	Aug 10, 2015	37,200
Detlev Louis Motorradvertriebs	Feb 20, 2015	450
Duracell	Nov 13, 2014	4700
Business Wire	Jan 18, 2006	n/d
CORT Business Services Corporation	Jan 14, 2000	467
NetJets	July 23, 1998	725
The Kansas Bankers Surety Co.	May 1, 1996	n/d
FlightSafety International	Oct 15, 1996	1,500
The Scott Fetzer Company	Oct 30, 1985	413
See's Candies	Jan 1, 1972	25
Total in billion US$		45,480

Source: https://www.crunchbase.com/organization/berkshire-hathaway-corp/acquisitions/acquisitions_list#section-acquisitions
*n/d: not disclosed

8.1%, Phillips 66 (energy), with 14.9% and General Motors, with a 3.2% stake (Berkshire Hathaway *Annual Report*, 2017, p.9).

While it invests in manufacturing and services companies, there is also a massive participation in others of a financial type, such as American Express (17.6% stake), Moody's Corporation (12.9%), Wells Fargo (9.9%), and Bank of America (6.8%), confirming the vocation of financial investments.

These holdings reflect what we have affirmed throughout our work that more and more manufacturing and production companies have their control associated with financial-type organizations, seeking to allocate their surplus capital and return consistent profits to their business. This is yet another characteristic of financialization, the formation of large economic groups that involve manufacturing companies, banks, investment funds, and other financial organizations.

The data reveal yet another confirmation of the financialization process in large companies and an investment reality that places Berkshire Hathaway as a major investor in several firms, but also a company that has large investors behind it, such as the "Big Three" mentioned: Vanguard, State Street, and BlackRock.

6.6 Origin of managers

Berkshire's small Board of Directors is made up of six people, starting with Warren Buffett, the president, and CEO. It is a group of "old school" managers, mainly from manufacturing companies. Coca-Cola, McDonald's, Columbia Pictures, Costco, and among others have integrated Berkshire Hathaway executives in recent years. Table 6.7 shows the members of the Board of Directors (Crunchbase, 2019).

Table 6.7 Berkshire Hathaway managers – 2018

Board of Directors	*No. of Boards they participate*	*Organizations in which they participated*
Warren Buffett President & CEO	2 The Kraft Heinz Company, Kraft Foods	Buffett Partnership, Susan Thompson Buffett Foundation, Bill & Melinda Gates Foundation Studied Business at University of Nebraska
Charles Munger Director – 1997 Vice-Chairman of the Board	4 Costco Wesco Financial Corporation Daily Journal Corporation Berkshire Hathaway	Costco, Wesco Financial Corporation, Daily Journal Corporation, Berkshire Hathaway
Donald Keough Director	6 Allen & Company, Convera Corporation, Berkshire Hathaway, IAC, YankeeNets, University of Notre Dame	The Coca-Cola Company, Columbia Pictures, Inc., McDonald's Corporation, The Washington Post Company, H. J. Heinz Company, The Home Depot. Honorary doctorates from University of Notre Dame, Creighton University, Emory University, Trinity University in Dublin, Clark University.
Howard Buffett Director	6 The Coca-Cola Company, Howard G. Buffett Foundation, Berkshire Hathaway, National Geographic, The ONE Campaign, Lindsay Corporation	The Coca-Cola Company, Buffett Farms, Howard G. Buffett Foundation, Berkshire Hathaway Inc., Lindsay Corporation
Sue Decker Director	4 Costco, Intel, LegalZoom, Berkshire Hathaway	Deck3 Ventures LLC, Save the Children, Harvard Business School (HBS), Yahoo!, Donaldson, Lufkin & Jenrette (DLJ), Pixar Animation Studios, The Stanford Institute for Economic Policy Research (SIEPR) B.S. from Tufts University, with a double major in computer science and economics, and an M.B.A. from HBS.

Ronald Olson Director	5 Washington Post, City National Bank, Berkshire Hathaway, Mayo Clinic, Edison International	Munger, Tolles & Olson LLP, Western Asset Trusts, RAND Corporation, California Institute of Technology, Nuclear Threat Initiative, Claremont University Center, BS from Drake University, JD from the University of Michigan, Diploma in Law from Oxford University, England

Source: www.crunchbase.com

They participate in several boards, but few financial ones, such as Ronald Olson, who is on the board of the City National Bank and Western Asset Trusts and Charles Munger, who is part of the Wesco Financial Corporation. Other than that, there is almost no participation in financial companies, apart from Berkshire itself.

The academic background is also extensive. Warren Buffett studied business at the University of Nebraska; Sue Decker graduated in Computer Science and Economics at Stanford and Tufts University; and Ronald Olson studied at the California Institute of Technology, Claremont University, Drake University, University of Michigan, and has a law degree from the University of Oxford, England.

Can we say that this educational trajectory helped to shape the business mentality geared to the dictates of financialization? Apparently, we can because even the directors studied computing, economics, and law. They have been in the insurance, investment, and divestment business for a long time, and do not have much experience in "production" itself. Nonetheless, they act in the way of maximizing value to the shareholder, acquiring companies, seeking to increase assets, and use them in the best way to better reward their investors. This is yet another indication that the trajectories alone today can no longer exemplify exactly what the conduct of the manager is, as the worlds of industry and finance increasingly merge together making decisions more homogeneous toward large shareholders' interests.

6.7 Compensation paid to executives

The compensation paid to executives is small compared to that paid by other companies analyzed by us in this work, at least for 2017. Except for Marc Hamburg, who received US$ 2.2 million in 2017, Warren Buffett and Charles Munger received only US$100,000, a symbolic value for the size and wealth of the company. See Table 6.8.

Table 6.8 Compensation payment to executives. Berkshire Hathaway

Annual salary in US$ – 2017				
Compensation to executives	*Total in cash*	*Stock options*	*Others*	*Total compensations*
Warren E. Buffett Chief Executive Officer/ Chairman of the Board	100,000	0	0	100,000
Marc D. Hamburg Senior Vice President/CFO	2,275,000	0	13,500	2,288,500
Charles T. Munger Vice Chairman of the Board	100,000	0	0	100,000

Source: https://www1.salary.com/BERKSHIRE-HATHAWAY-Executive-Salaries.html

The following year, 2018, the values rose considerably, including for Warren Buffett, who received US$ 388,968 in total compensation. Two other executives, Gregory Abel, Vice Chairman-Non-Insurance Operations, and Ajit Jain, Vice Chairman-Insurance Operations, each received more than US$ 18 million in total compensation in 2018 (Salary.com, 2020), much higher amounts to those previously paid to executives and close to the amounts paid by other large companies.

These values differ from most companies (with few exceptions as we saw in the case of Gregory Abel and Ajit Jain), and similarly to Amazon, the founders are not concerned with earning generous wages or compensation as they dominate large portions of the companies' shares, that is, they are large or medium-sized shareholders. The fact is that in this regard, Berkshire Hathaway distances itself from most companies that practice the millionaire payment of compensation to its executives, remaining as an old or traditional company. In addition to the indicator that follows, dividend payments to shareholders and the stock repurchases, which have not existed for a long time, we can say that it is a company with little financialization, although completely immersed in financial activities and not committed to the production itself. On the contrary, it uses the production of wealth of the manufacturing companies to generate their profits and to grow, becoming one of the ten largest companies in market capitalization in the world.

6.8 Dividend payments to shareholders and stock repurchases

As stated before, Berkshire has not paid dividends to shareholders since 1967, as described in its multiyear annual reports. According to the Investopedia website, the holding company

Table 6.9 Dividend payments to Berkshire Hathaway's shareholders

	2014	*2015*	*2016*	*2017*
Dividend payments in billion US$	0	0	0	0
Stock Repurchases in billion US$	0	0	0	0
Totals in billion US$	0	0	0	0

Sources: annual reports, several years

> believes that it is more beneficial to allocate the company's earnings in other ways. Buffett prefers to reinvest profits in the companies he controls to improve their efficiency, expand their reach, create new products and services, and improve existing ones. Buffett, like many business leaders, feels that investing back into the business provides more long-term value to shareholders than paying them directly because the company's financial success rewards shareholders with higher stock values.
>
> (Investopedia, 2018a)

Table 6.9 shows the absence of dividend payments and stock repurchases.

According to Investopedia, Berkshire only paid dividends once, in 1967, and points out that "Buffett claims that he must have been in the bathroom when the dividend was authorized" (Investopedia, 2018b). In other words, here we have a traditional position of retaining and reinvesting (Lazonick & O'Sullivan, 2000), which contradicts the current trend of decreasing and distributing resources to shareholders, one of the crucial points of the financialization process.

The fact that it does not repurchase shares, even though the company has launched a plan to do so, which has not yet been practiced (Berkshire Hathaway *Annual Report*, 2017, p.K-30), is another demonstration that the company has a different attitude from most of the large companies studied by us and from hundreds of others that strongly adhere to dividend payments and stock repurchases. This reflects that financialization does not happen equally in all companies, but these exceptions apparently only reinforce the rule. This financialization happens even if some do not fully practice it, as it seems to be the case we are seeing at Berkshire Hathaway.

6.9 Employee salaries

As for employee salaries, Berkshire follows the global trend: low and medium salaries compared to the average American income for all ethnic groups, which was US$ 61,000 in 2017 (Fontenot et al., 2018). Table 6.10 shows the salaries of several employees.

Table 6.10 Berkshire Hathaway

Annual salary in US$ – 2018			
Professional	*Minimum*	*Maximum*	*Salary average*
Realtor	20,424	90,724	55,574
Receptionist	20,716	38,459	29,587
Certified Nurse Assistant	22,108	37,604	29,856
Administrative Assistant	25,730	58,000	41,865
Marketing Coordinator	26,003	48,509	37,256
Executive Assistant	31,050	66,680	48,885
Accountant	32,701	72,890	52,795
Financial Controller	57,335	159,325	108,330
Senior Finance Analyst	64,800	101,772	83,286
Head of IT and Infrastructure	77,576	137,573	107,574
Associate General Counsel	97,988	222,170	160,079

Source: https://www.payscale.com/research/US/Employer=Berkshire_Hathaway_Inc/Salary/by_Job

As can be seen in Table 6.10, most of the starting and average salaries of the most representative professions of the company pay less than the average American salary, as mentioned before. This fact places the company as all the others that we are studying in this work. Even so, it is still a little better than Apple's starting salaries, for example, where employees are initially paid US$ 18,000 annually, while the lowest salary seen at Berkshire started at US$ 20,424 in 2018, for a realtor, slightly above, but still a small starting salary when we compared it with all American salaries.

When we compare employee salaries with CEO Warren Buffett's total earnings, we have the smallest difference between all the companies analyzed. Not because wages are much better than at other companies, but because the total compensation to the CEO is small, practically symbolic, as we have seen, of just US$ 100,000 in 2017. Even in 2018 (Buffett received US$ 388,000), the compensation to the CEO is much below the compensations paid to the CEOs in other companies.

Table 6.11 shows the ratio between CEO earnings and the rest of the employees.

This establishes a small difference between the employees and the CEO, ranging from one to five times, which is negligible in the business world today. But we must not forget that for the ongoing process of economic inequality between income brackets (Piketty, 2014), these data are not sufficient as Warren Buffett accumulates billions of dollars as a shareholder and his annual gain as CEO does not interfere in anything in the accumulation of wealth.

There is a development of a divergent situation here from other companies, which is a slight difference between employee earnings and the CEO, but taking into account the caveat made above that Buffett is one of the owners

Table 6.11 Ratio between employee salaries and total CEO earnings

Warren Buffett in 2017 - US$ 100,000.00			
Employee X CEO	*Minimum*	*Maximum*	*Average*
Realtor	5	1	2
Receptionist	5	3	3
Certified Nurse Assistant	5	3	3
Administrative Assistant	4	2	2
Marketing Coordinator	4	2	3
Executive Assistant	3	2	2
Accountant	3	1,5	2
Financial Controller	2	-	-
Senior Finance Analyst	1,5	-	1
Head of IT and Infrastructure	1,5	-	-
Associate General Counsel	1	-	-

Source: author, based on the values of the compensation table paid to the CEO and the workers' salary table

and every year his fortune grows exponentially. It can be said that income inequality is also present in Berkshire Hathaway.

6.10 Employment

In the indicator that deals with employment, we bring a small historical series, from 2012 to 2017. There was growth, from 288,462 employees in 2012 to 330,745 in 2013, 340,499 in 2014, 361,270 in 2015, 367,671 in 2016, and 377,291 in 2017 (Berkshire Hathaway *Annual Report*, several years).

This contingent refers to all employees of the holding company, including companies acquired by it, which remain with their legal personality but are part of the company. It reflects the company's acquisitions and expansion. In this case, there is also an expansion in employment, similar to Apple, Google, and Amazon.

In this company, financialization did not mean job cuts, but growth, confirming the two-way street of the financialization process, that is, there is no single way in which this phenomenon occurs, but it is diverse and full of specificities. We will analyze this in more depth when we look at the other companies.

In summary, we can see that Berkshire Hathaway is a company that mixes elements of financialization, such as not very high salaries, whose average is below the salaries of all North American ethnic groups (US$ 53,000 for Berkshire and US$ 61,000 for all ethnic groups in 2017) (Fontenot et al., 2018; Salary.com, 2019, 2020). It also contradicts some assumptions of financialization, such as the dividend payments to shareholders and stock repurchases, which are two fundamental elements in the current economic moment. This double condition reinforces our understanding that the financialization process is something heterogeneous, with different behaviors in each company when we analyze each indicator. Instead of questioning the phenomenon of financialization, this situation only shows that reality is more complex and dynamic than theories, which take decades to develop, while reality changes without warning in a matter of a few years and even months. For us, the study of concrete cases such as that of Berkshire Hathaway helps to better understand, in practice, how contemporary companies behave and how the financialization process takes place in them.

References

Berkshire Hathaway. 2014. *Annual Report*, 2014. Available at: https://www.berkshirehathaway.com/2014ar/2014ar.pdf. Accessed 06/20/2017.

Berkshire Hathaway. 2015. *Annual Report*, 2015. Available at: https://www.berkshirehathaway.com/2015ar/2015ar.pdf. Accessed 06/23/2017.

Berkshire Hathaway. 2016. *Annual Report*, 2016. Available at: https://www.berkshirehathaway.com/2016ar/2016ar.pdf. Accessed 06/23/2017.

Berkshire Hathaway. 2017. *Annual Report*, 2017. Available at: https://www.berkshirehathaway.com/2017ar/2017ar.pdf. Accessed 02/19/2018.

Davis, G.F. 2008. A new finance capitalism? Mutual funds and ownership re-concentration in the United States. *European Management Review*, 5, 11–21.

Erturk, I. 2016. Financialization, bank business models and the limits of post-crisis bank regulation. *Journal of Banking Regulation*, 17, 60–72. Available at: https://link.springer.com/article/10.1057/jbr.2015.23

Fichtner, J., Heemskerk, E.M., and Garcia-Bernardo, J. 2017. Hidden power of the Big Three? Passive index funds, re-concentration of corporate ownership, and new financial risk. *Business and Politics*, 19(2), 298–326.

Fligstein, N. 2001. *The Architecture of Markets: An Economic Sociology of Twenty-First-Century Capitalist Societies*. Princeton, NJ: Princeton University Press.

Fontenot, K., Semega, J., and Kollar, M., 2018. Income and poverty in the United States 2017. Available at: https://www.census.gov/content/dam/Census/library/publications/2018/demo/p60-263.pdf. Accessed 10/06/2019.

Investopedia, 2018a.Why doesn't Berkshire Hathaway pay a dividend? Available at: https://www.investopedia.com/ask/answers/021615/why-doesnt-berkshire-hathaway-pay-dividend.asp. Accessed 03/01/2019.

Investopedia, 2018b. How Warren Buffett made Berkshire Hathaway a Winner. Greg McFarlane. Available at: https://www.investopedia.com/articles/markets/041714/how-warren-buffett-made-berkshire-hathaway-worldbeater.asp. Accessed 04/17/2019.

Lazonick, W. and O'Sullivan, M. 2000. Maximizing shareholder value: a new ideology for corporate governance. *Economy and Society*, 29(1), 13–35.

Nasdaq. 2019a. Berkshire Hathaway institutional holdings. Available at: https://www.nasdaq.com/symbol/brk.b/institutional-holdings. Accessed 01/23/2019.

Nasdaq. 2019b. Berkshire Hathaway institutional holdings - increased. Available at: https://www.nasdaq.com/symbol/brk.b/institutional-holdings/increased. Accessed 01/27/2019.

Nasdaq. 2019c. Berkshire Hathaway Institutional Holdings - decreased. Available at: https://www.nasdaq.com/symbol/brk.b/institutional-holdings/decreased. Accessed 01/28/2019.

Piketty, T. 2014. *O Capital no século XXI*. Editora Intrínseca, Rio de Janeiro.

Salary.com. 2019. Berkshire Hathaway executive salaries. Available at: https://www1.salary.com/BERKSHIRE-HATHAWAY-Executive-Salaries.html. Accessed 01/12/2019.

Salary.com. 2020. Berkshire Hathaway executive salaries. Available at: https://www.salary.com/tools/executive-compensation-calculator/berkshire-hathaway-executive-salaries?year=2018. Accessed 03/10/2020.

Warren Buffett Archive. 2022. Available at: https://buffett.cnbc.com/. Accessed 03/03/2022.

7 Facebook

Facebook was founded in February 2004 in Cambridge, Massachusetts, USA, by Mark Zuckerberg, Andrew McCollum, Dustin Moskovitz, Eduardo Saverin, and Chris Hughes. Headquartered in Menlo Park, California, it was the sixth-largest company in market capitalization in December 2017, valued at US$ 512 billion (Companies Market Cap., 2018). In 2021, the company created the brand Metaverse, or Meta Platforms Inc., indicating an immersion in virtual reality, developing games, avatars, among other forms of interaction typical of science fiction.

Facebook's mission is to "give people the power to build community and bring the world closer together" (Facebook *Annual Report*, 2017, p.5). Its priority "is to build useful and engaging products that enable people to connect and share with friends and family through mobile devices, personal computers, and other surfaces". (They) also help people discover and learn about what is going on in the world around them, enable people to share their opinions, ideas, photos and videos, and other activities with audiences ranging from their closest friends to the public at large, and stay connected everywhere by accessing our products, including:

> **Facebook**. Facebook enables people to connect, share, discover, and communicate with each other on mobile devices and personal computers. There are a number of different ways to engage with people on Facebook, the most important of which is News Feed which displays an algorithmically-ranked series of stories and advertisements individualized for each person.
>
> (Facebook *Annual Report*, 2017, p.5)

"**Instagram**. Instagram is a community for sharing visual stories through photos, videos, and direct messages. Instagram is also a place for people to stay connected with the interests and communities that they care about" (Facebook *Annual Report*, 2017, p.5).

"**Messenger**. Messenger is a messaging application that makes it easy for people to connect with other people, groups, and businesses across a variety of platforms and devices" (Facebook *Annual Report*, 2017, p.5).

DOI: 10.4324/9781003309536-7

"**WhatsApp**. WhatsApp is a fast, simple, and reliable messaging application that is used by people around the world to connect securely and privately" (Facebook *Annual Report*, 2017, p.5).

"**Oculus**. Our Oculus virtual reality technology and content platform power products that allow people to enter a completely immersive and interactive environment to train, learn, play games, consume content, and connect with others" (Facebook *Annual Report*, 2017, p.5).

The all-powerful and controversial company, run by Mark Zuckerberg, has various problems in courts and with some governments, not only in the US but in Europe. User data leakage, the company's relationship with election campaigns, foreign exchange evasion, and tax evasion are some of the crimes that have been committed by the Californian technology company. In March 2016, it maintained more than US$ 1.8 billion of its US$ 15.8 billion reserve in offshores in an attempt to evade taxes in the United States (Srnicek, 2016, p.17).

Arvidsson (2016) suggests that Facebook

> embodies a new logic of capitalist governance, what has been termed the 'social logic of the derivative'. The logic of the derivative is rooted in the now dominant financial level of the capitalist economy, and is mediated by social media and the algorithmic processing of large digital data sets. This article makes three precise claims: First, that the modus operandi of Facebook mirrors the operations of derivative financial instruments. Second, that the algorithms that Facebook uses share a genealogy with those of derivative financial instruments – both are outcomes of the influence of the 'cyber sciences' on managerial practice in the post-war years. Third, that the future potential of Facebook lies in its ability to apply the logic of derivatives to the financial valuation of ordinary social relations, thus further extending the process of financialization of everyday life.
>
> (Arvidsson, 2016, *abstract*)

From this interesting analysis by Adam Arvidsson, we can see that the process of valuing Facebook is anchored in the continuous search for a greater number of users by using algorithms that set standards in the network and that allow the company to increase its revenues year by year, as we will see when we analyze the financialization indicators, starting with their sources of profitability. Furthermore, Facebook, similar to Google, are beneficiaries of an oligopolistic market situation, where few companies hold the majority of the market. Facebook ranks first accounting for 73.33% of the social media market share (Statcounter, 2022).

7.1 Comparison between the sources of profitability

Facebook's revenue in 2017 was US$ 40.65 billion, an increase of 47% over the previous year, and advertising revenue was US$ 39.94 billion, an increase of 49% compared to the previous year. Its revenues have been growing

Table 7.1 Facebook's revenues

	2013	*2014*	*2015*	*2016*	*2017*
Revenues in billions of US$	7872	12,466	17,928	27,638	40,653
Operating profit	2804	4994	6225	12,427	20,203
Net profit	1500	2940	3688	10,217	15,934
% of return on revenues	19.05	23.58	20.57	36.96	39.19
Earn per share US$	0.62	1.12	1.31	3.56	5.49
Total assets	17,858	39,966	49,407	64,961	84,524

Source: Facebook *Annual Report* 2017, p.32

steadily, year by year, since 2013. Net income went from US$ 1.5 billion in 2013 to US$ 15.934 billion in 2017, more than 1000% growth in just four years. This confirms the idea that Facebook's growth lies in gaining more users and based on this earning revenue from its advertisements. Earnings per share also grew by almost a thousand per cent, from US$ 0.62 in 2013 to US$ 5.49 in 2017, as can be seen in Table 7.1

Facebook's main source of profitability is based on monetization metrics that involves users who log in daily and monthly. Daily active users (DAUs) averaged 1.4 billion in December 2017, an increase of 14% over 2016. Monthly active users (MAUs) were 2.13 billion on December 31, 2017, an increase of 14% over the previous year (Facebook *Annual Report*, 2017, p.34).

The growth of daily active users went from 890 million in December 2014 to 1.4 billion in December 2017. The lowest growth was observed in the USA and Canada, which went from 157 million in December 2014 to 184 million in December 2017. Europe went from 217 million in 2014 to 277 million in 2017. Africa, Latin America, and the Middle East saw a substantial growth from 263 million daily active users in December 2014 to 441 million in December 2017. The largest growth in daily active users was found in the Asia-Pacific region, where data show that there was a growth from 253 million daily active users in 2014 to 499 million in 2017.

Another metric used by Facebook is the average revenue per user (ARPU). This reflects the volume of contribution per user, and this time, the US-Canada region was by far the most profitable, having an average revenue per user in 2015 of US$ 13.70 and rising to US$ 26.76 in December 2017, 100% growth in just two years. Meanwhile, in Europe, the average revenue per user was US$ 4.56 in 2015 to US$ 8.86 in 2017. The Asia-Pacific region had an average revenue per user of US$ 1.60 in 2015 and US$ 2.54 in 2017; and finally, Africa, Latin America, and the Middle East had an average revenue per user of US$ 1.10 in 2015 and US$ 1.86 in 2017 (Facebook *Annual Report*, 2017, p.37).

These data show that Facebook still has a great deal of the market to conquer, since almost half of the population is not yet connected to the Internet. Moreover, there is room for growth within the regions, increasing the average revenue per user in the Middle East, Asia/Pacific, Latin America regions, which has been growing in the number of users, including about 70% of them, but with weak average contribution to revenues.

As the company stated in its annual report:

> For 2017, worldwide ARPU was $20.21, an increase of 26% from 2016. Over this period, ARPU increased by 41% in Europe, 36% in United States & Canada, 33% in Rest of World, and 22% in Asia-Pacific. In addition, user growth was more rapid in geographies with relatively lower ARPU, such as Asia-Pacific and Rest of World. We expect that user growth in the future will be primarily concentrated in those regions where ARPU is relatively lower, such that worldwide ARPU may continue to increase at a slower rate relative to ARPU in any geographic region, or potentially decrease even if ARPU increases in each geographic region.
>
> (Facebook *Annual Report*, 2017, p.38)

This expectation from Facebook matches the numbers we found. In fact, revenues grow slower in lower income regions, but there is room to grow, as with the rise in average income in Asia and other poorer regions of the world, Facebook will undoubtedly be able to see its revenue grow without many difficulties.

7.2 Shareholding composition

Facebook's shareholding structure follows the same line as the other companies analyzed by us in this work. Large groups of institutional investors dominate their shareholding structure. Having issued more than 2.4 billion shares on September 30, 2018, 70.51% of them were in the hands of 2,420 institutional shareholders, who held 1.693 billion shares (Nasdaq, 2019a), and almost 1 billion shares are in the hands of just fifteen shareholders, as shown in Table 7.2.

Table 7.2 Facebook's largest shareholders on 9/30/2018

Financial groups	*Shares held*	*Value in thousands of US$*	*% of Institutional shares*
Vanguard Group Inc.	172,425,552	25,444,839	10.18
BlackRock Inc.	151,364,039	22,336,791	8.94
FMR LLC	124,255,610	18,336,400	7.33
State Street Corp.	85,300,828	12,587,843	5.03
Price T Rowe Associates Inc./MD	75,175,843	11,093,699	4.44
Capital Research Global Investors	60,314,380	8,900,593	3.56
Capital World Investors	33,201,516	4,899,548	1.96
Capital International Investors	30,540,615	4,506,879	1.80
Geode Capital Management LLC	29,569,123	4,363,515	1.74
Invesco LTD.	28,355,892	4,184,479	1.67
Northern Trust Corp.	26,788,215	3,953,137	1.58
Morgan Stanley	25,517,710	3,765,648	1.50
Bank of New York Mellon Corp.	22,083,692	3,258,890	1.30
Goldman Sachs Group Inc.	17,694,273	2,611,144	1.04
Baillie Gifford & Co.	16,994,166	2,507,829	1.00
Totals (15 biggest shareholders)	899,581,454	132,751,234	53.07%

Source: https://www.nasdaq.com/symbol/fb/institutional-holdings

Table 7.3 Groups that most acquired Facebook shares on 9/30/2018

Financial groups	*Shares acquired*	*% of change (+)*
FMR LLC	2,132,804	1.75
Capital Research Global Investors	25,147,288	71.51
Capital International Investors	26,317,366	623.15
Geode Capital Management LLC	499,429	1.72
Invesco LTD.	467,414	1.68
Morgan Stanley	799,081	3.23
Jennison Associates LLC	242,474	1.60
Magellan Asset Management LTD.	1,835,941	13.77
Loomis Sayles & Co. LP	3,077	0.02
UBS Asset Management Americas Inc.	194,601	1.77

Source: https://www.nasdaq.com/symbol/fb/institutional-holdings/increased

Table 7.2 shows that only the fifteen largest Facebook shareholders own almost 900 million shares, almost 40% of all shares (2.4 billion shares) and more than 50% of the amount that is held by 2,420 institutional investors (1.693 billion shares). Only the fifteen largest investors, which include our well-known Big Three from North American investment funds (Vanguard Group, State Street Corp., and BlackRock Inc.) and which represent 0.6% of total institutional shareholders, make up more than half of the shares and of the financial resources represented by these shares, which accounts for more than US$ 132 billion. Once again, it is a huge concentration of resources and decision-making power, as has already been widely debated in this work.

7.3 Shareholding acquisitions

Those who acquired the most shares on Facebook were also large groups of investors, such as Capital International Investors, which acquired more than 26 million shares, increasing its presence in the company by 623%. Capital Research Global Investors also bought more than 25 million shares and increased its shareholding by 71%. Magellan Asset Management Ltd. bought more than 1.8 million shares and grew its investments in Facebook shares by 13.7% (Nasdaq, 2019b). Table 7.3 shows the groups that most acquired Facebook shares.

Nevertheless, all the biggest buyers in this period were financial institutions, which are predominant in buying and selling shares, confirming what we have seen, in the sense of the increasing participation of these institutions.

7.4 Share sales

Following the same line of buying and selling, the main institutional investors have slightly decreased their positions in Facebook shares. The Big Three (Vanguard, BlackRock and State Street) sold only a fraction of what they

Table 7.4 Groups that most sold Facebook shares on 9/30/2018

Financial groups	*Sold shares*	*% of change (−)*
Vanguard Group Inc.	481,667	0.28
BlackRock Inc.	491,958	0.32
State Street Corp.	3,070,325	3.47
Price T Rowe Associates Inc./MD	10,215,716	11.96
Capital World Investors	23,432,423	41.38
Northern Trust Corp.	121,764	0.45
Bank of New York Mellon Corp.	18,479	0.08
Goldman Sachs Group Inc.	98,695	0.56
Baillie Gifford & Co.	2,155,096	11.25
Ameriprise Financial Inc.	1,273,059	7.19

Source: https://www.nasdaq.com/symbol/fb/institutional-holdings/decreased

own in the company. Capital World Investors sold the most, which gave up more than 23 million shares, reducing its share in the business by 41.38%. Table 7.4 shows the groups.

Price T Rowe Associates also sold more than 10 million shares and decreased its stake in 11.96% in Facebook shares. The most interesting thing to note is that out of the 2,420 institutional investors, 1,129 increased their participation, buying more than 122 million shares. Another 1,097 decreased their share, selling more than 182 million shares. However, the bulk of the shares, 1.3 billion, were in the hands of 194 institutional investors, or 8% of the shareholders (Nasdaq, 2019c). These determine the buying and selling transactions and, in a way, share prices, as they often prefer to play at a standstill, selling little or buying shares, in a typical medium- and long-term strategy, which contradicts the option for the short term, typical of financialization. These data confirm the notion that financialization is a complex process full of specificities, not occurring in a similar or mechanically way as many may think.

7.5 Mergers and acquisitions

Facebook had acquired 77 companies from 2007 to 2018. Table 7.5 shows fifteen companies purchased since 2009. Many do not show the value of the business done.

The most iconic company acquisitions were WhatsApp, acquired on February 9, 2014, for US$ 19 billion, Instagram, purchased on April 9, 2012, for US$ 1 billion, and the content and virtual reality platform Oculus, purchased for US$ 2 billion on March 25, 2014.

Haeruddin (2017) states that

> In general, mergers and acquisitions activities do not based on the similar reasons. There are several different reasons for organizations in getting other organizations. For example, to penetrate and to expand into market

Table 7.5 Facebook's acquisitions of companies – 2007 to 2018

Company	*Data of purchase*	*Value in millions of US$*
Vidpresso	Aug 14, 2018	n/d
LiveRail	July 2, 2014	500
Ascenta (UK)	Mar 28, 2014	20
Oculus	Mar 25, 2014	2,000
WhatsApp	Feb 19, 2014	19,000
Branch	Jan 13, 2014	15
Onavo	Oct 14, 2013	120
Parse	Apr 25, 2013	85
Instagram	Apr 9, 2012	1000
Gowalla	Dec 2, 2011	3
Snaptu	Mar 20, 2011	70
Nextstop	Sept 25, 2010	2
Chai Labs	Aug 15, 2010	10
Hot Potato	July 28, 2010	10
FriendFeed	Aug 10, 2009	50
Totals in billions of US$		22.885

Source: https://www.crunchbase.com/organization/facebook/acquisitions/acquisitions_list#section-acquisitions

> in particular area, to strengthen current products by uniting complementary product portfolios; and vertically or horizontally integrate into new potential growth or low-cost technologies and market segment.
>
> (Haeruddin, 2017, p.85)

According to the author, this happened when Facebook purchased WhatsApp because "to strengthen current products, Facebook, was focused on finding an existing partner within a similar market by uniting complementary product portfolios, WhatsApp (...) integration was completely successful in terms of the original reasons for the deal" (Haeruddin, 2017, p.85).

As we can see in the numbers and existing bibliography on the topic of mergers and acquisitions, there is always an interest in expanding markets, dominating existing ones, increasing the number of people reached by the business and, by doing that, increasing profitability. The goal is to increase profits and maximize shareholder value, a fundamental conduct of the financialization process.

7.6 Origin of managers

As already mentioned, the question of the leaders' trajectory is important to recognize their current trends and behaviors. Facts, such as where they studied and which organizations have already participated or participate, are data that speak volumes about the decisions made and the mentality expressed today, as Fligstein (1991) pointed out. Although we have also positioned ourselves in favor of a progressive merger of the industrial, financial, banking, and services worlds, which were previously more watertight, and which are now moving toward a more homogeneous understanding of the tasks and objectives posed by businesses today. The ideology of financialization seems to be well developed, in terms of maximizing value and return to the shareholder. Even if the company does not pay dividends to shareholders, as we have seen in the cases of Google, Amazon, and Berkshire Hathaway, and now in the case of Facebook, the fact is that the objective is still to maximize investor value as a fundamental premise.

In the case of Facebook directors, there are Board members who have worked at several business organizations, in a number of different positions, as can be seen in Table 7.6.

Board members went through all kinds of organizations from technology, which was to be expected, to banks, investment funds, the United States Air Force, Medical Centers, government officials at the White House, among others. They studied at renowned universities such as Harvard, Stanford, University of California at Berkeley, Columbia University, to name a few. They also participated in several other boards in various other companies. Paul Madera, for example, who has been an observer board member since 2006, currently participates in thirty boards, while Marc Andreessen, a full member since 2008, participates in sixteen boards. Many connections and relationships are established between these leaders, who start to form networks and merge the performance in organizations of various types, significantly contributing to a more homogeneous financialized mentality.

Table 7.6 Facebook executives – Board of Directors – 2019

Directors	*No. of Boards in which they participate*	*Organizations in which they participated*
Peter Thiel Board Member Apr 2005	9 Halcyon Molecular, Powerset, Nanotronics Imaging, Zenreach, Mithril Capital Management	PayPal, Clarium, Palantir Technologies, Founders Fund, Committee to Protect Journalists, Seasteading Institute, Human Rights Foundation, BA in Philosophy from Stanford University and a J.D. from Stanford Law School
Mark Zuckerberg Board Member	3 CHORD, Facebook, Breakthrough Prize	Facebook Attended Harvard University and studied Computer Science

(*Continued*)

Directors	*No. of Boards in which they participate*	*Organizations in which they participated*
Sue Desmond-Hellmann Board Member Mar 2013	3 Facebook, Procter & Gamble, California Academy of Sciences	Genentech University of California at San Francisco (UCSF), Undergraduate degree in Education and Medical studies at the University of Nevada, Reno, Master's degree in Public Health from the University of California, Berkeley
Guy Rosen Board Member Oct 2013	2 Facebook, Maayan Ventures	Onavo
Erskine Bowles Board Member Sep 2011	6 BDT Capital Partners, Morgan Stanley, Carousel Capital, Belk, Norfolk Southern Corporation	University of North Carolina, National Commission on Fiscal Responsibility and Reform, Forstmann Little & Co., Bowles Hollowell Connor & Co., Kitty Hawk Capital, White House Chief of Staff, BSc in Business from the University of North Carolina at Chapel Hill and an MBA from Columbia University Graduate School of Business.
Marc Andreessen Board Member Jun 2008	16 Pindrop, Dialpad, OpenGov, Arimo, Anki, Qik, Honor, Hewlett-Packard, Lytro, Mori	Andreessen Horowitz, Netscape, Loudcloud, BSc in Computer Science from the University of Illinois at Urbana-Champaign.
Roi Tiger Board Member Oct 2013	1 Facebook	Onavo, Modu, IDF, Vircado
Sheryl Sandberg Board Member	2 Facebook, Lean In	Google, United States Treasury Department, McKinsey & Company, World Bank, BA summa cum laude from Harvard University and an MBA with the highest distinction from Harvard Business School.

Kenneth Chenault Board Member 2018	8 Airbnb, Procter & Gamble, American Express, IBM, Bloomberg Philanthropies, Harvard Law School, National Academy Foundation	Bain & Co, American Express, Co-Chairman of The Partnership for New York City, Inc., Mount Sinai NYU Medical Center and Health System, National Center on Addiction and Substance Abuse, National September 11 Memorial & Museum at the World Trade Center Foundation, Inc., American Express Bank Ltd, Council of National Museum of African American History and Culture, BA in History from Bowdoin College and a JD from Harvard Law School.
Paul Madera Board Observer Mar 2006	30 Braze, Glaukos, Wonga, OPENLANE, 21viaNet, BlueArc, Force10 Networks, MuleSoft, Sonendo	Montgomery Securities/Bank of America, Meritech Capital Partners, Morgan Stanley & Co., United States Air Force, MBA from the Stanford Graduate School of Business and BSc in Political Science from the United States Air Force Academy.

Source: https://www.crunchbase.com/organization/facebook/people

7.7 Compensation paid to executives

Regarding the payment of compensation to executives, Facebook followed the trend of millionaire compensation. In 2017, it paid around US$ 20 million to US$ 30 million to its main executives, except for Mark Zuckerberg, who received US$ 8,852 million, the lowest amount, until this year. He also received US$ 1.00 in cash wages, as Google's founders did, repeating the symbolism of the owner that does not want to make money in cash, but grow the share price of the company. Table 7.7 shows the payment of compensation to executives in 2017.

However, in 2018, 2019, and 2020, Mark Zuckerberg received US$ 22 million, US$ 23 million, and US$ 25 million, respectively, growing exponentially his gains (Salary.com, 2022). It seems that the promise of not earning so much from salaries and cash is a thing of the past, and the multimillionaire dollar compensations to executives, including him, are in full swing at Facebook.

Table 7.7 Compensation payment to executives. Facebook annual salary in US$ – 2017

Compensation to executives	*Total in cash*	*Stock options*	*Others*	*Total Compensations*
Sheryl K. Sandberg COO	1,436,147	21,072,431	2,687,643	25,196,221
Mike Schroepfer CTO	1,344,856	21,072,431	9000	22,426,287
David M. Wehner CFO	1,344,856	21,072,431	9000	22,426,287
Christopher K. Cox CPO	1,278,943	21,072,431	9000	22,360,374
Mark Zuckerberg CEO	1,00	0	8,852,365	8,852,366

Source: https://www1.salary.com/FACEBOOK-INC-Executive-Salaries.html

As in the other companies we analyzed, Facebook pays a sum of money, shares, other remuneration, such as refunds, for example. The cash salary is one of the lowest observed, but it follows the tendency to pay relatively little in cash, including for a lower incidence of income tax, and significant amounts in shares, a phenomenon known as stock compensation, which is the payment of salary through the company's shares. This is an aspect of financialization, which is to make the executive also a shareholder, a minority, but as someone who will be more than just the manager of the business, obscuring that separation that existed between ownership and control. According to this idea, the large existing publicly traded organizations would strive for the separation between ownership and control, so that "the agents of the most important decisions are not the same agents who have a significant share of value to lose due to the effects of their decisions" (Fama & Jensen, 1983).

The payment of millionaire compensation, and through the shares of companies, is a fact to be recognized in this change in the conception of corporate control, precisely confirming the financialization process.

7.8 Dividend payments to shareholders and stock repurchases

Facebook has not been paying dividends to shareholders (Bourgi, 2017; Ervin, 2017; Caplinger, 2019; Seeking Alpha, 2019). However, it has been making increasing stock repurchases of the company (Frier, 2018; Reuters, 2018, Sparks, 2018). This is the first case analyzed by us in this work of a company that does not pay dividends to shareholders but that practices stock repurchases (Table 7.8).

Facebook follows the same strategy as Google, of not paying dividends to its shareholders, retaining its profit for reinvestments, such as the acquisition of complementary companies, as we saw in the case of WhatsApp, Instagram,

Table 7.8 Dividend payments and stock repurchases to Facebook's shareholders

	2015	*2016*	*2017*	*2018*	*2019*	*2020*	*2021*
Dividend Payment in billions of US$	0	0	0	0	0	0	
Stock Repurchases in billions of US$	0	0	1.976	12.879	4.212	6.272	44.538
Total in billions of US$	0	0	1.976	12.879	4.212	6.272	44.538

Sources: https://www.nasdaq.com/symbol/fb/financials and https://ycharts.com/companies/FB/stock_buyback

and Oculus Virtual Reality. This strategy enables us to assess that one of the assumptions of financialization, which is dividend payments to shareholders, is absent in another company, such as Google, Amazon, and Berkshire Hathaway.

However, the Siamese sibling of dividend payouts to shareholders is stock repurchases, which are also rapidly increasing on Facebook. Until 2016, neither dividends nor stock repurchases were practiced. In 2017, buybacks began, with disbursements of US$1.9 billion in 2017, US$12.8 billion in 2018, US$4.2 billion in 2019, US$6.2 billion in 2020, and a significant US$44.5 billion in 2021, resulting in US$59.6 billion in stock repurchases in just five years (Ycharts, 2022). These numbers show the progressive integration of Facebook to the principles of maximizing shareholder value, because if the company refuses to pay dividends, it has been forced to pour massive amounts of dollars every year into stock repurchases.

On the other hand, this fact helps to confirm the occurrence of financialization, as the stock repurchase process is an artifice to raise the price of shares, by repurchasing millions of them, as already widely discussed in this work. Thus, when it comes to paying dividends to shareholders, Facebook takes a step away from financialization but fully embraces it in the case of stock repurchases. This shows, once again, that the financialization process of contemporary companies is very complex and varied, full of specificities and very interesting to observe in practice, through real numbers found by our research.

7.9 Employee salaries

Facebook employee salaries are, so far, the highest among the companies that we are analyzing in this work. Amazon was the champion in the crunch and low initial payments, with starting salaries of US$ 15,825 annually. Apple and Google showed starting salaries of US$ 18,000 annually, Microsoft of US$ 19,000, and Berkshire Hathaway of US$ 20,000 annually. Facebook has its lowest starting salaries paid to the Consumer Services Representative, who starts his career with US$ 28,168 annually, almost double the lowest initials

Table 7.9 Facebook. Annual salary in US$ – 2018

Professional	*Minimum*	*Maximum*	*Average salary*
Consumer Services Representative	28,168	58,789	43,478
IT Specialist	32,706	98,763	65,734
Customer Service Specialist	34,815	77,845	56,330
Web Content Specialist	35,616	108,967	72,291
Human Resources Specialist	37,273	93,208	65,240
Data Center Technician	41,664	90,747	66,205
Intelligence Analyst	57,217	162,340	109,778
Electric Engineer	94,538	222,100	158,319
Senior Software Engineer	100,000	208,140	154,070
Leading Software Engineer	116,182	224,845	170,513
Associate General Counsel	131,409	310,627	221,018

Source: https://www.payscale.com/research/US/Employer=Facebook_Inc/Salary/by_Job

on Amazon, for example, and reaches an average of US$ 43,478 annually, a good salary for the least valued position. Table 7.9 shows eleven professions that are representative of the company's staff and their minimum, maximum, and average wages.

Engineers' averages are also higher than at other companies, which range from US$ 80,000 to US$ 100,000 annually. On Facebook, the average salary of engineers ranges from US$ 154,000 to US$ 170,000 annually. Nevertheless, even because it has few employees, only around 25,000, compared to other larger companies, it is possible to pay more for each worker. When the total earnings of CEO Mark Zuckerberg, who received US$ 8.8 million in 2017, are compared to employee earnings, a smaller difference than that seen in other companies can be observed, such as Apple and Google, for example, which reached thousands of times.

On Facebook, compensation to the CEO was also lower than at Apple and Google and the wages found were higher, hence an inequality was also found, as can be seen in Table 7.10.

The difference between the CEO earnings and the salaries of the least paid employees was 314 times for the novice consumer services representative and only forty times between the CEO and the Associate General Counsel. These differences are much smaller than those found at Apple and Google, as previously mentioned. In this chapter, we consider the amounts earned by CEO Mark Zuckerberg in 2017, US$ 8,8 million. If we consider the amounts earned by Zuckerberg in 2018, 2019, and 2020, as we highlighted earlier on in this text, the differences between the salary earnings of employees in relation to the CEO increase significantly, even tripling, and where we observed a difference of 314 times in 2017, it may have reached 900 times the ratio between workers' earnings and the total CEO earnings in the following years. The most correct strategy in future analyses would be to establish an average gain for a certain period (for example, five years) for both workers

Table 7.10 Ratio between employee salaries and total CEO earnings Mark Zuckerberg in 2017 – US$ 8,852,366.00

Employees X CEO	*Minimum*	*Maximum*	*Average Ratio*
Consumer Services Representative	314	150	203
IT Specialist	270	89	134
Customer Service Specialist	254	113	157
Web Content Specialist	248	81	122
Human Resources Specialist	237	94	135
Data Center Technician	212	97	133
Intelligence Analyst	154	54	80
Electric Engineer	93	39	55
Senior Software Engineer	88	42	57
Leading Software Engineer	76	39	51
Associate General Counsel	67	28	40

Source: authors, based on the values of the compensation table paid to the CEO and the workers' salary table

and the CEO as a single year alone can distort the true inequality existing between income groups within a given company.

7.10 Employment

The volume of employment on Facebook has been growing slowly and presents two moments, at least. From 2004, the foundation date, with only seven employees, until 2009 (Figure 7.1).

In 2009, the company was over a thousand, reaching 1,218 employees. The second period is from 2010, with 2,127 employees, until the present moment, where it has been growing year by year, more consistently and with a greater numerical growth. In 2014, it reached 9,199 employees, reaching 2017 with a workforce of 25,105 employees. Although it had a rapid growth from 2010 to 2017, the number of workers is still small compared to Amazon (566,000), Microsoft (131,000), Apple (123,000), and Google (88,000). This fact confirms the thesis contained in the study by Srnicek (2016, p.41) that the sector of communications services, information technology, Internet hosting, cloud, etc., does not employ more than 1% of the workforce in the USA and the world. If it is true that the digital platform companies have revolutionized communications and the way many companies produce, and even allowing many people to take advantage of these technologies and work autonomously, from home, etc., this is a sector with low job creation and high added value.

For those who believe that platform capitalism is the lifeline for the problems of the unemployed at present, it is important to observe these numbers to know that, if there is no greater job creation in traditional industry, in services, retail, commerce, among others, it will not be the communications sector that comes to the rescue of many anxious, unemployed, exasperated people with no prospects for a better life in the short term.

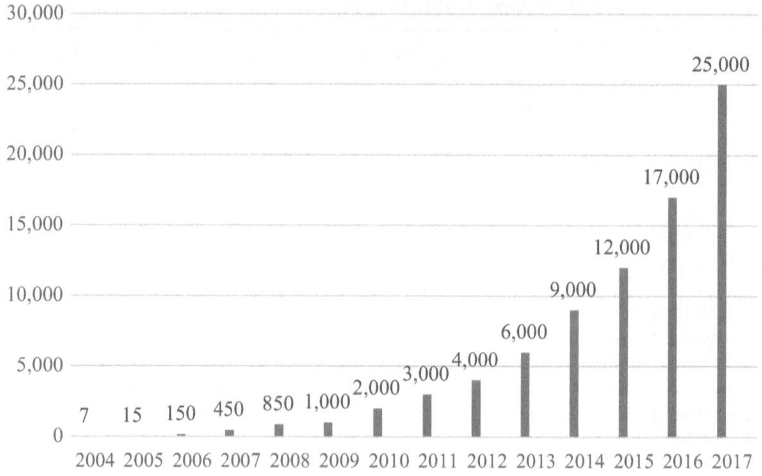

Figure 7.1 Evolution of employment at Facebook – 2004 to 2017

References

Arvidsson, A. 2016. Facebook and finance: on the social logic of the derivative. *Theory, Culture & Society*, 33(6), 3–23. Available at: https://doi.org/10.1177/0263276416658104

Bourgi, S. (22 Dec 2017). Why doesn't Facebook pay dividends? Available at: https://www.dividend.com/news/2017/12/22/why-doesnt-facebook-pay-dividend/. Accessed 05/14/2019.

Caplinger, D. (21 Jan 2019). Will Facebook start paying a dividend in 2019? Available at: https://www.fool.com/investing/2019/01/21/will-facebook-start-paying-a-dividend-in-2019.aspx. Accessed 05/14/2019.

Companies Market Cap. 2018. Facebook market capitalization. Available at: https://companiesmarketcap.com/facebook/marketcap/. Accessed 11/20/2018.

Ervin, E. (26 Jan 2017). If these 4 stocks declared dividends in 2017, it could mean billions in payouts. Available at: https://www.forbes.com/sites/ericervin/2017/01/26/if-these-4-stocks-declared-dividends-in-2017-it-potentially-could-mean-billions-in-payouts/#483. Accessed 05/14/2019.

Facebook. 2017. *Annual Report*, 2017. Available at: https://www.sec.gov/Archives/edgar/data/1326801/000132680118000009/fb-12312017x10k.htm. Accessed 08/12/2018.

Fama, E.F. and Jensen, M.C. 1983. Separation of ownership and control. *The Journal of Law and Economics*, 26(2). Available at: https://www.journals.uchicago.edu/doi/10.1086/467037

Fligstein, N. 1991. The structural transformation of American industry: an institutional account of the causes of diversification in the largest firms, 1919–1979. *The New Institutionalism in Organizational Analysis*. Paul J. DiMaggio and Walter W. Powell (eds.), 311–336. Chicago, IL: University of Chicago Press.

Frier, S. (7 Dec 2018). Facebook plans to repurchase $9 billion more of its shares. Available at: https://www.bloomberg.com/news/articles/2018-12-07/facebook-plans-to-repurchase-9-billion-more-of-its-shares. Accessed 05/14/2019.

Haeruddin, M.I.M. 2017. Mergers and acquisitions: Quo Vadis? *Management*, 7(2), 84–88. Available at: http://article.sapub.org/10.5923.j.mm.20170702.02.html

Nasdaq. 2019a. Facebook institutional holdings. Available at: https://www.nasdaq.com/symbol/fb/institutional-holdings. Accessed 01/23/2019.

Nasdaq. 2019b. Facebook institutional holdings - increased. Available at: https://www.nasdaq.com/symbol/fb/institutional-holdings/increased. Accessed 01/23/2019.

Nasdaq. 2019c. Facebook institutional holdings - decreased. Available at: https://www.nasdaq.com/symbol/fb/institutional-holdings/decreased. Accessed 01/28/2019.

Reuters. (7 Dec 2018). Facebook to buy back additional $9 billion of shares. Available at: https://www.reuters.com/article/us-facebook-buyback/facebook-to-buy-back-additional-9-billion-of-shares-idUSKBN1O62IT. Accessed 05/14/2019.

Salary.com. 2022. Facebook executive salaries. Available at: https://www1.salary.com/FACEBOOK-INC-Executive-Salaries.html. Accessed 02/12/2022.

Seeking Alpha. 2019. FB does not currently pay a dividend. Available at: https://seekingalpha.com/symbol/FB/dividends/no-dividends. Accessed 05/14/2019.

Sparks, D. (9 Dec 2018). Why Investors should Cheer Facebook's Stock Buyback. Available at: https://www.fool.com/investing/2018/12/09/why-investors-should-cheer-facebooks-stock-buyback.aspx. Accessed 05/14/2019.

Srnicek, N. 2016. *Platform Capitalism*. Cambridge: Polity Press.

Statcounter, 2022. Social media stats worldwide. Available at: https://gs.statcounter.com/social-media-stats. Accessed 03/07/2022.

Ycharts. 2022. Facebook stock buyback. Available at: https://ycharts.com/companies/FB/stock_buyback. Accessed 03/08/2022.

8 Johnson & Johnson

Johnson & Johnson is the oldest and largest American pharmaceutical company, founded in 1886. According to the company's annual report

> Johnson & Johnson and its subsidiaries (the Company) have approximately 134,000 employees worldwide engaged in the research and development, manufacture and sale of a broad range of products in the health care field. Johnson & Johnson is a holding company, which has more than 260 operating companies conducting business in virtually all countries of the world. The Company's primary focus is products related to human health and well-being. Johnson & Johnson was incorporated in the State of New Jersey in 1887. (...)

"The Company is organized into three business segments: Consumer, Pharmaceutical and Medical Devices" (Johnson & Johnson *Annual Report*, 2017, p.1).

> The Consumer segment includes a broad range of products used in the baby care, oral care, beauty, over-the-counter pharmaceutical, women's health and wound care markets. These products are marketed to the general public and sold both to retail outlets and distributors throughout the world. The Pharmaceutical segment is focused on six therapeutic areas, including immunology, infectious diseases, neuroscience, oncology, pulmonary hypertension, and cardiovascular and metabolic diseases. Products in this segment are distributed directly to retailers, wholesalers, hospitals and health care professionals for prescription use.
>
> (Johnson & Johnson *Annual Report*, 2017, p.1)

> The Medical Devices segment includes a broad range of products used in the orthopaedic, surgery, cardiovascular, diabetes care and eye health fields. These products are distributed to wholesalers, hospitals and retailers, and used principally in the professional fields by physicians, nurses, hospitals, eye care professionals and clinics. They include orthopaedic products; general surgery, biosurgical, endomechanical and energy products; electrophysiology products to treat cardiovascular disease;

DOI: 10.4324/9781003309536-8

sterilization and disinfection products to reduce surgical infection; diabetes care products, such as blood glucose monitoring; and vision care products such as disposable contact lenses and ophthalmic products related to cataract and laser refractive surgery.

(Johnson & Johnson *Annual Report*, 2017, p.1)

Having such a wide range of products in the area of health and well-being, the company is a giant and was considered the seventh company in market capitalization on December 15, 2017, estimated at US$c 338 billion (companiesmarketcap, 2022).

Presenting ever increasing revenues, the sector that has grown the most is the pharmaceutical segment, offering a wide range of medicines that are produced and sold all over the world. Although we do not have more in-depth knowledge in the health field to make a direct link between financialization and drug consumption, the fact is that the increase in the volume and variety of medicines in the world today is also a phenomenon concomitant to that of financialization. The idea of always selling products at a more expensive price to obtain more profit and, consequently, greater shareholder value comes from the strategic thinking of the company, whose main product is to create value, mainly medicines. Apple sells smartphones, Berkshire sells insurance, and Facebook offers social media, while Johnson & Johnson has medicines as a source of value, which will be delivered to shareholders in the form of dividend payments and stock repurchases, for example.

Having said that, we will move on to analyzing financialization at Johnson & Johnson starting by making a comparison among the sources of profitability.

8.1 Comparison between the sources of profitability

Johnson & Johnson's revenues have been growing year by year but at a steady pace and without many highs or lows. Total revenues were in the range of US$ 70 billion in the 2010s. What draws attention here is the profitability of the business, which exceeds 20% of net profit, which is very high for a manufacturing company. We saw in the automotive sector that production profits ranged from 4% to 11%, depending on the automaker (Carmo, 2017; Carmo et al., 2021). In 2016, Johnson & Johnson's net income reached 23% of revenues, as shown in Table 8.1.

The segment that has been growing the most in the business is the Pharmaceutical one, selling a wide range of medicines every year. The segment went from US$ 28 billion in revenue in 2013 to US$ 36 billion in 2017, a 21% growth in just four years. Its share of total revenues went from 39.43% in 2013 to 47.42% in 2017, accounting for almost half of Johnson & Johnson's revenues. It is important to inform the reader that in a more detailed analysis of the annual report, it was observed that the drugs related to Neuroscience and Oncology have been responsible for strong increases in the revenues of the pharmaceutical segment. The drugs Invega, Sustenna, Xeplion, Trinza,

Table 8.1 Revenue by segment – J&J

	2013	2014	2015	2016	2017
Total revenue in billions of US$	71,312	74,331	70,074	71,890	76,450
Net profit in billions of US$	13,831	16,323	15,409	16,540	1300*
% of net income over revenue	19.39	21.95	21.98	23	1.7*
Consumer in billions of US$	14,697	14,496	13,507	13,307	13,602
% of revenue	20.6	19.5	19.27	18.51	17.79
Pharmaceutical in billions of US$	28,125	32,313	31,430	33,464	36,256
% of revenue	39.43	43.47	44.85	46.54	47.42
Medical devices in billions of US$	28,490	27,522	25,137	25,119	26,592
% of revenue	39.95	37.02	35.87	34.94	34.78

Source: Johnson & Johnson *Annual Report*, 2015, 2016 and 2017

* In 2017, there was an income tax expense of more than US$ 16 billion, while the normal annual average is US$ 3 billion, depending on the revenue. Hence the drop in net profit (2017, p.14)

and Trevicta, belonging to the area of Neuroscience, went from a revenue of US$ 1.830 billion in 2015 to US$ 2.569 billion in 2017, more than a 30% increase in just two years (J&J *Annual Report*, 2017, p.18).

In the area of Oncology, the medicine Imbruvica went from a revenue of US$ 689 million in 2015 to US$ 1.893 billion in 2017, almost 300% growth in two years. In the Cardiovascular and Metabolism area, the drug Xarelto increased its revenues from US$ 1.868 billion in 2015 to 2.5 billion in 2017, an increase of more than 30% in just two years (Johnson & Johnson *Annual Report*, 2017, p.18).

In the Consumer segment, the Beauty area was responsible for an improvement in revenues, which went from US$ 3.633 billion in 2015 to US$ 4.2 billion in 2017, an increase of 16% in two years. The Baby Care area dropped, which had revenues of US$ 2.157 billion in 2015 and fell to US$ 1.916 billion in 2017, a 10% drop in two years (Johnson & Johnson *Annual Report*, 2017, p.17).

These figures show that there is a progressive tendency toward an increase in the sale of medicines related to neuroscience, mainly in the fight against depression and other disorders, and in the area of oncology, where there was an increase in the number of cancer cases worldwide and, consequently, the increased research and development of new products. The issue of beauty also proved to be very important as the concern with aesthetics and appearance is increasing, expressed in a society that values celebrities, the cult of a well-defined body, among other concerns that people have in a contemporary society. All of this helps to develop this market, producing inputs. On the one hand, for the concept of beauty that sells a great deal and makes money. On the other hand, cancer, depression, cardiovascular diseases, hypertension and obesity, which destroy human beings, also sell copious amounts of medicine and make a profit, like any other commodity in the market economy.

Ultimately, what matters is generating revenue and high profits to maximize shareholder value, a fundamental part of this socioeconomic gear. This is where the financialization process is shown with all its power, as the need to create value in any way also occurs in the area of health, which is very sensitive to everyone and very profitable.

8.2 Shareholding composition

The shareholding structure of J&J portrays the same large institutional investors that participate in the other companies that we are analyzing in this work. Here, The Big Three (Fichtner et al., 2017) have an outstanding participation. Vanguard Group has more than 213 million shares worth more than US$ 27 billion. BlackRock Inc. holds 179 million shares, valued at US$ 22 billion. Furthermore, State Street Corp brings together 152 million shares at a value of US$ 19 billion. After the Big Three, the fourth largest investor appears to gather 37 million shares and US$ 4.8 billion in values, much lower than that of the top three (Nasdaq, 2019a), as shown in Table 8.2.

Having 2,650 institutional investors, J&J holds 66% of its shares in the hands of these shareholders. Having issued more than 2.6 billion shares, 1.7 billion shares are held by these institutional investors. The rest of the shares are held by individuals. More than half of the 1.7 billion shares (885 million or 52.01%) are in the hands of only the fifteen largest shareholders, as can be seen in Table 8.2. These fifteen largest shareholders make up US$ 112 billion, half of the total value held by institutional investors, which reaches US$ 227 billion.

Table 8.2 Johnson & Johnson's largest shareholders as of September 30, 2018

Financial groups	*Shares held*	*Value in thousands of US$*	*% of institutional shares*
Vanguard Group Inc.	213,433,449	27,112,451	12.55
BlackRock Inc.	179,416,420	22,791,268	10.55
State Street Corp.	152,444,054	19,364,968	8.96
State Farm Mutual Automobile Insurance Co.	37,878,592	4,811,718	2.22
Bank of New York Mellon Corp.	33,892,560	4,305,372	1.99
Geode Capital Management LLC	33,623,523	4,271,196	1.97
Northern Trust Corp.	33,612,887	4,269,845	1.97
Bank of America Corp/DE	33,253,764	4,224,226	1.95
Massachusetts Financial Services Co/MA	29,789,154	3,784,116	1.75
Capital International Investors	24,984,249	3,173,749	1.46
JPMorgan Chase & Co.	24,569,333	3,121,042	1.44
Wellington Management Group LLP	24,187,044	3,072,480	1.42
Morgan Stanley	22,920,470	2,911,587	1.34
FMR LLC	20,907,980	2,655,941	1.22
Wells Fargo & Company/MN	20,903,552	2,655,378	1.22
Totals (15 biggest shareholders)	885,817,031	112,525,337	52,01%

Source: https://www.nasdaq.com/symbol/jnj/institutional-holdings

Table 8.3 Groups that most acquired Johnson & Johnson shares on September 30, 2018

Financial groups	*Acquired shares*	*% of change (+)*
Vanguard Group Inc.	3,235,861	1.54
BlackRock Inc.	1,106,155	0.62
State Street Corp.	3,479,261	2.34
Bank of New York Mellon Corp.	435,564	1.30
Geode Capital Management LLC	541,642	1.64
Bank of America Corp/DE	4,796,282	16.85
Capital International Investors	18,768,905	301.98
JPMorgan Chase & Co.	1,756,783	7.70
Wellington Management Group LLP	299,517	1.25
Morgan Stanley	1,352,484	6.27

Source: https://www.nasdaq.com/symbol/jnj/institutional-holdings/increased

When we note that only the three largest shareholders hold US$ 70 billion, this corresponds to at least 30% of the total held by institutional investors. It is a huge concentration of economic resources and power within the organization, as can be seen from analyzing other companies and it is one of the central and well-highlighted points of the financialization process.

8.3 Shareholding acquisitions

Similar to the other companies studied here, the biggest buyers of Johnson & Johnson's shares were financial groups. The Big Three acquired shares that kept them in their leadership positions, without changing their situation, as shown in Table 8.3.

Capital International Investors was the one who bought the most shares, accounting for 18.7 million shares, and consequently increasing its position by 301% and becoming Johnson & Johnson's tenth-largest institutional investor. Bank of America bought 4.7 million shares and increased its stake by 16.8%. JPMorgan Chase bought 1.7 million shares and grew 7.7% in the company's shares. Furthermore, Morgan Stanley acquired 1.3 million shares, leading to a 6.2% increase in its share in the pharmaceutical company's shares (Nasdaq, 2019b). These data reinforce what we have been saying throughout this study, that more and more financial organizations, banks, investment funds, etc., participate in the shareholding structure of manufacturing firms, withdrawing billions of dollars from them every year. Although this is not exactly a novelty, what we find is an ever-increasing trend in this phenomenon, and the numbers increasingly corroborate this reality.

8.4 Sale of shares

Regarding the sale of shares, the same is true at Johnson & Johnson. Financial groups were the most responsible for the sale of shares. However, those that

Table 8.4 Groups that most sold Johnson & Johnson shares on September 30, 2018

Financial groups	*Sold shares*	*% of change (−)*
Northern Trust Corp.	614,012	1.79
Massachusetts Financial Services Co/MA	514,118	1.7
Wells Fargo & Company/MN	719,933	3.33
Deutsche Bank AG	19,597	0.16
Franklin Resources Inc.	99,925	0.94
Capital World Investors	16,656,063	61.79
Clearbridge Investments, LLC	325,686	3.17
Swiss National Bank	338,000	3.43
PNC Financial Services Group, Inc.	539,884	5.79
LSV Asset Management	210,942	2.43

Source: https://www.nasdaq.com/symbol/jnj/institutional-holdings/decreased

sold the most were secondary groups of institutional investors, compared to the Big Three, as can be seen in Table 8.4.

Capital World Investors sold the most, which gave up more than 16 million shares, reducing its participation in the J&J shares by 61% (Nasdaq, 2019c). The other biggest sellers slightly decreased their participation, from 2% to 6%, which are common numbers for those who buy and sell constantly, as is the case of the stock market. This item listed by us, sale of shares, may have various interpretations. We have already offered some here and the main one was the short term. In the short term, the concern is to earn as much as possible and any sign of a drop in the share price proceeds to massive sales. However, the most common part of large investors, as we have found in our study, is to stay in the company for long periods, because in the long run, the trend is for the share price to be appreciated. Thinking along these lines, buying and selling quickly sends out the wrong signal to the market that such a company is not sustainable in the long run and a constant withdrawal of investments would make the very existence of the company unfeasible, which is contrary to the interests of these large investors.

8.5. Mergers and acquisitions

Following the trend of large companies, Johnson & Johnson has acquired thirty-eight companies since 1994 (Crunchbase, 2022). In the case of Johnson & Johnson, the issue of purchases followed the prescription of mergers and acquisitions of the other companies analyzed here, such as the quest to dominate its market and complementary products, expand sales, and seek greater synergy in the health and personal care sector. Table 8.5 shows these data.

As defined by Haeruddin (2017), the idea of mergers and acquisitions, in general, is "to penetrate and to expand into the market in a particular area, to strengthen current products by uniting complementary product portfolios; and vertically or horizontally integrating into new potential growth or

Table 8.5 Johnson & Johnson's acquisitions

Company	*Date of Purchase*	*Value in millions of US$*
Momenta Pharmaceuticals	Aug 19, 2020	6500
Auris Health, Inc.	Feb 13, 2019	3400
Ci:z Holdings	Oct 23, 2018	2300
Actelion Pharmaceuticals	Jan 26, 2017	30,000
Abbott Medical Optics	Sept 16, 2016	4300
Vogue International	June 2, 2016	3300
Alios BioPharma	Sept 30, 2014	1800
Aragon Pharmaceuticals	June 17, 2013	1000
Crucell	Feb 22, 2011	2300
Acclarent	Dec 17, 2009	785
Omrix Biopharmaceuticals	Nov 23, 2008	432
Peninsula Pharmaceuticals Inc.	Apr 19, 2005	245
Transform Pharmaceuticals	Mar 10, 2005	230
LXN Corporation	May 9, 2001	1300
BabyCenter	Mar 2, 2001	10
Menlo Care	Oct 18, 1994	n/d
Totals in billions of US$		57,902

Sources: https://www.crunchbase.com/organization/johnson-johnson/acquisitions/acquisitions_list#section-acquisitions; https://www.crunchbase.com/organization/johnson-johnson/company_financials

low-cost technologies and market segments" (Haeruddin, 2017, p.85). That is, vertical integration is still a recurring phenomenon in contemporary companies, which is widely practiced, although the focus is currently on integrating products related to the core business, unlike in previous periods, when groups bought any type of company, even those that they had nothing to do with their vocation. This is another aspect of financialization, which changed an old practice of corporate strategies, vertical integration, in a new type of vertical integration, which focuses on creating value in what the company dominates, to better create shareholder value. The companies acquired by Johnson & Johnson are, in their overwhelming majority, pharmaceutical companies that were acquired for billions of dollars, as shown in Table 8.5, confirming in practice the theoretical assumptions presented by us here.

8.6 Origin of managers

In the indicator that discusses the origin of the directors, Johnson & Johnson has representatives from different sectors of the economy and full integration of boards, as shown in Table 8.6.

The Board of Directors members studied at several major universities, such as the Massachusetts Institute of Technology (MIT), Cornell University, University of North Carolina, etc., and participated in government entities and banks, such as Charles Prince, a board member since 2006. Charles Prince has participated in Citigroup Inc., US Steel Corporation, Council on Foreign

Table 8.6 Johnson & Johnson executives – Board of Directors

Director	*No. of Boards in which they participate*	*Organizations in which they participated*
Charles Prince Board Member 2006	2 Xerox, Johnson & Johnson	Citigroup Inc., U.S. Steel Corporation, Council on Foreign Relations, The Council of Chief Executives
Anne Mulcahy Board Member 2012	6 LPL Financial, Johnson & Johnson, Washington Post, Graham Holdings, Target, Save the Children	Xerox Corporation, Bachelor of arts degree in English/journalism from Marymount College in Tarrytown, NY.
Alex Gorsky Board Member Apr 2012	3 IBM, Johnson & Johnson, Travis Manion Foundation	Janssen Pharmaceutical Inc., Johnson & Johnson, Novartis Pharmaceuticals Corporation, Medical Devices and Diagnostics Group.
Susan Lindquist Board Member 2004	1 Johnson & Johnson	Whitehead Institute for Biomedical Research; Professor of Biology, Massachusetts Institute of Technology, FoldRx Pharmaceuticals, Inc.
Mary Coleman Board Member 2003	4 Johnson & Johnson, Meredith Corporation, Kavli Foundation, Mayo Clinic	University of Michigan, American Academy of Arts & Sciences, Society for Science & the Public, Gates Cambridge Scholars, University of Iowa, American Association for the Advancement of Science, Ph.D. in Biochemistry from the University of North Carolina and a BSc in Chemistry from Grinnell College.
William Perez Board Member 2007	4 Whirlpool, Johnson & Johnson, Greenhill & Co, Northwestern Memorial HealthCare	Greenhill & Co., Inc., Wm. Wrigley Jr. Company, Nike, Inc. S.C. Johnson & Son, Inc., Cornell University, Northwestern Memorial Hospital

(*Continued*)

Director	*No. of Boards in which they participate*	*Organizations in which they participated*
	7	
Mary Beckerle Board Member Jun 2015	Huntsman Corporation, American Association for Cancer Research, The Mechanobiology Institute, The Howard Hughes Medical Institute, Tata Institute of Fundamental Research, The Coalition for Life Sciences	University of Utah, NIH Advisory Committee, Professor of Biology and oncological sciences, holding the Ralph E. and Willia T. Main Presidential Professorship
	8	
Ian Davis Board Member 2010	Rolls-Royce Motor Cars Ltd, BP, Majid Al Futtaim Holdings LLC., Teach for All, Apax Partners, Cabinet Office – GOV.UK, McKinsey & Company	Bowater, McKinsey & Company,
	5	
Scott Davis Board Member 2014	United Parcel Service (UPS), EndoChoice, Johnson & Johnson, Honeywell International, Annie E. Casey Foundation	UPS, II Morrow, President's Intelligence Advisory Board, Carter Center Board of Councilors, Federal Reserve Bank of Atlanta, BSc in Accounting from Portland State University
	8	
Ron Williams Board Member 2011	Envision Healthcare, The Boeing Company, American Express, NaviHealth, Committee for Economic Development, Massachusetts Institute of Technology – MIT	RW2 Enterprises, LLC, Aetna Inc.,

Source: https://www.crunchbase.com/organization/johnson-johnson/advisors/current_advisors_image_list#section-board-members-and-advisors

Relations, The Council of Chief Executives, among other organizations, in addition to participating on the boards of Xerox and J&J. Ron Williams, a member of the board since 2011, participates in at least eight boards, in different organizations, such as Boeing, Envision Healthcare, American Express, MIT, among others. The cross participation of Board members in various company boards shows that large investors have a "portfolio" of directors they can trust, as the directors have shown a spectacular convergence of purposes with the large shareholders, a phenomenon that has been expressed through dividend payments to shareholders and stock repurchases, which have made institutional investors satisfied, while for senior executives, a generous share of what is produced by business for them is distributed through substantial total compensation packages, in cash or in shares, as we will see in the next topic.

8.7 Compensation paid to executives

The compensation paid to Johnson & Johnson executives follows an average standard of contemporary companies, neither excessive, such as Apple and Google (more than US$ 100 million in compensation to the CEO in one year), nor low, such as Berkshire Hathaway (US$ 100,000/US$ 388,000 to the CEO). They were between US$ 9 million for Dominic Caruso and US$ 22 million for CEO Alex Gorsky. They maintained the practice of paying less in wages in cash than in stock options, as shown in Table 8.7.

CEO Alex Gorsky received US$ 5.1 million in cash and US$ 17.4 million in stock options in 2017, triple in shares than in cash. We have already stated in this work that one of the characteristics of financialization is to privilege the financial aspect over the physical, the real. Compensation payment

Table 8.7 Compensation payment to executives. Johnson & Johnson

Annual salary in US$ – 2017				
Compensation to executives	*Total in cash*	*Stock options*	*Others*	*Total compensations*
Alex Gorsky Chairman, CEO	5,198,382	17,408,759	236,279	22,843,420
Sandra Peterson EVP, Group Worldwide Chairman	2,327,500	13,887,776	128,780	16,344,056
Joaquin Duato EVP, Worldwide Chairman Pharmaceuticals	2,825,516	13,133,019	71,726	16,030,261
Paulus Stoffels EVP, CSO	3,312,211	6,490,302	443,139	10,245,652
Dominic Caruso EVP, CFO	3,089,280	6,020,485	159,172	9,268,937

Source: https://www1.salary.com/JOHNSON-JOHNSON-Executive-Salaries.html

through stock options favors the financial aspect in at least two issues: does it increase the stock price, as a large purchase pushes the price upward, and leaves a smaller margin for income taxation, which will be US$ 5.1 million, in the case of CEO Alex Gorsky and not the total compensation, of US$ 22 million, further concentrating income at the top. Generally, income tax on wages on stock options is lower compared to income tax on cash wages. Moreover, salaries based on stock options are only subject to income tax when the person exercises the option to buy or sell those shares and not at the time of immediate credit in shares as a form of salary. In other words, at least it is a way to momentarily escape, that is, from the collection of income tax on wages.

8.8 Dividend payments to shareholders

We now return to companies that have been paying dividends and practicing stock repurchases. Johnson & Johnson has been distributing almost all net income, and sometimes more than net income to shareholders, as can be seen in Table 8.8.

The company has been on an upward trend in paying dividends to shareholders since 1973 when it paid US$ 0.010 per share. In 2004, it paid US$ 1.09 per share and never stopped, year after year. In 2014, it was US$ 2.74 per share, in 2015 US$ 2.95 per share, in 2016 US$ 3.15 per share, in 2017 US$ 3.32 per share, in 2018 US$ 3.54 per share, reaching US$ 4.19 per share in 2021. This is a movement that does not depend on net income, which, as we have seen, may be higher or lower each year, but earnings per share are growing steadily (J&J Dividend History, 2022).

In the case of stock repurchases, it has already reached US$ 12 billion in just one year, 2013, (Seeking Alpha, 2018) and then it fell until it launched a US$ 5 billion stock repurchase plan, which was badly received by the shareholders. In fact, the company faces several lawsuits for tests on women's health, use of asbestos, among other issues that increase the risk of financial losses, currently considered at more than US$ 20 billion (Seeking Alpha, 2018).

Table 8.8 Dividend payment to Johnson & Johnson's shareholders

	2014	*2015*	*2016*	*2017*
Net profit in billions of US$	16,323	15,409	16,540	1,300*
Dividend payments in billions of US$	7,914	8,451	8,907	n/d
Stock Repurchases in billions of US$	4,00	8,00	5,00	n/d
Totals in billions of US$	11,914	16,451	13,907	n/d

Source: Johnson & Johnson Annual Report, several years

* In 2017, there was an income tax expense of more than US$ 16 billion, while the normal annual average is US$ 3 billion, depending on the revenue. Hence the drop in net profit (2017, p.14). https://johnsonandjohnson.gcs-web.com/stock-information/dividends-splits; https://seekingalpha.com/article/4229179-johnson-and-johnson-weak-sign?dr=1

The fact is that the pharmaceutical giant responds well to maximizing shareholder value policies, always concerned about allocating its net profit to shareholders, whether by paying dividends or stock repurchases, which help to artificially increase the price of shares, as already widely debated in this study.

8.9 Employee salaries

In this indicator, we see that Johnson & Johnson pays its employees reasonably well when compared to the other companies analyzed by us. We saw earlier that Amazon pays an initial US$ 15,825 annually for the lowest position (Cashier). Apple and Google reported starting salaries of US$ 18,000 annually; Microsoft, US$ 19,000; Berkshire Hathaway pays an initial US$ 20,000 annually. An intern starts at Johnson & Johnson earning US$ 16 an hour, which is multiplied by 1,700 hours (average in the USA) reaching an annual value of US$ 27,200, which is well above all other companies. It is second only to Facebook, which pays lower starting salaries of US$ 28,000, as we saw earlier. Table 8.9 shows some Johnson & Johnson professions and salaries.

In most other jobs, the average salary exceeds the average for all North American ethnic groups, which was US$ 61,000 in 2017 (Fontenot et al., 2018), as we have already seen before and can be seen in the analysis of Table 8.9.

This slightly higher salary than in other companies, coupled with the issue of compensation for executives that are within an average value among large companies, means that wage differences within Johnson & Johnson are not on an extremely unequal level, as we can see in the cases of Apple and Google, where the differences between the salaries of the less paid employees and the total CEO earnings reached 8,000 or 11,000 times the relation with each other. Table 8.10 shows this relationship between the biggest and smallest gains at Johnson & Johnson.

Because CEO Alex Gorsky was paid $22.8 million in 2017, which can be considered average compared to the highest compensation paid at other companies such as Apple and Google, and the salaries of the lowest paid workers were higher than in other companies, as we saw earlier, the differences

Table 8.9 Johnson & Johnson. The hourly and annual salary in US$ – 2018

Professional	*Minimum*	*Maximum*	*Average salary*
Intern	16,00/hour	41,00/hour	21,00/hour
Finance Intern	18,00/hour	23,00/hour	21,00/hour
Sales Representative	30,000	105,000	67,339
Analyst	46,000	110,000	71,647
Financial Analyst	50,000	85,000	65,098
Scientist	60,000	128,000	99,827
Senior Analyst	65,000	114,000	86,330
Project Manager	72,000	158,000	115,459
IT Manager	100,000	160,000	137,160
Director	127,000	232,000	180,000

Source: https://www.glassdoor.com/Salary/Johnson-and-Johnson-Salaries-E364.htm

Table 8.10 Relationship between employee salaries and total CEO earnings

Alex Gorsky. 2017 – US$ 22,843,420.00			
Employees X CEO	*Minimum*	*Maximum*	*Average*
Intern	713	278	543
Finance Intern	634	496	543
Sales Representative	761	217	339
Analyst	496	207	318
Financial Analyst	456	268	350
Scientist	380	178	228
Senior Analyst	351	200	264
Project Manager	317	144	197
IT Manager	228	142	166
Director	179	98	126

Source: Author, based on the values of the compensation table paid to the CEO and the workers' salary table

reached 713 times, which we cannot consider as an island of equality, but much smaller, between the initial intern and the CEO. The average between the Intern and the CEO was 543 times between them. When we compare the earnings of an initial Financial Analyst to the total CEO earnings, we see a difference of 456 times, in which the average was 350 times between one and the other. The further up the salary scale, the difference narrows. The Scientist showed an average difference of 228 times compared to CEO earnings, while the IT Manager 166 times. The Director earned "only" 126 times on average less than the CEO. If we talk about the Director at the end of his/her career, the difference was ninety-eight times.

These numbers confirm the correctness of our analysis in the sense of affirming that financialization is a process that widens the income inequality between the salary ranges, as already postulated by several authors, among which the most prominent is Thomas Piketty (2014). In our study, we want to make this phenomenon clear that is growing every year and is still seen as natural and immutable for certain schools of economic thought, such as the neoclassical mainstream, which advocates that the value of wages is strictly a matter of economic laws of supply and demand, with no possibility of changing this on the part of the actors involved. Just the fact that the initial Johnson & Johnson worker earns almost twice as much as the Amazon worker is already a sign that something can be done to improve the income of the least paid and thus combat wage and economic inequality.

8.10 Employment

Finally, we have the employment indicator, which, as stated several times in this study, does not behave the same as in all the companies. In fact, in these ten largest companies in market capitalization chosen in our sample, the majority increased their number of employees, differently from the automotive sector, as we studied in our previous book (Carmo et al., 2021). Even in the automotive sector, there was a fall in the North American Ford and GM but hiring in the others, such as Volkswagen, Toyota, and Hyundai. Figure 8.1 shows the number of Johnson & Johnson employees from 2007 to 2017.

Not many people were hired in the ten years between 2007 and 2017, as we can see in Figure 8.1. The increase was also due to the acquisitions of companies made by Johnson & Johnson, probably without adding new jobs. But the fact is that job posts grew from 119,000 in 2007 to 134,000 in 2017, having only fallen due to the financial global crisis of 2008, recovering from 2011.

As we insisted in this work, financialization is not a process that affects companies in the same way, and the data we found cannot be overlooked in the name of supposedly weakening the theory. It would be a crime against science to seek to distort the data to try to defend the theory at any cost. That is not our goal. The fact is that in the employment indicator, the reality is more complex than the simple statement made by activists and nonscientists that financialization linearly decreases employment worldwide, when we know that millions of people have left a situation of unemployment and misery in Asia or Southeast Asia, in Eastern Europe (previously stagnated economically by seventy years of communism and central planning economies) for a situation of job creation and improvement of living conditions.

Therefore, we cannot avoid the facts and figure. We must/have a duty to show reality. While there is greater inequality between the salary ranges, there is also precarious work in the richest countries, but there is also job creation where there was not, and this must be emphasized. However, that

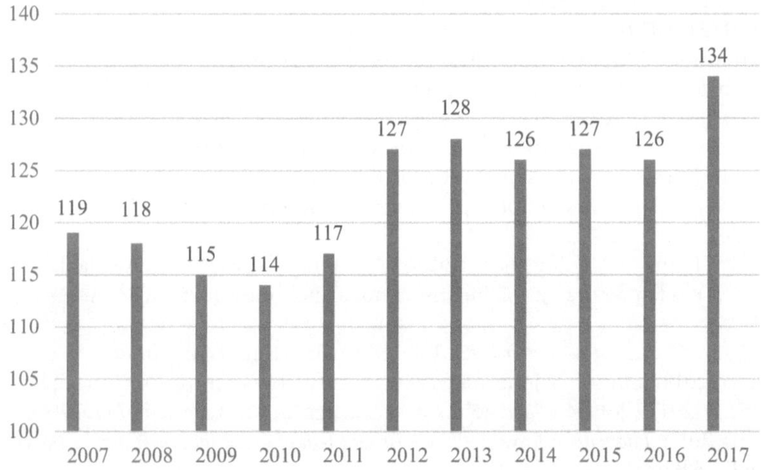

Figure 8.1 Evolution of employment at Johnson & Johnson – 2007 to 2017

stable, long-term job, with various benefits and labor rights, as explained by Wartzman (2017), is increasingly difficult to find and that is where the most visible face of financialization comes in when we talk about employment indicators.

References

Carmo, M.J. 2017. Análise do processo de financeirização do setor automotivo. *Dissertação de Mestrado apresentada ao programa de Pós-Graduação em Engenharia de Produção da Universidade Federal de São Carlos*- UFSCar, 135 f. Available at: https://repositorio.ufscar.br/handle/ufscar/8917

Carmo, M.J., Sacomano Neto, M., and Donadone, J.C. 2021. *Financialization in the Automotive Industry: Capital and Labour in Contemporary Society*. London and New York: Routledge. Available at: https://www.routledge.com/Financialisation-in-the-Automotive-Industry-Capital-and-Labour-in-Contemporary/Carmo-Neto-Donadone/p/book/9780367751395

Companiesmarketcap. 2022. Market capitalization of Johnson & Johnson (JNJ). Available at: https://companiesmarketcap.com/johnson-and-johnson/marketcap/

Crunchbase. 2022. Johnson & Johnson company acquisitions. Available at: https://www.crunchbase.com/organization/johnson-johnson#section-acquisitions. Accessed 03/08/2022.

Fichtner, J., Heemskerk, E.M., and Garcia-Bernardo, J. 2017. Hidden power of the Big Three? Passive index funds, re-concentration of corporate ownership, and new financial risk. *Business and Politics*, 19(2), 298–326.

Fontenot, K., Semega, J., and Kollar, M. 2018. Income and poverty in the United States 2017. Available at: https://www.census.gov/content/dam/Census/library/publications/2018/demo/p60-263.pdf. Accessed 10/06/2019.

Haeruddin, M.I.M. 2017. Mergers and acquisitions: Quo Vadis? *Management*, 7(2), 84–88. Available at: http://article.sapub.org/10.5923.j.mm.20170702.02.html

Johnson & Johnson *Annual Report*, 2017. Available at: https://www.investor.jnj.com/_document/2017-annual-report?id=00000162-2469-d298-ad7a-657fef1c0000. Accessed 01/21/2019.

Johnson & Johnson. 2022. Dividend history. Available at: https://johnsonandjohnson.gcs-web.com/stock-information/dividends-splits. Accessed 03/09/2022.

Nasdaq. 2019a. Johnson & Johnson institutional holdings. Available at: https://www.nasdaq.com/symbol/jnj/institutional-holdings. Accessed 01/25/2019.

Nasdaq. 2019b. Johnson & Johnson institutional holdings - increased. Available at: https://www.nasdaq.com/symbol/jnj/institutional-holdings/increased. Accessed 01/27/2019.

Nasdaq. 2019c. Johnson & Johnson institutional holdings - decreased. Available at: https://www.nasdaq.com/symbol/jnj/institutional-holdings/decreased. Accessed 01/28/2019.

Piketty, T. 2014. *O Capital no século XXI*. Rio de Janeiro: Editora Intrínseca.

Seeking Alpha. 2018. Johnson & Johnson weak sign. Available at: https://seekingalpha.com/article/4229179-johnson-and-johnson-weak-sign?dr=1. Accessed 12/19/2018.

Wartzman, R. 2017. *The End of Loyalty: The Rise and Fall of Good Jobs in America*. New York: Public Affairs.

9 JPMorgan Chase & Co.

JPMorgan Chase & Co. is the result of the merger that took place at the end of 2000 between JPMorgan & Co. and Chase Manhattan, the former Bank of Manhattan, founded by David Rockefeller. The merger created the largest US bank and sixth largest in the world, with a market capitalization in December 2017 of US$ 306 billion and which manages assets above US$ 2 trillion worldwide (Smartasset, 2019).

Discussing the financialization process involving a bank may seem odd as the bank is a financial organization *par excellence* and its main concern is finance. However, it is not that simple. We remember that Ertürk (2015) had already mentioned that the financialized mentality was the product of a progressive inculcation in all companies, including banks. The idea of maximizing shareholder value as a basic premise of the new orientation resulting from the change in the conceptions of control, as described by Fligstein (1990, 2001), was also an increasing process in banks and not something whose adhesion has been automatic.

In the case of banks, what is happening in at least two issues is raised by us here. The dividend payments to shareholders and the increasing collection of fees and services are novelties in banking activities, in which the core business is (funding, loans, and spread) progressively surpassed by fees, collection charges, administration services, mortgages, insurance, and other banking "products". Apparently, this is a novelty in the activity that we will analyze now. The comparison between the sources of profitability is one of the most important characteristics of the financialization process as it examines the changes in the sources of profits, whether through financial activities in manufacturing firms, or other activities in banking and financial companies.

9.1 Comparison between the sources of profitability

JPMorgan Chase & Co. has at least eight segments, in addition to interest-generating activities. As mentioned earlier, these segments have meant a large part of their profitability. One of them is *Investment bank fees*. These fees refer mainly to consultancies and investments in subscribed shares. Another segment is *Principal transactions*, which refer to operations with derivatives,

DOI: 10.4324/9781003309536-9

brokerage, currency, and commodities. *Lending- and deposit-related fees*, relating to deposits and loans, excluding interest. *Asset management, administration, and commissions*, which are its main source of earnings. *Investment securities*, which in fact are not very profitable and have even led to losses in recent years. *Mortgage fees and related income* are a lucrative segment but declining. *Card income* is lucrative but stagnant or declining. Finally, *Other income* that refers to leasing, Visa Europe, etc. Table 9.1 shows the bank's total revenues and by segment.

As we can see in Table 9.1, the highest revenues come from principal transactions, asset management, administration and commissions, and the investment banking fees segments. These segments have been growing year by year in total revenues. If we take the bank's net profit, compared to revenues, it went from 22.65% in 2014 to 29.78% in 2018, which meant an increase of 30% in four years. When we look at five years (2014 to 2018), in at least four of them, noninterest revenue was higher than the net interest income (the bank's core business). It was only in 2018 that interest income was higher, reaching US$ 55 billion compared to US$ 53 billion from noninterest revenue, that is, fees and other "products" that are not included in the central activity of the banking organization.

This was the trend observed by Ertürk (2015) in his study on the regulation process of banks in the postglobal crisis period of 2008. According to the author, bank regulations did not rule out the possibility of future crises, as they did not affect shareholder value maximization, whose main objective in service is to increase revenues in general and increase revenues in segments not related to interest in particular. That is, when a bank starts to have more profits in activities that are not related to interest, loans, its reason of being, we can question what the process is that presides over this conduct, and we

Table 9.1 Total and segment revenues at JPMorgan Chase & Co.

	2014	*2015*	*2016*	*2017*	*2018*
Total revenues in billions of US$	95,994	94,440	96,569	100,705	109,029
Net profit	21,745	24,442	24,733	24,441	32,474
% of net income over revenue	22,65	25,88	25,61	24,26	29,78
Investment banking fees	6542	6751	6572	7412	7550
Principal transactions	10,531	10,408	11,566	11,347	12,059
Lending- and deposit-related fees	5801	5694	5774	5933	6052
Asset management, administration, and commissions	15,931	15,509	15,364	16,287	17,118
Investment securities	0,077	202	141	−0,066	−0,395
Mortgage fees and related income	3563	2513	2491	1616	1254
Card income	6020	5924	4779	4433	4989
Other income	3013	3032	3799	3646	5343
Noninterest revenue	51,478	50,033	50,486	50,608	53,970
Net interest income	43,634	43,510	46,083	50,097	55,059

Source: JPMorgan Chase & Co. *Annual Report* 2018, pp.40 and 48; 2017, p.44; 2016, p.40.

can say that it is indeed the financialization process that is in full effect, where the most important thing is to extract value from wherever it comes from as much as possible to meet the demands of shareholders, the main stakeholders of today's corporate world. The shareholding composition of JPMorgan Chase demonstrates the strength that large shareholders have in defining the company's strategies.

9.2 Shareholding composition

The configuration of the shareholding structure in JPMorgan Chase & Co. is practically the same as that of the nonfinancial companies we are analyzing in this study. Table 9.2 shows the bank's fifteen largest shareholders, according to data from Nasdaq (2019a).

The top three and largest shareholders are the already known Big Three of North American investment funds: the Vanguard Group, BlackRock, and State Street Corp., which are the largest shareholders in all ten companies we analyzed. In addition to them, there are other investment funds, such as FMR LLC, Berkshire Hathaway, Price T. Rowe, among others. Banks also participate in this composition, such as Bank of America, Morgan Stanley, and New York Mellon, confirming the practice of cross-participation between them, as one shareholder is of the other.

Having launched more than 3.3 billion shares on the market, 72.84% of JPMorgan Chase bank's shareholders were made up of institutional investors,

Table 9.2 JPMorgan Chase's largest shareholders on September, 30, 2018

Financial groups	*Shares held*	*Value in thousands of US$*	*% of institutional shares*
Vanguard Group Inc.	254,920,409	26,190,523	10.62
BlackRock Inc.	217,485,728	22,344,484	9.06
State Street Corp.	156,770,281	16,106,579	6.53
FMR LLC	84,572,976	8,689,028	3.52
Capital World Investors	64,026,119	6,578,043	2.66
Price T Rowe Associates Inc./MD	63,968,443	6,572,118	2.66
Wellington Management Group LLP	57,695,190	5,927,604	2.40
Bank of America Corp/DE	53,569,950	5,503,777	2.23
Northern Trust Corp.	45,851,569	4,710,790	1.91
Massachusetts Financial Services Co/MA	39,247,725	4,032,311	1.63
Geode Capital Management LLC	38,759,505	3,982,152	1.61
Morgan Stanley	37,518,967	3,854,699	1.56
Bank of New York Mellon Corp.	36,045,712	3,703,336	1.50
Berkshire Hathaway Inc.	35,664,767	3,664,198	1.48
Ameriprise Financial Inc.	32,419,409	3,330,770	1.35
Total (15 biggest shareholders)	1,218,516,750	125,190,412	50.72%

Source: https://www.nasdaq.com/symbol/jpm/institutional-holdings

one of the highest percentages among the companies studied here. These shareholders, numbering 2,528, held 2.4 billion shares. Moreover, as in other companies, the shareholding concentration is large, although no single shareholder holds more than 8% of the shares. This is the case of the Vanguard Group, which held on September 30, 2018 the amount of 254 million shares, 8% of the bank's total shares, and 10.62% of the total shares held by institutional investors.

BlackRock held 217 million shares and State Street Corp. held 156 million shares. These three shareholders alone held more than 600 million shares, or 20% of the total shares and 26.21% of the total institutional shareholders. When we increase the sample to the fifteen largest institutional investors, they hold 1.2 billion shares, 50.72% of the total shares held by institutional investors. That means 0.59% of shareholders holding half of the shares at a value of more than US$ 125 billion (Nasdaq, 2019a).

These data make it clear that the process of concentrating shares in a few hands is current and leaves no room for doubt. As Davis (2008) and Fichtner et al. (2017) have pointed out, there is a process of reconcentration of properties and shareholding control, as opposed to the idea that there would be a growing dispersion of shareholders, with no one really having control of companies. What we see, on the contrary, is that these institutional investors hold huge sums of money invested in companies and, therefore, enormous decision-making power.

9.3 Shareholding acquisitions

Regarding shareholding acquisitions, the same groups that were already part of the group of shareholders were the ones that most practiced share purchases. The exception was Berkshire Hathaway, which held no shares in JPMorgan Chase, and which bought over 35 million shares, becoming the bank's fourteenth largest shareholder. Table 9.3 presents these data.

Table 9.3 Groups that most acquired JPMorgan Chase shares on September 30, 2018

Financial groups	*Shares purchased*	*% of change (+)*
Vanguard Group Inc.	66,051	0.03
State Street Corp.	2,370,968	1.54
Price T Rowe Associates Inc./MD	1,332,470	2.13
Wellington Management Group LLP	36,655	0.06
Bank of America Corp/DE	1,500,905	2.88
Morgan Stanley	3,247,181	9.48
Berkshire Hathaway Inc.	35,664,767	New
Wells Fargo & Company/MN	112,123	0.40
Capital International Investors	7,296,691	37.85
UBS Group AG	417,198	2.30

Source: https://www.nasdaq.com/symbol/jpm/institutional-holdings/increased

Table 9.4 Groups that sold most JPMorgan Chase shares on September, 30, 2018

Financial groups	*Sold shares*	*% of change (−)*
BlackRock Inc.	5,554,008	2.49
FMR LLC	6,636,589	7.28
Capital World Investors	2,345,788	3.53
Northern Trust Corp.	907,327	1.94
Massachusetts Financial Services Co/MA	2,145,602	5.18
Geode Capital Management LLC	253,346	0.65
Bank of New York Mellon Corp.	606,501	1.66
Ameriprise Financial Inc.	1,434,265	4.24
Dodge & Cox	130,450	0.52
Franklin Resources Inc.	673,595	2.76

Source: https://www.nasdaq.com/symbol/jpm/institutional-holdings/decreased

Capital International Investors acquired 7.2 million shares, increasing its stake by 37.85%. Morgan Stanley bought 3.2 million shares and increased its stake in the bank by 9.48% and State Street Corp. acquired 2.3 million shares, growing just over 1.5%. The Bank of America bought 1.5 million shares and increased its participation by 2.88% in the shares of the competing bank (Nasdaq, 2019b), an interesting fact of how this cross-participation works at the current moment.

9.4 Share sales

The groups that sold the most shares did not do so very intensely. Sales fluctuated between a 0.52% reduction in the shares held by Dodge & Cox, for example, up to 7.28% in the shares held by FMR LLC, which sold more than 6.6 million shares. However, in the latter case, despite the significant number of shares sold, FMR LLC still holds over 84 million shares of the JPMorgan Chase bank, as shown before. Table 9.4 presents these numbers.

BlackRock Inc. also sold a good number of shares, 5.5 million of them, decreasing its participation in the bank's shares by 2.49%, but it remains the second largest shareholder, with more than 217 million shares. The sale of shares, as we have said several times in this work, has to do with the issue of the short term, but in the case of the bank. there are more investors buying shares than selling. On January 25, 2019, there were 107 new purchases, totaling 42 million shares, and eighty-one sales, totaling just 3.3 million shares, which proves the great demand for bank shares. It can be observed that purchases far outpaced sales (Nasdaq, 2019c).

9.5 Mergers and acquisitions

Just like the other companies analyzed by us in this work, JPMorgan Chase & Co. also practices acquisitions of companies but in a much smaller number. From 1999 to 2017, the bank had acquired nine companies. Most of them did not have their purchase price disclosed, as shown in Table 9.5.

Table 9.5 JPMorgan Chase's acquisitions

Company	*Date of purchase*	*Value in millions of US$*
WePay	Oct 17, 2017	400
J.P. Morgan Cazenove	Nov 19, 2009	n/d
Washington Mutual	Sep 26, 2008	n/d
Bear Stearns	Mar 17, 2008	n/d
Xspand	Mar 1, 2008	n/d
Collegiate Funding Services	Dec 15, 2005	n/d
Neovest Holdings	June 23, 2005	n/d
Bank One	Jan 15, 2004	58,000
Hambrecht & Quist	Sept 28, 1999	1,400
Totals in billions of US$		59,800

Source: https://www.crunchbase.com/organization/jpmorgan-chase-co#section-acquisitions

As with other companies, JPMorgan Chase's acquisitions were from companies complementary to its business, such as banks, investment funds, and payment companies. The biggest acquisition came on January 15, 2004, when it bought Bank One for US$ 58 billion. The last disclosed acquisition was on October 17, 2017, when it bought WePay, a payment services company, for US$ 400 million. The difference in the current process of company acquisitions and the previous process lies in the fact that large companies have acquired companies that are directly related to their core business, as discussed earlier in this work. In a period before financialization, companies acquired any type of company they deemed worthy of investment. Considering financialization, the focus was on complementary companies that bring synergy to the business, always, of course, thinking about the return that such businesses will give institutional investors.

9.6 Origin of executives

JPMorgan Chase & Co. has nineteen members of Board of Directors. Here, we selected ten executives, at random, to analyze their business and academic trajectories. As in other companies, the relationship is strong among the executives, who participate in several other boards. Furthermore, they have a very varied trajectory, going through financial, industrial, public, and entertainment organizations. Table 9.6 shows where these officers went and how many and which boards they comprise or have already made up.

James Crown, for example, has been a member since 2010 and has participated in several companies, such as Henry Crown and Company, General Dynamics Corporation, JPMorgan Chase Bank, NA, Sara Lee Corporation, Salomon Brothers Inc., Capital Markets Service Group, Museum of

Table 9.6 JPMorgan Chase officers – Board of Directors

Director	*No of Boards in which they participate*	*Organizations in which they participated*
Laban P. Jackson, Jr. Board Member	1 JP Morgan Chase & Co.	Clear Creek Properties, Inc., J.P. Morgan Securities plc., JPMorgan Chase Bank, N.A., The Home Depot, Federal Reserve Bank of Cleveland, Graduated from the United States Military Academy
Jamie Dimon Board Member	1 JP Morgan Chase & Co.	Bank One Corporation, Citigroup Inc., Travelers Group, Commercial Credit Company; American Express Company, Graduated from Tufts University; MBA from Harvard Business School
William Weldon Board Member 2005	5 Chubb, CVS Health, ExxonMobil, JP Morgan Chase & Co., JPMorgan Partners (JPMP)	Johnson & Johnson, ExxonMobil, JP Morgan Chase & Co.,
Linda B. Bammann Board Member	1 JP Morgan Chase & Co.	Bank One Corporation, JPMorgan Chase, UBS Warburg LLC, The Federal Home Loan Mortgage Corporation (Freddie Mac), Manulife Financial Corporation, Loan Syndications and Trading Association, BSc from Stanford University and an MA in public policy from the University of Michigan.
Stephen B. Burke Board Member	1 JP Morgan Chase & Co.	Comcast Cable, The Walt Disney Company, ABC Broadcasting, The Children's Hospital of Philadelphia, C-SPAN, Phi Beta Kappa graduate of Colgate University, MBA from the Harvard Business School

(*Continued*)

Director	*No of Boards in which they participate*	*Organizations in which they participated*
James Bell Board Member	7 The Dow Chemical Company, The Economic Club of Chicago, The Chicago Urban League, CDW Corporation, Apple, Chicago Infrastructure Trust	The Boeing Company, Dow Chemical Company, Space Station Electric Power System, Rockwell, BA in Accounting from California State University
Lee Raymond Board Member	7 Wisconsin Alumni Research Foundation, Mayo Clinic, University of Texas Southwestern Medical School, National Academy of Engineering, Business Council for International Understanding	ExxonMobil, Graduated from the University of Wisconsin in 1960 and received a PhD from the University of Minnesota in Chemical Engineering
James Crown Board Member 2010	10 General Dynamics, The University of Chicago, DocuSign, World Business Chicago, Chicago Symphony Orchestra	Henry Crown and Company, General Dynamics Corporation, JPMorgan Chase Bank, N.A., Sara Lee Corporation, Salomon Brothers Inc., Capital Markets Service Group, Museum of Science and Industry, The Aspen Institute, Graduated from Hampshire College, Law degree from Stanford University Law School
Donald Dickerson Board Member	1 JP Morgan Chase & Co.	Worked in several management and accounting positions and has experience with companies in the technology, manufacturing, and health sciences area. Mr. Dickerson's experience includes leadership positions at BioRasi, Dell, Boeing Capital, and Medistem, Inc. Master of Business Administration, Finance from the University of Southern California

Glenn Tilton Board Member	6 Skills for Chicagoland's Future, World Business Chicago, AbbVie, Phillips 66, Abbott	United Continental Holdings, Inc., UAL Corporation, Lincoln National Corporation, TXU Corporation, Corning Incorporated, Chevron Texaco, Dynegy, Inc.

Source: https://www.crunchbase.com/organization/jpmorgan-chase-co/people

Science and Industry, The Aspen Institute, among others. He graduated from Hampshire College and has a law degree from Stanford University Law School. He currently participates in ten boards, among which are General Dynamics, The University of Chicago, DocuSign, World Business Chicago, Chicago Symphony Orchestra, etc.

CEO Jamie Dimon's career has mostly been in financial organizations, including Bank One Corporation, Citigroup Inc., Travelers Group, Commercial Credit Company, and American Express Company. Graduated from Tufts University, he has an MBA from Harvard Business School.

There are also, on the other hand, managers who have predominantly passed through the world of industry, such as James Bell, who previously worked at the Boeing Company, Dow Chemical Company, Space Station Electric Power System, Rockwell, etc., that is, large manufacturing companies. He holds a BA in Accounting from California State University and currently serves on seven boards, including The Dow Chemical Company, The Economic Club of Chicago, The Chicago Urban League, CDW Corporation, Apple, and Chicago Infrastructure Trust.

These life trajectories, both academic and professional, show the complex network of relationships established in today's corporate world. It recruits leaders from various worlds, including the financial, industrial, public sector, entertainment, communications and technology, as well as various segments of civil society, such as economy clubs, universities, museum curators, employers "and sometimes even workers" unions.

This true mixture of origins does not seem to influence the logic of financialization, in terms of maximizing shareholder value and the current conception of control (Fligstein, 1990, 1991, 2001). These professionals seem to behave in a very similar way, regardless of their origin, whether it be industrial, financial, or services. They act according to the prevailing conception of control and their professional origin does not seem to have any weight in their decisions made today.

9.7 Compensation paid to executives

The compensation paid to the executives of JPMorgan Chase & Co. is at an average level among the companies that we are analyzing in this work. It is

Table 9.7 Compensation payment to executives. JPMorgan Chase

Annual salary in US$ – 2017				
Compensations to executives	*Total in cash*	*Stock options*	*Others*	*Total compensations*
Jamie Dimon Chairman and CEO	6,500,000	21,500,000	278,278	28,278,278
Gordon Smith CEO CCB	8,450,000	10,950,000	0	19,400,000
Mary Callahan Erdoes CEO AWM	8,250,000	10,950,000	0	19,200,000
Daniel Pinto CEO CIB	8,238,628	10,696,766	80,384	19,015,778
Marianne Lake Chief Financial Officer	5,850,000	7,050,000	60,969	12,960,969

Source: https://www.salary.com/tools/executive-compensation-calculator/jpmorgan-chase-and-co-executive-salaries?year=2017

not as high as Apple and Google, which paid more than US$ 100 million to the CEO in a single year, nor as low as Berkshire Hathaway, which paid US$ 100,000/US$388,000 to CEO Warren Buffett. Table 9.7 shows the payment of compensation to the main executives in 2017.

CEO Jamie Dimon received US$ 28 million in 2017, comprising US$ 6.5 million in cash wages and US$ 21.5 million in shares, through the so-called stock options (SO). Stock options are also practiced at JPMorgan Chase bank and share payments are higher than cash payments, although in a more balanced way than in other companies. Cash wages are more significant and closer to the amounts paid in shares, as can be seen in Table 9.7. The average cash wage in 2017 was US$ 7.5 million and the average payment in stock options was US$ 12 million, which is closer to Google, for example, which paid CEO Sundar Pichai in 2016 only US$ 650,000 in cash and US$ 198 million in stock options. As we have already stated, this practice has two objectives: to increase the price of shares through large purchases, including these payments to executives through stock options, which are thousands, and to avoid taxation on income, which will end up focusing only on the time of exercising the options. In our view, these are typical movements in tune with the financialization process, also in this indicator of compensation to executives.

9.8 Dividend payments to shareholders

JPMorgan Chase & Co. regularly practices the policy of paying dividends to shareholders and repurchasing shares of the company, the so-called stock repurchases. The interesting thing to note is that among the companies that pay dividends to shareholders, the bank does not allocate all its net profit to these payments but leaves a small reserve, as can be seen in Table 9.8.

Table 9.8 Dividend payment and stock repurchases to JPMorgan Chase's shareholders

	2014	*2015*	*2016*	*2017*	*2018*
Net profit in billions of US$	21,745	24,442	24,733	24,441	32,474
Dividend payment in billions of US$	15,317	17,035	13,752	7,157	10,726
Stock repurchases in billions of US$	4,760	5,616	9,082	15,410	19,983
Total in billions of US$	20,077	22,651	22,834	22,567	30,709
Total held in reserve in billions of US$	1668	1791	1899	1874	1765

Sources: https://www.nasdaq.com/symbol/jpm/financials?query=income-statement. JPMorgan Chase *Annual Reports*, 2016, p.84 and 2018, p.92.

In the past five years, around US$ 2 billion has been left in the bank and has not been earmarked for dividend payments or stock repurchases (Nasdaq, 2019d). This situation differs from most companies that pay dividends and repurchases, as they practically drain all the net profit on these disbursements.

Regarding stock repurchases, the bank bought back more than US$ 55 billion in just five years. 82 million shares were repurchased in 2014, 89 million in 2015, 140 million shares in 2016, 166 million in 2017, and 181 million shares repurchased in 2018 (JPMorgan Chase & Co. *Annual Reports*, 2016, p. 84; 2018, p.92). In addition to showing a growth trend, this movement was responsible for the repurchase of more than 658 million shares, almost 20% of the total issued shares, which add up to 3.3 billion shares.

These figures show that this policy is in full effect in most of the companies studied by us in this work. Dividend payments to shareholders implements the policy of maximizing shareholder value as the main concern of the business and the stock repurchases aims to increase the unit price of the shares through a massive purchase of them, artificially, as we can see. This is in addition to valuing the remaining shares even more, which in smaller numbers will represent a market capitalization that will be higher over time.

9.9 Employee salaries

Table 9.9 shows some professions and their starting salaries, the maximum and the average.

The bank is not a big payer, as we can see in Table 9.9. There were starting salaries of US$ 9.00 an hour for a bank teller, which can reach US$ 18.00 an hour, and their average is US$ 12.00. This average gives an annual salary of US$ 24,000 if we consider 2,000 hours worked per year, but in the USA, this number of hours is lower, around 1,700 hours, which gives an average value

Table 9.9 JPMorgan Chase. The hourly and annual salary in US$ – 2018

Professional	*Minimum*	*Maximum*	*Average salary*
Bank teller	9,00/hour	18,00/hour	12,00/hour
Trainee – Technology Analyst	17,00/hour	38,00/hour	32,00/hour
Licensed Personal Banker	29,000	60,000	35,327
Personal Banker II	28,000	57,000	35,384
Associate	28,000	176,000	97,804
Banker for private clients	32,000	84,000	39,610
Financial Analyst	44,000	121,000	66,147
Subsidiary manager	46,000	96,000	64,473
Vice President of Technology	92,00	211,000	141,980
Executive Director	120,000	330,000	197,461

Source: https://www.glassdoor.com/Salary/J-P-Morgan-Salaries-E145.htm

Table 9.10 Ratio between employee salaries and total CEO earnings Jamie Dimon in 2017 – US$ 28,278,278.00

Employees X CEO	*Minimum*	*Maximum*	*Average salary*
Bank teller	1571	785	1178
Trainee – Technology Analyst	831	372	441
Licensed Personal Banker	975	471	800
Personal Banker II	1009	496	799
Associate	1009	160	289
Banker for private clients	883	336	713
Financial Analyst	642	233	427
Subsidiary manager	614	294	438
Vice President of Technology	307	134	199
Executive Director	235	85	143

Source: Authors, based on the values of the compensation table paid to the CEO and the workers' salary table

of US$ 21,360 and US$ 16,020 for early stage bank tellers. This figure is at least three times lower than the average wages for all North American ethnic groups, which stood at US$ 61,000 in 2017 (Fontenot et al., 2018).

The relationship between the CEO's total earnings and employee salaries can be seen in Table 9.10.

We can see that the lowest salary, that of the initial bank teller, is up to 1,571 times lower than the earnings of CEO Jamie Dimon, who received more than US$ 28 million in 2017. The smallest difference can be seen for the executive director with a maximum salary of US$ 330,000 annually, reaching eighty-five times. The wage issue, for us in this work, represents a financialization indicator as there is an increasing inequality between wage brackets, as defined by Piketty (2014) and it has to do with power within organizations, as they defined Bebchuk and Fried (2004). This policy of paying millions in compensation to executives and low salaries to employees has, over time, contributed to the increase in economic inequality, which could be reversed if a more balanced decision were taken in favor of better remuneration for basic workers and lower remuneration for top executives. This is a recommendation that our work can bring to the actors involved, aiming for a more economically balanced and more egalitarian society for all, where income can help develop a greater number of people.

9.10 Employment

The level of employment at JPMorgan Chase has varied considerably since 2008, as shown in Figure 9.1.

In ten years, the number of employees jumped from 225,000 to 253,000 workers, an increase of 11%. After the 2008 crisis, the number dropped to 222,000, a small retraction, to rise by 18,000 from 2009 to 2010. It reached 260,000 in 2011, dropped to 234,000 in 2015 and 2016, and rose to 253,000 in 2017. This movement, at first, does not reflect the bank's financial problems as we saw that from 2014 to 2018 its revenues only increased. There would be no reason for a drop in revenues to justify the drop in the number of employees from 2014 to 2016, which were 7,000 layoffs. Nevertheless, from 2016 to 2017, there were more than 18,000 hires. We would need more studies to make a better assessment of what happened in the bank to understand such a fluctuation without a very apparent cause. But this fact only corroborates what we have been saying throughout this work, that financialization does not happen in the same way in all companies and all countries. And this aspect is one of the most intriguing when we analyze the financialization indicators in contemporary companies.

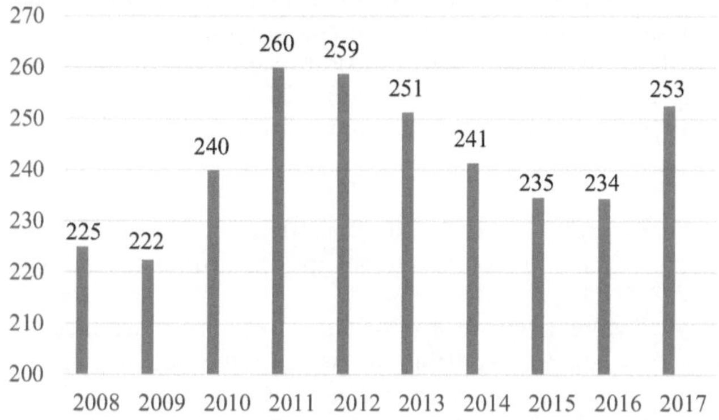

Figure 9.1 Evolution of employment at JPMorgan Chase – 2008 to 2017

References

Bebchuk, L.A. and Fried, J.M. 2004. Pay without performance, the unfulfilled promise of executive compensation, part II: power and pay, draft of the book *Pay without Performance, The Unfulfilled Promise of Executive Compensation*. Available at: http://www.law.harvard.edu/faculty/bebchuk/pdfs/Performance-Part2.pdf. Accessed 09/10/2021.

Davis, G.F. 2008. A new finance capitalism? Mutual funds and ownership re-concentration in the United States. *European Management Review*, 5, 11–21.

Ertürk, I. 2015. Financialization, bank business models and the limits of post-crisis bank regulation. *Journal of Banking Regulation*, 17(1–2), 60–72.

Fichtner, J., Heemskerk, E.M., and Garcia-Bernardo, J. 2017. Hidden power of the Big Three? Passive index funds, re-concentration of corporate ownership, and new financial risk. *Business and Politics*, 19(2), 298–326.

Fligstein, N. 1990. *The Transformation of Corporate Control*. Cambridge, MA: Harvard University Press.

Fligstein, N. 1991. The structural transformation of American industry: an institutional account of the causes of diversification in the largest firms, 1919–1979. *The New Institutionalism in Organizational Analysis*. Paul J. DiMaggio and Walter W. Powell (eds.), 311–336. Chicago, IL: University of Chicago Press.

Fligstein, N. 2001. *The Architecture of Markets: An Economic Sociology of Twenty-First-Century Capitalist Societies*. Princeton, NJ: Princeton University Press.

Fontenot, K., Semega, J., and Kollar, M., 2018. Income and poverty in the United States 2017. Available at: https://www.census.gov/content/dam/Census/library/publications/2018/demo/p60-263.pdf. Accessed 10/06/2019.

JPMorgan Chase & Co, 2016. JPMorgan Chase & Co. *Annual Report* 2016. Available at: https://reports.jpmorganchase.com/investor-relations/2016/pdf/2016-annualreport.pdf. Accessed 08/27/2018.

JPMorgan Chase & Co, 2017. JPMorgan Chase & Co. *Annual Report* 2017. Available at: https://www.jpmorganchase.com/content/dam/jpmc/jpmorgan-chase-and-co/investor-relations/documents/annualreport-2017.pdf. Accessed 08/27/2018.

JPMorgan Chase & Co, 2018. JPMorgan Chase & Co. *Annual Report* 2018. Available at: https://www.jpmorganchase.com/content/dam/jpmc/jpmorgan-chase-and-co/investor-relations/documents/annualreport-2018.pdf. Accessed 05/22/2019.

Nasdaq, 2019a. JPMorgan Chase & Co. institutional holdings. Available at: https://www.nasdaq.com/symbol/jpm/institutional-holdings. Accessed 01/25/2019.

Nasdaq, 2019b. JPMorgan Chase & Co. institutional holdings - increased. Available at: https://www.nasdaq.com/symbol/jpm/institutional-holdings/increased. Accessed 01/27/2019.

Nasdaq, 2019c. JPMorgan Chase & Co. institutional holdings - decreased. Available at: https://www.nasdaq.com/symbol/jpm/institutional-holdings/decreased. Accessed 01/28/2019.

Nasdaq, 2019d. JPMorgan Chase & Co. Net income and net income applicable to common shareholders. Available at: https://www.nasdaq.com/symbol/jpm/financials?query=income-statement. Accessed 01/28/2019.

Piketty, T. 2014. *O Capital no século XXI*. Rio de Janeiro: Editora Intrínseca.

Smartasset, 2019. The top ten banks in America. Available at: https://smartasset.com/checking-account/the-top-ten-banks-by-assets-held. Accessed 05/28/2019.

10 Tencent Holdings

Tencent Holdings Limited is a company that was created in 1998 by Hua Teng Ma and Zhang Zhidong, specializing in mobile and internet services, as well as online advertising. Its headquarters are in Nanshan District, Shenzhen, Guangdong, in the People's Republic of China. Tencent's services include social networks, portals, e-commerce, and multiplayer online games. It manages the instant messaging service Tencent QQ, operates one of China's largest portals, QQ.com, and the instant messaging app WeChat.

In 2015, there were 853 million active Tencent QQ accounts, making Tencent QQ the fourth largest online community in the world, and 697 million WeChat users (Jia & Winseck, 2018, p.34). The number of QQ accounts connected simultaneously sometimes exceeds 100 million. In January 2017, Tencent entered the capital of Skydance Media in a proportion of 5% to 10% (Tencent Holdings *Annual Reports*, 2010, 2017).

The Chinese giant was considered the ninth-largest company in market capitalization, worldwide, in December 2017, estimated at US$ 277 billion (Statista, 2018). It has stakes in several companies, such as Riot Games (69%); Bizzard Entertainment (12%); Supercell (84%); Epic Games (40%); Kingston Network Technology (18%); South Korea´s CJ Games (28%); JD.com (15%); GLU Mobile (14%); PUBG (32%); Snap (12%); Grinding Gear Games (80%); Via Varejo (36%); Level Up! Games (49%), among others (Tencent Holdings *Annual Report*, 2017).

Tencent sells virtual objects for use in its multiplayer online games, instant messaging clients, social networks, and cell phones. Revenues from the sale of virtual items represent a large proportion of Tencent's revenues. Tencent's online currency, Q Coins, can be used to purchase virtual goods. These range from virtual pets, clothes, jewelry, and virtual cosmetics needed to personalize an avatar in an online game, to the most banal, such as storage space, screen, larger photo albums, and ringtones. Tencent Holdings is undoubtedly an innovative company in every way, taking advantage of its immense market to become, in just twenty-one years, the ninth-largest company in market cap in the world and the fifth largest in the field of communication and internet. It is the product, above all, of the union between "state, internet companies and international finance capital" (Jia & Winseck, 2018, p.30).

DOI: 10.4324/9781003309536-10

Table 10.1 Tencent Holdings' revenues

	2013	*2014*	*2015*	*2016*	*2017*
Revenues in billions of US$	9,3	11,6	15,6	22,4	35,1
Gross margin	4,8	7,1	9,05	12,4	17,2
Operating profit	2,8	4,2	5,3	7,6	13,04
Net profit	2,7	3,2	6,6	7,1	11,6
% of net profit on revenue	29	27	42	31	33
Net income available to shareholders	2,7	3,2	6,6	7,1	11,5
VAS – value added services – games in billions of US$	6,6	9,3	11,9	15,9	22,7
Online advertising in billions of US$	0,744	1,2	2,5	3,9	5,9

Source: Tencent *Annual Reports*, 2017, pp.3 and 13; 2015, p.13. On 1/11/2019 the exchange rate was $ 1 = CNY 6.76

10.1 Comparison between the sources of profitability

Tencent Holdings' revenue growth is undisputed, as shown in Table 10.1. It went from US$ 9.3 billion in total revenues in 2013 to US$ 35.1 billion in 2017, a 376% growth in just four years. The percentage of net profit on revenue is also very high, reaching 42% of net profit in revenue in 2015 and an average of 32.4% in the five years, between 2013 and 2017. Table 10.1 shows the data.

As in other communications and internet companies, such as Google and Facebook, for example, Tencent Holdings has been growing its margin in value-added services (VAS), which went from US$ 6.6 billion in 2013 to US$ 22.7 billion in 2017, an increase of 343% in four years. Furthermore, online advertising went from US$ 744 million in 2013 to US$ 5.9 billion in 2017, multiplying its online advertising revenue by eight in just four years. The monthly active users (MAUs) and daily active users (DAUs), which we explored when analyzing Facebook, are the main drivers of this growth, since Tencent is the largest Chinese company in games and users and the fourth largest in population of users in the world and has been growing year by year (Jia & Winseck, 2018, p.34). And therein lies the financialization in this indicator that compares the sources of profitability, as it is in the growth in the number of users and advertisements, which are more expensive each year and which take more resources, either from users or from those who pay for the advertisements, which company revenues are growing at a rapid pace. As Google and Facebook, the average revenue per user has been increasing year by year, indicating that this is a tactic of these companies, which drain public resources for themselves, reinforcing a trend in the financialization process worldwide.

10.2 Shareholding composition

Having launched more than 9.5 billion shares on the market, Tencent Holdings has a greater shareholding concentration than all the other companies analyzed by us in this research. When it went public on the Hong Kong stock exchange in 2004, the company's largest shareholder was the conglomerate Naspers Ltd., which

> provides platforms, print media, internet services, technology products and book publishing. It operates through the following business segments: B2C, Classifieds, Corporate, Naspers Ventures, Payments, Press and Digital Media and Video Entertainment. The company was founded on May 12, 1915, and is headquartered in Cape Town, South Africa.
>
> (Marketscreener, 2018a)

Naspers Ltd. remained the largest shareholder in Tencent Holdings at least until 2019, with 31.1% of the shares, as shown in Table 10.2.

Note to the reader that only the ten largest shareholders of Tencent hold almost half of the shares, that is, 47.37%, and they are large groups of foreign institutional investors, and cannot fail to figure among them Vanguard Group and BlackRock Inc., two of the Big Three of the U.S. investment funds. International banks such as Norges Bank (Central Bank of Norway) and JPMorgan Investment also participate in its shareholding control.

CEO Hua Teng Ma held 8.61% on January 25, 2019, but has seen his share fall since the IPO in 2004. "At Tencent, founder Hua Teng Ma's share in 2015 was 9.1%, down from 13.1% in 2004. This is very interesting because the trajectory in the maturation of capitalism over time has been the eclipse of owner-controlled companies in favor of commercial companies controlled by shareholders and specialist managers" (Noam, 2016, pp. 1190–1200 *apud* Jia & Winseck, 2018, p.44).

That is, banks, venture capital funds, and other institutional investors also obtained significant equity stakes in Tencent Holdings, although Naspers Ltd. is still its largest shareholder. However, large investment funds and institutional shareholders are also large shareholders of Naspers itself. It is the worldwide trend of cross-participation between large companies and one of

Table 10.2 Tencent Holdings' largest shareholders on January 25, 2019

Financial groups	*Shares held*	*%*
Naspers LTD.	2,961,223,600	31.1
Hua Teng Ma	819,507,500	8.61
Vanguard Group, Inc.	197,042,711	2.07
BlackRock Fund Advisors	133,074,931	1.40
T. Rowe Price Associates, Inc.	99,488,340	1.05
Norges Bank	79,924,685	0.84
Schroder Investment Management LTD	58,893,110	0.62
Capital World Investors	58,111,411	0.61
JPMorgan Investment Management, Inc.	51,053,633	0.54
Capital Global Investors	50,690,718	0.53
Totals (ten biggest shareholders)	4,509,010,639	47.37%

Source: https://www.marketscreener.com/TENCENT-HOLDINGS-LTD-3045861/company/

the characteristics of the financialization process, as we have been advocating since the beginning of this research.

The most interesting thing to note, in our opinion, is that this process also arrives in full force in China, albeit a little late, compared to the financialization in the West. However, it arrives and confirms, through the numbers and references we found, the financialization process in the largest companies in market value, regarding the indicator that reveals the shareholder composition of companies, including Chinese ones.

10.3 Mergers and acquisitions

Tencent Holdings has been acquiring companies at a fast pace, having acquired thirteen companies from 2011 to 2019, announcing a value of more than US$ 11.7 billion in only three of them, China Music Corp., acquired in 2016 for US$ 2.7 billion; Supercell, also in 2016 for US$ 8.6 billion, and Riot Games, the first to be acquired, in 2011, for US$ 400 million (Crunchbase, 2018). This movement is happening in several Chinese companies, following the world trend.

Since 2013, "Baidu, Alibaba and Tencent – referred to in the sector as BAT – have made a combined total of US$ 75 billion in investments in the acquisition of strategic partners, according to an HSBC research report" (Perez, 2016). Table 10.3 shows the acquisitions of Tencent Holdings, until May 2019, although our source does not have more information on the values of all transactions.

In addition to Tencent, Chinese companies are in full swing in the acquisition of companies.

> The BAT (Baidu, Alibaba and Tencent) group has emerged as the dominant force in mergers and acquisitions on the continent, with deals last

Table 10.3 Tencent Holdings' company acquisitions

Company	*Date of purchase*	*Value in millions of US$*
Sharkmob	May 21, 2019	n/d
Cat Cake	Aug 22, 2018	n/d
Grinding Gear Games	May 21, 2018	n/d
Sanook Thailand	Dec 22, 2016	n/d
China Music Corp.	July 14, 2016	2700
Supercell	June 21, 2016	8600
Miniclip SA	Feb 18, 2015	n/d
Cloudary	Jan 27, 2015	n/d
Linktech Navi	Jan 26, 2014	n/d
Zam	Mar 1, 2012	n/d
Riot Games	Feb 2011	400
Totals in billions of US$		11,700

Source: https://www.crunchbase.com/organization/tencent/acquisitions/acquisitions_list#section-acquisitions

> year in highly competitive segments, including mobile-hailing apps, where Alibaba is an investor in Lyft and Baidu invested in the US operator Uber.

"Moreover, a survey by the bank BNP Paribas estimates that Alibaba could spend another US$ 38 billion in 2016, Tencent US$ 35 billion and Baidu US$ 15 billion in acquisitions" (Perez, 2016).

In short, company mergers and acquisitions crown the financialization process as they further concentrate ownership on a few gigantic companies, such as the Chinese communications and internet ecosystem.

> Consolidation, in turn, has resulted in high levels of concentration in many core segments of the internet economy. While greater precision is needed, it is safe to say that the market for internet services in China is now a tight oligopoly, with Baidu, Alibaba and Tencent occupying much of the field.
>
> (Jia & Winseck, 2018, p.50)

10.4 Origin of managers

The directors of Tencent Holdings come predominantly from the media world. Except for CEO Hua Teng Ma, who is a politician and deputy member of the 5th Shenzhen Municipal People's Congress and the 12th National People's Congress, that is, a member of the Chinese Communist Party, all other members of the Board of Directors are from the media, communication, or finance (Jia & Winseck, 2018, p.47). Table 10.4 shows the Tencent's leaders.

The relationship between these professionals, as already seen in the other companies that we are analyzing, is very important to establish power within the network in which they operate. In the case of Tencent, its largest owner, Naspers, has long been represented on the board and, similar to Mail.ru, a Russian internet company in which Tencent invested heavily, each company also has interconnected relationships with several Chinese Communist Party members. "As Arsenault and Castells observe (2008, p.731), media networks do not exist in a vacuum, but they leverage connections with other critical networks: in finance, technology, cultural industries, in social networks and in politics" (Jia & Winseck, 2018, p.46).

This entire relationship network is not exclusive to Western companies, as we have seen in the largest companies in market value studied here, almost all of which are North American. They exist strongly in Chinese capitalism and their participants have been learning fast, as in a movement of mimetic isomorphism. That is, everyone is copying successful models over time and establishing ties between companies, Boards, sectors of the broader economy. Hence, financialization has been developing as a very homogeneous process

Table 10.4 Tencent Holdings' executives

Directors	*Organizations in which they participate or participated*
Hua Teng Ma Chairman and Chief Executive Officer	Tencent Holdings Ltd., Tencent Technology (Shenzhen) Co., Ltd., Advance Data Services Ltd., Undergraduate degree from Shenzhen University.
Martin Chi Ping Lau President and Executive Director	JD. Com Inc. (ADR), Vipshop Holdings Ltd – ADR, Kingsoft Corporation Limited, Leju Holdings Ltd (ADR), Meituan Dianping, Undergraduate degree from the University of Michigan, a graduate degree from Stanford University and an MBA from Kellogg School of Management.
Yu Xin Ren COO and President-Interactive Entertainment Group	Tencent Holdings Ltd., Sea Ltd. (ADR), Sogou Inc., Undergraduate degree from the University of Electronic Science & Technology of China and an MBA from China Europe International Business School.
Shek Hon Lo EMBA Chief Financial Officer and Senior Vice President	PricewaterhouseCoopers LLP (Hong Kong), Tencent Holdings Ltd., Undergraduate degree from Curtin University and an MBA from The Hong Kong University of Science & Technology.
Chen Ye Xu Chief Information Officer	Tencent Holdings Ltd., Tencent Technology (Shenzhen) Co., Ltd., Undergraduate degree from Shenzhen University and a graduate degree from the University of Nanjing.
Charles St. Leger Searle Nonexecutive Director	Tencent Holdings Ltd., Mail Ru Group Ltd., MakeMyTrip Limited, Naspers Limited, The Institute of Chartered Accountants in Australia, Institute of Chartered Accountants of New Zealand, Chartered Accountants Australia & New Zealand, Undergraduate degree from the University of Cape Town.
Dong Sheng Li Independent Nonexecutive Director	Tencent Holdings Ltd., Legrand SA, TCL Corporation, TCL Electronics Holdings Ltd., Fantasia Holdings Group Co., Limited, TTE Technology, Inc. (California), TCL Communication Tech Holdings Ltd., Huizhou TCL Mobile Communication Co., Ltd., Guangdong Household Electrical Appliances Chamber of Commerce, China Video Industry Association, China Electronic Imaging Industry Association,

	Guangdong Chamber of Commerce for Household Appliances, Shenzhen Flat Panel Display Industry Association, China Chamber of International Commerce, Guangdong Provincial Federation of Industry & Commerce, Undergraduate degree from South China University of Technology.
Iain Ferguson Bruce Independent Nonexecutive Director	KPMG Hong Kong, KCS Ltd., KPMG Asia Pacific Ltd, Tencent Holdings Ltd, Wing On Company International Ltd, Goodbaby International Hldg Ltd, South Shore Holdings Ltd, Yingli Green Energy Holding Co Ltd (ADR), Citibank NA (Hong Kong Branch), MSIG Insurance (Hong Kong) Ltd., Paul Y. Engineering Group Ltd., The Institute of Chartered Accountants of Scotland, Hong Kong Securities & Investment Institute
Ian Charles Stone Independent Nonexecutive Director	UK Broadband Ltd., SmarTone Mobile Communications Ltd., Pacific Link Communications Ltd., Pilipino Telephone Corp., Tencent Holdings Ltd., CSL Mobile Ltd., Saudi Integrated Telecom Co., The Hong Kong Institute of Directors.
Jacobus Petrus Bekker Nonexecutive Director	Tencent Holdings Ltd., Naspers Limited, Media24 Ltd., MIH (Mauritius) Ltd., MIH BV, Undergraduate degree from the University of Stellenbosch, a graduate degree from the University of the Witwatersrand and an MBA from Columbia University.

Source: https://www.marketscreener.com/TENCENT-HOLDINGS-LTD-3045861/company/

within companies, with the increasing participation of financial organizations, managers who have passed through financial companies, banks, etc., and with dividend payment practices to shareholders in most of them. This is also the case when analyzing the origin of the directors in this great Chinese company, Tencent Holdings.

Table 10.5 Compensation payment to executives. Tencent Holdings' annual salary in US$ – 2017

Compensation to executives	*Total in cash*	*Stock options*	*Others*	*Total compensations in millions of US$*
Martin Chi Ping Lau President and Executive Director	7510	30,240	n/d	37,750
Unidentified director 1	n/d*	n/d	n/d	78
Unidentified director 2	n/d	n/d	n/d	60,5
Unidentified director 3	n/d	n/d	n/d	54,9

Sources: https://finance.yahoo.com/news/does-tencent-holdings-limiteds-hkg-230405998.html and https://ir.didiglobal.com/leadership-and-governance/board-of-directors/person-details/default.aspx?ItemId=e25e8c66-0da8-4b48-93cc-5694cb3f7a5e*n/d: not disclosed

10.5 Compensation paid to executives

Tencent Holdings pays millions in compensation to top executives, in line with the other companies we are analyzing, reaching US$ 37,750 million for its president and CEO Martin Chi Ping Lau in 2017, including US$ 30 million in stock options. Interestingly, in the company's annual report, there is no reference to the total compensation received by its executives. It was necessary for us to research articles in economy newspapers to find that there were even higher compensations, but that they did not mention the name of the executive in question. This is a transparency problem that China has never been concerned with, and very slowly, it is adapting to the compliance standards required for publicly traded companies and listed on stock exchanges. Table 10.5 shows the compensations.

As Tencent Holdings is listed on the Hong Kong stock exchange, which is part of the Chinese territory, the concern to disclose the data as widely as possible does not yet exist. At least that is our perception. We can see in Table 10.5 that there were compensations of US$ 54.9 million, US$ 60.5 million, and US$ 78 million, intermediate values between the companies that we are analyzing in this work, but enormous if we take into account the per capita income of the country, which was US$ 15,200 in 2018, placing China in 102th place in per capita income worldwide (Ciafactbook, 2019).

These values reinforce what we are saying throughout this work, which is the tendency to pay millionaire compensation to executives as one of the aspects and indicators of the financialization of companies, and we can conclude that they also affect Chinese companies, at least in the case of Tencent Holdings.

10.6 Dividend payments to shareholders

This indicator also shows that Tencent Holdings follows the largest companies in terms of market capitalization. It is interesting to note that its closest competitors, such as Google, did not pay dividends to shareholders,

Table 10.6 Dividend payment to Tencent Holdings' shareholders

	2013	*2014*	*2015*	*2016*
Net profit in billions of US$	2,7	3,2	6,6	7,1
Dividend payment in billions of US$	n/d	n/d	n/d	n/d
Stock repurchases in billions of US$	n/d	n/d	n/d	n/d
Totals in billions of US$	2,7	3,2	6,6	7,1

Source: Tencent Holdings *Annual Report*, 2017. pp.121 and 122

and Facebook, only practiced share repurchases, as we saw earlier. Tencent destined 100% of net income to shareholders, as shown in Table 10.6. Also due to the lack of data, we cannot say how much was distributed in dividend payments and in the stock repurchases, if any, because it is not detailed in its report yearly. The only information available to us is the total amount available to shareholders each year, which rises continuously.

Here we see that one of the basic premises of financialization, dividend payments to shareholders, is in full operation, in the same way, that we have seen the payment of compensation to executives include payment in stock options, a modern tactic and much used by Western companies. We would need more data to be able to analyze this situation at Tencent Holdings more accurately, but the set of indicators allows us to infer that this is a company that quickly adheres to the principles of financialization, with several indicators pointing in this direction.

10.7 Employee salaries

The salaries of Tencent Holdings employees vary from country to country. They are low in China and higher abroad, for example, in the USA, from where we can obtain more reliable data. A management assistant in the US in his/her early career earns US$ 48,000 annually and an average of US$ 50,000 annually. The North American web developer receives an average of US$ 62,000 annually, a good salary and above the average salary for all North American ethnic groups, which was US$ 61,000 in 2017 (Fontenot et al., 2018). Engineer positions range from US$ 76,000 to US$ 90,000 annually in the U.S., as shown in Table 10.7.

When we see wages in China, they are much lower for similar positions, including among Chinese cities themselves. The same software engineer receives an average of US$ 20,700 annually in Guangzhou, US$ 29,000 annually in Shanghai and US$ 31,000 in Beijing, and what is more interesting is that this engineer has his/her starting salary in Beijing fixed at just US$ 2,000 a year, which is negligible for a professional of this level.

Table 10.7 Tencent Holdings. Annual salary in US$ – 2018

Professional	*Minimum*	*Maximum*	*Average salary*
Management Assistant – USA	48,000	52,000	50,000
Web Developer – USA act	60,000	64,000	62,000
Business Development Associate – USA	64,000	68,000	66,000
Automation Engineer – USA	73,000	79,000	76,000
Solutions Engineer – USA	87,000	94,000	90,500
Software Engineer – Beijing *	14,000 (CNY) 2,000 (USD)	250,000 (CNY) 36,990 (USD)	210,000 (CNY) 31,070 (USD)
Software Engineer – Guangzhou *	100,000 (CNY) 14,800 (USD)	220,000 (CNY) 32,550 (USD)	140,000 (CNY) 20,710 (USD)
Software Engineer – Shanghai *	108,000 (CNY) 15,980 (USD)	400,000 (CNY) 59,180 (USD)	196,000 (CNY) 29,000 (USD)
Senior Software Engineer – Beijing	280,000 (CNY) 41,430 (USD)	700,000 (CNY) 103,570 (USD)	425,000 (CNY) 62,880 (USD)
IT Administrator – USA	80,000	87,000	83,500

Source: https://www.glassdoor.com/Salary/Tencent-Salaries-E38281.htm
* Wages in Chinese yuan (CNY) converted to the US dollar (USD). On 11/1/2019, the exchange rate was US$ 1 = CNY 6.76

Table 10.8 Ratio between employee salaries and total earnings of President-Martin Chi Ping Lau – US$ 37.7 million in 2017

Employees X President	*Minimum*	*Maximum*	*Average*
Management Assistant – USA	786	725	755
Web Developer – USA	629	589	608
Business Development Associate	589	555	571
Automation Engineer – USA	517	477	496
Solutions Engineer – USA	433	401	419
Software Engineer – Beijing	18875	1020	1217
Software Engineer –Guangzhou	2690	1179	1887
Software Engineer – Shanghai	2360	639	1301
Senior Software Engineer – Beijing	920	366	608
IT Administrator – USA	471	433	454

Source: authors, based on the values of the compensation table paid to the President and the workers' salary table

When we compare employee salaries with the total earnings of the company's president, Martin Chi Ping Lau, who received US$ 37.7 million in 2017, there is a significant difference, especially in China itself. If we take into account the initial engineer in Beijing, who we think is not representative of most employees, the difference can be more than 18,000 times between the salary of one and the total earnings of the president of the company. However, this initial salary should not be prevalent and we prefer to analyze the average, which is US$ 31,000 in Beijing, and that difference drops to 1,217 times. Table 10.8 shows the relationship between the total earnings of the President of Tencent Holdings and his employees.

The smallest relative difference is between the senior software engineer with the highest salary in Beijing and the company's president, 366 times. Such discrepancies accompany those existing among the other companies analyzed by us in this study and also confirm the thesis that financialization widens inequality between income groups and economic inequality in general and is an economic phenomenon of extreme concern today.

10.8 Employment

In the last indicator applied to the company Tencent Holdings, we once again observed that the increase in the number of jobs does not contradict the financialization process. In ten years, from 2008 to 2017, the number of employees went from just over 6,000 to more than 44,000 in 2017, a jump of more than seven times. Figure 10.1 shows these data.

Although this is a proportionately impressive growth, the absolute numbers are small, confirming what Srnicek (2016) said, that the platform capitalism sector employs very few people, compared to the rest of the economy. Moreover, as we have seen in the framework of employee salaries, these are low-paid jobs, especially in China, with very low wages, compared to wages created in the USA.

This is a demonstration of financialization, which, even creating jobs, creates them in a precarious, underpaid way and without the advantages and incentives of other times (Wartzman, 2017). Moreover, it consists of a process that affects not only the West but also Asian countries and their companies.

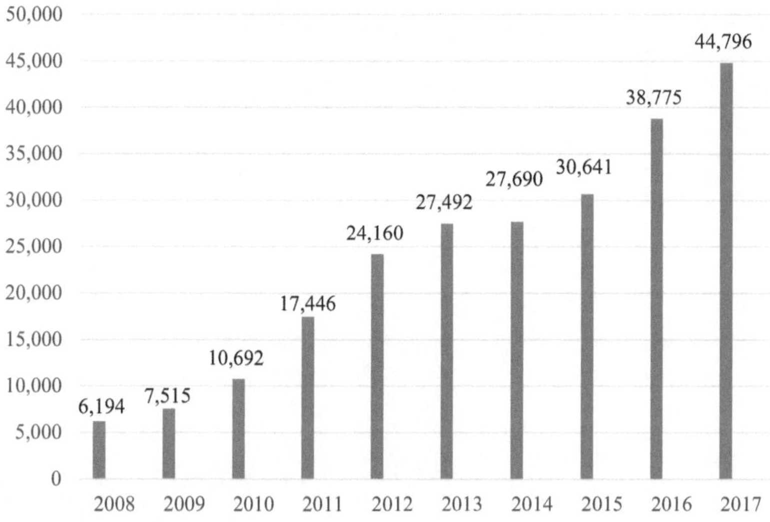

Figure 10.1 Evolution of employment at Tencent Holdings – 2008 to 2017

References

Central Intelligence Agency. The World Factbook 2019. Available at: https://www.cia.gov/the-world-factbook/countries/china/#economy. Accessed 12/11/2019.

Crunchbase, 2018. Tencent holdings acquisitions. Available at: https://www.crunchbase.com/organization/tencent/acquisitions/acquisitions_list#section-acquisitions. Accessed 08/30/2018.

Fontenot, K., Semega, J., and Kollar, M., 2018. Income and poverty in the United States 2017. Available at: https://www.census.gov/content/dam/Census/library/publications/2018/demo/p60-263.pdf. Accessed 10/06/2019.

Jia, L. and Winseck, D. 2018. The political economy of Chinese internet companies: financialization, concentration, and capitalization. *International Communication Gazette*, 80(1), 30–59. Available at: https://doi.org/10.1177/1748048517742783

Marketscreener, 2018a. Naspers Limited. Available at: https://www.marketscreener.com/NASPERS-LIMITED-1413396/company/. Accessed 08/30/2018.

Noam E. (ed.) (2016). *Who Owns the World's Media*. New York: Oxford University.

Perez, B. (7 Apr 2016). BAT- Baidu, Alibaba and Tencent – lead charge in China mergers and show no sign of slowing down. Available at: http://www.scmp.com/business/companies/article/1934083/bat-baidu-alibaba-and-tencent-lead-charge-china-mergers-and-show. Accessed 11/09/2018.

Tencent Holdings *Annual Report*, 2010. Available at: https://www.annualreports.com/HostedData/AnnualReportArchive/t/OTC_TCEHY_2010.pdf. Accessed 11/25/2018.

Tencent Holdings *Annual Report*, 2017. Available at: https://www.annualreports.com/HostedData/AnnualReportArchive/t/OTC_TCEHY_2017.pdf. Accessed 11/25/2018.

Srnicek, N. 2016. *Platform Capitalism*. Cambridge: Polity Press.

Statista, 2018. Top companies in the world by market value. Available at: https://www.statista.com/statistics/263264/top-companies-in-the-world-by-market-value/. Accessed 12/15/2017.

Wartzman, R. 2017. *The End of Loyalty: The Rise and Fall of Good Jobs in America*. New York: Public Affairs.

11 ExxonMobil

ExxonMobil Corporation is an oil group formed by the merger between Exxon and Mobil, which took place in 1999. Exxon was the new name given to the Standard Oil Company of New Jersey, and Mobil was the name given to the former Standard Oil Company of New York. Previously, the two were the same company, Standard Oil, founded by tycoon John Davison Rockefeller in 1870, who was dismembered in 1911. It is an oil group organized around three areas of activity:

1 *Refining and distribution*: (79.3% of sales): 5.5 million barrels of oil products (diesel oil, gasoline, fuel oil, lubricants, engine oils, etc.) sold per day. At the end of 2018, the group operated a network of 20,806 service stations under the Exxon, Mobil, Esso, etc.
2 *Petrochemicals*: (11.6%): especially oils, aromatics, alcohols, ethylene, elastomers, propylene, and polymers (26.9 million tons sold in 2018) for the pharmaceutical, cosmetic, textile, electrical, and other industries.
3 *Exploration and production of hydrocarbons*: (9.1%, world number 1): 2.3 million barrels of crude oil and natural gas produced per day.

The geographic distribution of sales is as follows: United States (34.7%), Canada (8.1%), United Kingdom (6.7%), Belgium (5.6%), Singapore (4.9%), France (4.9%), Italy (4.8%), Germany (3.4%), and others (26.9%) (Boursorama, 2019).

It is the largest revenue company among the ten largest that we are analyzing in our research, but it is the one that provides the lowest proportional profits concerning revenues, as we will see further ahead. This fact proves our thesis that financialization is an economic process that makes the financial pole of society increasingly more important than the productive pole. ExxonMobil is a good example of how production profits are low concerning profits from financial activities, but also about profits from service, Internet, communication, etc., as we saw in the cases of other companies. The analysis of the ExxonMobil case is positive in having stayed last in this work because it crowns a set of analyses that begins with companies in the information technology, Internet, and communications sector, named by Srnicek (2016)

DOI: 10.4324/9781003309536-11

as belonging to *platform capitalism*, whose profits on revenues are quite high, passing through another pharmaceutical manufacturer, namely Johnson & Johnson, which also has good returns on revenue. Amazon helps reinforce this thesis, as it also has low profitability as a percentage of revenues in the retail segment and high profitability in the cloud and Internet segment, as we saw earlier. Now, we will see the profits and the sources of profitability in the ExxonMobil company.

11.1 Comparison between the sources of profitability

In the case of ExxonMobil, we will not analyze its profitability from comparisons between business segments. The simple fact that we find a return on revenue of less than 9% and well below all the other companies we analyzed (except for the Amazon retail segment, as we have already pointed out) already helps to prove in numbers what we are trying to demonstrate since the beginning of this research that profits from productive activities are mediocre in the main productive sectors worldwide. We had already done this in the automotive industry (Carmo et al., 2021) and found empirical data that confirmed our suspicion. Table 11.1 shows revenue data.

Now, at ExxonMobil, we can see in Table 11.1 that the percentage of return on revenue was 6.97% on average over the past five years. It is clear that the price of oil fell incredibly mainly between 2015 and 2016, which justifies a decrease in revenues from US$ 385 billion in 2014 to US$ 208 billion in 2016, but the percentage of return in 2014 was only 8.72%, even lower than in some car manufacturers that we studied previously (Carmo et al., 2021).

The ExxonMobil case, however, is more complex than we might think, as it is a powerful company that has been changing its risk assessment continuously, and this influences its profitability. From the Exxon Valdez disasters in 1989 to its relations with power, not only in the United States, but around the world (Curriden, 2011; Ducey, 2014), the institutional dimension is a strong component in explaining its revenues and profits.

Table 11.1 ExxonMobil's revenues

	2014	*2015*	*2016*	*2017*	*2018*
Revenues in billions of US$	385,481	249,248	208,114	244,363	290,212
Profit before tax – in billions of US$	51,630	21,966	7969	18,674	30,953
Net Income – in billions of US$	33,615	16,551	8375	19,848	21,421
% of return over revenue	8.72	6.64	4.02	8.12	7.38
Cash dividends per share – US$	7,60	3,85	1,88	4,63	4,88

Source: ExxonMobil *Annual Report*, 2018, p.93

11.2 Shareholder composition

In terms of shareholder composition, ExxonMobil does not escape the rule of the ten largest companies analyzed in our research. The same large institutional investors dominate their shareholder structure. At the top are the Big Three from US investment funds, the Vanguard Group, BlackRock Inc., and State Street Corp. Together they hold more than 800 million shares, valued at almost US$ 60 billion. On September 30, 2018, ExxonMobil had a total of 4.234 billion shares issued on the market and 53% of them were in the hands of 2,534 institutional investors, for a total of 2,283,486,696 shares (Nasdaq, 2018).

Only the three largest companies hold 35% of the shares of institutional investors and 20% of the total shares. Table 11.2 shows ExxonMobil's fifteen largest shareholders.

They are all large financial groups and organizations that dominate the shareholding structure of the oil company: banks, pension funds, insurance companies, and investment funds of all kinds. The fifteen largest investors hold 1.3 billion shares or 55.54% of the shares held by institutional shareholders, the highest percentage found by us among the ten largest companies analyzed in our work. Again, it is worth remembering that there is an enormous concentration of resources and decision-making power that can be found within a business organization.

Table 11.2 ExxonMobil's largest shareholders on September 30, 2018

Financial groups	*Shares held*	*Value in thousands of US$*	*% of institutional shares*
The Vanguard Group Inc	329,558,203	23,635,914	14.43
BlackRock Inc.	267,190,408	19,162,896	11.70
State Street Corp.	208,622,266	14,962,389	9.13
Northern Trust Corp.	54,938,250	3,940,171	2.40
Wellington Management Group LLP	53,342,250	3,825,706	2.33
Bank of New York Mellon Corp	52,890,862	3,793,333	2.31
Capital Research Global Investors	49,762,289	3,568,951	2.17
Geode Capital Management LLC	48,602,488	3,485,770	2.12
Bank of America Corp/DE/	44,442,370	3,187,407	1.94
Price T Rowe Associates Inc /MD/	41,668,670	2,988,477	1.82
FMR LLC	41,616,726	2,984,752	1.82
State Farm Mutual Automobile Insurance Co	37,126,800	2,662,734	1.62
Dimensional Fund Advisors LP	32,074,706	2,300,398	1.40
Wells Fargo & Company/MN	25,324,083	1,816,243	1.10
Schwab Charles Investment Management Inc	24,496,120	1,756,862	1.07
Totals (15 biggest shareholders).	1,311,656,491	94,072,003	55.54%

Source: https://www.nasdaq.com/symbol/xom/institutional-holdings

Table 11.3 Groups that most acquired Exxon Mobil shares on September 30, 2018

Financial groups	*Shares purchased*	*% of change (+)*
Vanguard Group Inc	3,269,684	1.00
BlackRock Inc	1,984,204	0.75
State Street Corp	998,936	0.48
Wellington Management Group LLP	19,985,111	59.91
Geode Capital Management LLC	831,301	1.74
Price T Rowe Associates Inc /MD/	5,439,082	15.01
FMR LLC	7,661,385	22.56
Dimensional Fund Advisors LP	459,785	1.45
Schwab Charles Investment Management Inc	755,741	3.18
Morgan Stanley	3,614,568	19.64

Source: https://www.nasdaq.com/symbol/xom/institutional-holdings/increased

11.3 Shareholding acquisitions

The share acquisitions were made by the financial groups that already participated in the share control of ExxonMobil, focusing on the Wellington Management Group LLP, which acquired almost 20 million shares, increasing its participation by 59.91%. Table 11.3 shows the ten groups that most acquired shares in the oil company.

The FMR LLC fund increased its participation by 22.56% by acquiring 7.6 million shares, followed by Morgan Stanley bank, which acquired 3.6 million shares, an increase of 19.64% in the participation in the shares of the company. The Vanguard Group also acquired 3.2 million shares, increasing its stake by 1%, which is Exxon's largest shareholder. These data reveal what we have said throughout this research work, that more and more financial groups acquire shares in manufacturing companies, influencing the destinations of companies and having an increasing weight in their shareholding composition.

11.4 Sale of shares

The sale of shares was small compared with purchases. The ten groups that sold the most shares in ExxonMobil lost 0.08% to 7.97% of their positions. Capital Research Global Investors sold 4.3 million shares on September 30, 2018, down nearly 8% in its stake in the oil company. Goldman Sachs Group sold more than 1.7 million shares and decreased its stake by 7.63%. Table 11.4 shows these numbers.

The biggest sold-out movements also came from financial groups, which shows nothing new in our study, as we have seen that in other companies this has also happened. Here, we are able to state that it is a short-termism issue, but at the same time we have a great deal of data confirming that many groups have been holding shares in the oil company for a long time. We must assume that the issue of short or long termism is also a distinctive feature of

Table 11.4 Groups that sold most ExxonMobil shares on September 30, 2018

Financial groups	*Sold shares*	*% of change (-)*
Northern Trust Corp	951,972	1.7
Bank of New York Mellon Corp	1,210,498	2.24
Capital Research Global Investors	4,308,139	7.97
Bank of America Corp/DE/	1,112,777	2.44
Wells Fargo & Company/MN	759,584	2.91
Goldman Sachs Group Inc	1,799,222	7.63
JPMorgan Chase & Co	17,456	0.08
PNC Financial Services Group, Inc	446,776	2.84
Swiss National Bank	526,100	3.49
UBS Asset Management Americas Inc	519,715	3.5

Source: https://www.nasdaq.com/symbol/xom/institutional-holdings/decreased

Table 11.5 ExxonMobil's acquisitions

Company	*Date of purchase*	*Value in millions of US$*
MPM Lubricants	Apr 29, 2018	n/d*
Jurong Aromatics Corporation Pte Ltd	Aug 27, 2017	n/d
InterOil Corporation	July 21, 2016	2500
Celtic Exploration Ltd	Oct 17, 2012	n/d
XTO Energy	Dec 14, 2009	41,000
Totals in billions of US$		43,500

Source: https://www.crunchbase.com/organization/exxonmobil#section-acquisitions
*n/d -not disclosed

financialization because both strategies are intertwined, and this occurs more often than we may think, and multiple dynamics are observed by companies in some indicators we used in this work. What we know so far is that the long term is more common than the short term as investors generally leave the bulk of the shares for long periods, only selling small parts of them at any time, otherwise, they themselves would lose with the devaluation of their own shares. However, this question is certainly very interesting to show how financialization can be a more heterogeneous process than we may have assumed at the beginning of this book.

11.5 Mergers and acquisitions

ExxonMobil has acquired only five companies throughout its history and, following the trend of mergers and acquisitions, all are complementary. Table 11.5 shows what they were.

The acquired company that drew the most attention was XTO Energy, in 2009, purchased for US$ 41 billion, one of the highest values of acquired companies presented in our research. In the same way as in the other companies analyzed by us, the acquisitions of companies by ExxonMobil have the same characteristic as the others, allowing a supposed greater synergy through the purchase of competitors or complementary ones. However, in most of the cases observed here, what they really want is to seek to eliminate competition and dominate even larger markets and revenue slices.

11.6 Origin of managers

We believe that ExxonMobil is the company that most has a set of directors on its board of directors from different areas of activity and with greater connections and participation in other boards. Except for Larry Faulkner, a member since 2008 and who only sits on the board of Exxon, all other members have a dense participation on the boards of directors in several companies in various sectors of the economy, in addition to having studied at important and renowned universities. Table 11.6 shows the trajectory of the directors at ExxonMobil.

Table 11.6 Exxon Mobil – Board of directors

Directors	*No. of Boards in which they participate*	*Organizations in which they participate or participated*
Rex Tillerson Board Member 2006	4 ExxonMobil, Center for Strategic and International Studies Pacific Forum, Nepal Holiday Treks and Tours Pvt. Ltd, American Petroleum Institute	Exxon Yemen Inc, Esso Exploration and Production Khorat Inc., Exxon Neftegas Limited, Business Council for International Understanding, Emergency Committee for American Trade, Ford's Theatre Society, United Negro College Fund, Bachelor of science degree in Civil Engineering at the University of Texas at Austin
Henrietta Fore Board Member Mar 2012	8 General Mills, Millennium Challenge Corporation, Clinton Bush Haiti Fund, Holsman International, Theravance Biopharma	Asia Society, Women Corporate Directors, Aspen Institute and the Center for Strategic and International Studies, Coca-Cola Company, U.S. Agency for International Development, Studied International Politics at Oxford University and studied at Stanford University Graduate School of Business

Douglas Oberhelman Board Member 2015	7 Caterpillar, Inc, UI LABS, The Business Council, Eli Lilly, National Association of Manufacturers	Ameren Corporation, The Business Council, Business Roundtable
Samuel Palmisano Board Member 2006	4 American Express, ExxonMobil, Bloomberg Philanthropies, The Center for Global Enterprises	IBM, Personal Systems Group, Enterprise Systems, Graduate of The Johns Hopkins University
Larry Faulkner Board Member 2008	1 ExxonMobil	President of Houston Endowment, President of The University of Texas at Austin. Served on the chemistry faculties of The University of Texas, the University of Illinois, and Harvard University. At the University of Illinois, Provost and Vice Chancellor for Academic Affairs.
Peter Letmathe Board Member	10 Delta Topco, Credit Suisse, Nestle, Dreyer's, Winterthur Instruments, 2030 Water Resources Group, The World Economic Forum	Nestlé Group, Winterthur, Alcon, Inc., AXA Leben AG, AXA Versicherungen AG, L'Oreal India Pvt. Ltd, Dreyer's Grand Ice Cream Holdings Inc., Graduated from the University of World Trade in Vienna with a Degree in Economics.
Darren Woods Board Member 2016	2 ExxonMobil, Imperial Oil	ExxonMobil Refining & Supply Company, ExxonMobil Chemical Company, Exxon Company International
	7 Walmart, American Express, Marriott International, United States Naval Academy Alumni Association & Foundation, Furman University, The Cooper Institute	Wake Forest University, PepsiCo, Inc., Pizza Hut, Frito-Lay

(*Continued*)

Directors	*No. of Boards in which they participate*	*Organizations in which they participate or participated*
Michael Boskin Board Member 1996	4 The Nomination and Governance Committee, The Finance and Audit Committee – US, ExxonMobil, Oracle	Tully M. Friedman Professor of Economics and Hoover Institution Senior Fellow at Stanford University, Boskin & Co., Inc., Oracle, ExxonMobil
William Weldon Board Member 2013	5 Chubb, CVS Health, ExxonMobil, JP Morgan Chase & Co., JPMorgan Partners (JPMP)	Johnson & Johnson, JPMorgan Chase & Co, Chubb Corporation
Kenneth Frazier Board Member 2009	6 Merck & Co., Inc., Cornerstone Christian Academy, Weill Cornell Medical College, PhRMA (Pharmaceutical Researcher and Manufacturers of America), Pennsylvania State University	Drinker Biddle & Reath, Merck & Co., Inc., Graduate School of Medical Sciences, American Academy of Arts and Sciences, the President's Export Council, The Business Council, the Council of the American Law Institute and the American Bar Association, BSc from The Pennsylvania State University and a J.D. from Harvard Law School.
Ursula Burns Board Member 2012	10 Uber, Ford Foundation, Xerox, American Express, Massachusetts Institute of Technology – MIT, Change the Equation, Cornell Tech	Teneo Holdings, VEON, Nestlé, Diageo, Xerox Corporation, Conduent Incorporated, National Academy of Engineers, American Academy of Arts and Sciences, Master's degree in Mechanical Engineering from Columbia University and a bachelor's in Mechanical Engineering from Polytechnic Institute of New York University.

Source: https://www.crunchbase.com/organization/exxonmobil/people

This diversity of origins and the cross participation in different Boards are fundamental. According to Jia and Winseck (2018)

> Boards of Directors are important because this is the situation in which property can be transformed into control (or power and influence). This is because the boards shape the development of corporate policies and strategies and the allocation of resources (money, technology, people, knowledge, etc.).

Moreover, the authors claim that "these decisions affect the markets that companies enter (or don´t) and their responses to new technologies and government policies, laws, and regulations – i.e., to embrace them enthusiastically, hesitantly or not at all. This is a form of 'structural power'" (Jia & Winseck, 2018, p.46).

This structural power quoted by the authors mentioned before is given by investors, who influence the choice of board members and this directs decisions toward what we call financialization, with millionaire compensation to executives and dividend payments to shareholders, resulting in a joint effort where executives and shareholders win. Furthermore, this mentality forged in typical economic interests is the one that has been predominant in the last forty years, with the change in the conception of corporate control, as already widely explained by Fligstein (1990, 1991, 2001) and mentioned several times in this work.

11.7 Compensation paid to executives

Compensation paid to executives is not as high as at other companies, such as Google (US$ 199 million to the CEO in a single year) or Apple (US$ 145 million) and were around US$ 7 million to US$ 14 million, which were paid to CEO Darren Woods. At Exxon, the same formula used in other companies is repeated, of a cash payment, which was not very high, around US$ 3 million per year, and the remainder in stock options (SO), in much higher amounts, such as that shown in Table 11.7.

We do not have much to discuss here, as we have already exhaustively debated this subject throughout this book. However, it is worth repeating that the payment in cash in smaller amounts aims at lower taxation on a lower income, and the rest paid in stock options is subject to different taxation, and only when an executive exercises his/her right over the share. Besides, when you pay for shares, you help to raise their price, as mentioned before. In short, this policy of paying millionaire compensation to executives has increased the existence of a layer of super-executives awarded with super salaries (Piketty, 2014, pp.259 and 295), which has nothing to do with their performance, but with internal power that they enjoy in the organization (Bebchuk & Fried, 2004).

Table 11.7 Compensation payment to executives. ExxonMobil annual salary in US$ – 2017

Compensation to executives	*Total in cash*	*Stock options*	*Others*	*Total compensation*
D. W. Woods Chairman and CEO	3,048,000	10,809,810	282,544	14,140,354
M.J. Dolan Senior Vice President	3,033,000	8,123,736	158,215	11,314,951
M. W. Albers Senior Vice President	2,940,500	8,123,736	166,875	11,231,111
A.P. Swiger Senior Vice President; PFO	2,940,500	8,123,736	151,738	11,215,974
N. W. Duffin Vice President; President, ExxonMobil Production Company	2,084,250	5,675,150	120,349	7,879,749

Source: https://www1.salary.com/EXXON-MOBIL-CORP-Executive-Salaries.html

11.8 Dividend payments to shareholders and stock repurchases

ExxonMobil has been increasing the proportion of dividends paid to shareholders for at least thirty-five years. The values have been growing year by year, as can be seen in Table 11.8. Even with the decrease in revenues caused mainly by the drop in the price of a barrel of oil, from 2015 to 2016, the amounts of dividends paid per share only increased. It was US$ 2.70 per share in 2014, US$ 2.88 in 2015, US$ 2.98 in 2016 (dividends paid that year were higher than the net income – as we saw in the case of Microsoft) US$ 3.06 in 2017 and US$ 3.23 in 2018. For an amount of 4.234 billion of shares issued (Exxon Mobil *Annual Report*, 2018, p.93). Table 11.8 shows these data.

Stock repurchases are being practiced every year and rescued US$ 13,1 billion in shares in the 2014 fiscal year. CEO Darren Woods stated that "we can do all of this in a wide variety of pricing environments so that the additional money from divestments we can use for repurchases" (DiChristopher, 2019). In other words, there is a decision to sell assets to be able to repurchase shares, as competitors Chevron, Shell, British Petroleum, among others, continue to practice stock repurchases.

> Few phenomena in the stock market are more predictable than ExxonMobil Corp's massive share buyback program. The company, which has spent about $210 billion over the last decade buying back its own stock, is bowing to the reality that crude's sharp downturn is hurting its bottom line. It surprised investors on Tuesday by dramatically ratcheting back share repurchases, and for the first time in fifteen years, ExxonMobil will only buy back shares to offset dilution as opposed to return cash to shareholders.
>
> (Gaffen, 2016)

Table 11.8 Dividend payments to ExxonMobil's shareholders and stock repurchases

	2014	*2015*	*2016*	*2017*	*2018*
Net profit applicable to common shareholders in billions of US$	32,520	16,150	7,840	19,710	20,840
Dividend Payment in billions of US$	11,4	12,1	12,6	12,9	13,6
Stock Repurchases in billions of US$	13,153	4034	0971	0747	0626
Total in billions of US$	24,553	16,150	13,571	13,674	14,226

Sources: https://www.nasdaq.com/symbol/xom/financials?query=income-statement. Exxon Mobil Annual Report, 2018, p.93; https://corporate.exxonmobil.com/en/investors/investor-relations/dividend-information; https://ycharts.com/companies/XOM/stock_buyback

This can be seen in Table 11.8, when, from the low oil price in 2015 and 2016, the company was obliged to reduce stock repurchases to volumes of less than US$ 1 billion in 2016, 2017, and 2018.

Even with this momentaneous reduction in the level of stock repurchases, the company acts in a very coherent way with the financialization process, with the main mission of maximizing shareholder value, through billionaire dividend payments and stock repurchases for several years. Even with low profitability in proportion to revenues, as we saw earlier, the company is firmly concerned with meeting the demands of its shareholders, the most important and fundamental stakeholders of its business.

11.9 Employee salaries

While compensation to executives is in the millions and the dividend payments to shareholders are in the billions, employee salaries are not very substantial. Starting with a gas station cashier, whose starting salary is US$ 16,352 per year and an average of US$ 19,800 per year, several other positions have low salaries. A convenience store manager has an initial salary of US$ 20,900 annually and an average of US$ 39,700 per year. There are several wages below the average salaries for all North American ethnic groups, which stood at US$ 61,300 annually in 2017 (Fontenot et al., 2018). Table 11.9 shows some of ExxonMobil's most numerous professions in 2018.

A civil engineer receives an annual average of US$ 73,000 and a chemist US$ 91,000 per year. When we move up the scale of professions, those most related to the company's core business, such as the oil engineer, receive an average of US$ 161,000 annually, reaching a maximum salary of US$ 249,000 annually. A novice geologist receives US$ 73,000 and can reach US$ 331,000 annually, with an average salary of US$ 202,000. A senior geologist starts at US$ 111,000 and averages US$ 242,000, with a maximum salary of US$ 374,000 annually. We should recall that these professionals comprise the minority of the company's staff, the most numerous of whom are electricians (average of US$ 62,000 per year) and industrial painters (US$ 47,000 per year, below the average of American salaries).

Table 11.9 ExxonMobil. Annual salary in US$ – 2018

Professional	*Minimum*	*Maximum*	*Average salary*
Cashier	16,352	23,409	19,880
Assistant Store Manager	17,757	35,004	26,380
Convenience Store Manager	20,940	58,604	39,772
Industrial painter	28,104	67,316	47,710
Electrician	35,147	90,003	62,575
Civil Engineer	40,116	105,940	73,028
Chemist	46,435	136,978	91,706
Software Engineer	53,525	125,190	89,357
Data Engineer	66,339	109,256	87,797
Geologist	73,170	331,463	202,316
Petroleum Engineer	74,464	249,165	161,814
Senior Geologist	111,406	374,080	242,743

Source: https://www.payscale.com/research/US/Employer=ExxonMobil_Corporation/Salary/by_Job

Table 11.10 Ratio between employee salaries and total CEO earnings Darren W. Woods in 2017 – US$ 14,140,354.00

Employees X CEO	*Minimum*	*Maximum*	*Average*
Cashier	864	604	711
Assistant Store Manager	796	403	536
Convenience Store Manager	675	241	355
Industrial painter	503	210	296
Electrician	402	157	225
Civil Engineer	352	133	193
Chemist	304	103	154
Software Engineer	264	112	158
Data Engineer	213	129	161
Geologist	193	42	69
Petroleum Engineer	189	56	87
Senior Geologist	126	37	58

Source: Author, based on the values of the compensation table paid to the CEO and the employee salary table

Moreover, when we compare the difference between the total earnings of the CEO and the employee salaries, the ratio can reach 864 times, when comparing the CEO and the cashier. Table 11.10 shows the ratio between employee salaries and total CEO earnings in 2017.

The smallest difference found was between the total CEO earnings and the maximum salary of the senior geologist, only thirty-seven times. This is because the total compensation to the CEO, which was US$ 14 million in 2017, is not as high as at Apple and Google, for example, as previously discussed. Hence, the differences were less than a thousand times, which is already a considerable gap. These differences have confirmed the thesis that there is increasing inequality between income groups, and this inevitably causes an increase in inequality in general. Without control on compensation for executives and an increase in salaries, the movement of inequality will not slow down, but on the contrary, it will always be greater.

11.10 Employment

In the last financialization indicator of the tenth company in market capitalization analyzed by us in this book, we see that ExxonMobil was the only company to decrease its workforce over the years. Figure 11.1 shows the changes in the number of workers in the oil company, according to data from Statista (2020).

ExxonMobil decreased from 97,900 workers in 2001 to 69,600 in 2017, almost a 30% decrease. This did not directly have to do with the fall in the price of oil and a supposed decrease in activity, as it went from 2015 to 2016. Even in times of high oil barrel prices, the company reduced staff, as from 2001 to 2008, whose reduction reached almost 20,000 jobs. This seems to be a reduction in labor cost savings, an increase in technology and an increase in productivity, all of which are elements that are very consistent with the financialization process, which favors the financial pole over the productive pole and human capital. Although, as we have seen in all the other companies analyzed, the question of the relationship between employment and financialization is much more complex, and there are more specificities than we may think.

In summary, in the case of ExxonMobil, we can see that this is a traditional company of North American capitalism that is quite old and has old relationships with the financial sector of the economy, banks, and investment funds. All major institutional investors are major asset managers and have their demands met by the company. ExxonMobil behaves consistently

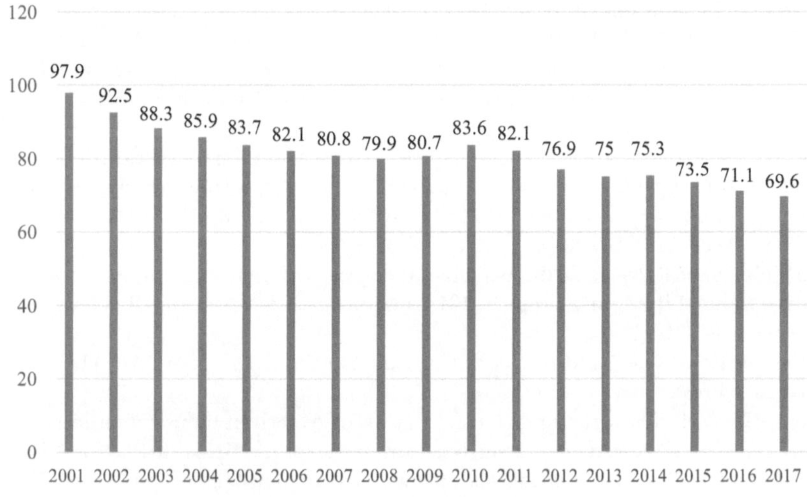

Figure 11.1 Evolution of employment at ExxonMobil – 2001 to 2017

across all the financialization indicators and exists as a company that seeks to maximize shareholder value, reward its executives well, pay little for most of its employees, and all that from a low basis profitability, which is very small in relation to its revenue, as we can also see in the automotive industry (Carmo et al., 2021). The study of these companies helps us to better understand, based on real numbers, what actually happens in large contemporary corporations, which is an accelerated financialization process of production, leading to significant and harmful consequences and impacts for most stakeholders, workers, consumers, and society as a whole, in order to satisfy the desires of a minority of shareholders and executives who are getting richer every day at the expense of an enterprise that exists because of the efforts of many other people.

References

Bebchuk, L.A. and Fried, J.M. 2004. Pay without performance, the unfulfilled promise of executive compensation, part II: Power and Pay, draft of the book *Pay without Performance, the Unfulfilled Promise of Executive Compensation*. Available at: http://www.law.harvard.edu/faculty/bebchuk/pdfs/Performance-Part2.pdf. Accessed 9/10/2021.

Boursorama, 2019. Exxon Mobil profile. Available at: https://www.boursorama.com/cours/societe/profil/XOM/. Accessed 6/12/2019.

Carmo, M.J., Sacomano Neto, M., and Donadone, J.C. 2021. *Financialization in the Automotive Industry: Capital and Labour in Contemporary Society*. London and New York: Routledge. Available at: https://www.routledge.com/Financialisation-in-the-Automotive-Industry-Capital-and-Labour-in-Contemporary/Carmo-Neto-Donadone/p/book/9780367751395

Curriden, M. 2011. Holding Chavez over a barrel: Exxon Mobil's dispute with Venezuela has global implications. *ABA Journal*, 97(4), 18+. *Gale Academic OneFile*. Available at: https://go.gale.com/ps/i.do?p=AONE&u=capes&id=GALE|A257216787&v=2.1&it=r&sid=AONE&asid=0cbd70ab. Accessed 1/07/2019.

DiChristopher, T.D. (7 Mar 2019). The road to Exxon's long-awaited stock buybacks is paved with billions in asset sales. Available at: https://www.cnbc.com/2019/03/07/the-road-to-exxons-buybacks-is-paved-with-billions-in-asset-sales.html. Accessed 6/14/2019.

Ducey, R. 2014. Coll, Steve. Private empire: Exxon Mobil and American power. *Naval War College Review*, 156+. *Academic OneFile*. Available at: http://link.galegroup.com/apps/doc/A363191728/AONE?u=capes&sid=AONE&xid=111f31ae. Accessed 1/07/2019.

ExxonMobil *Annual Report*, 2018. Available at: https://corporate.exxonmobil.com/-/media/Global/Files/annual-report/2018-Financial-and-Operating-Review.pdf. Accessed 4/05/2019.

Fligstein, N. 1990. *The Transformation of Corporate Control*. Cambridge, MA: Harvard University Press.

Fligstein, N. 1991. The structural transformation of American industry: an institutional account of the causes of diversification in the largest firms, 1919–1979. *The New Institutionalism in Organizational Analysis*. Paul J. DiMaggio and Walter W. Powell (eds.), 311–336. Chicago, IL: University of Chicago Press.

Fligstein, N. 2001. *The Architecture of Markets: An Economic Sociology of Twenty-First-Century Capitalist Societies.* Princeton University Press.

Fontenot, K., Semega, J., and Kollar, M., 2018. Income and poverty in the United States 2017. Available at: https://www.census.gov/content/dam/Census/library/publications/2018/demo/p60-263.pdf. Accessed 10/06/2019.

Gaffen, D. (2 Feb 2016). Exxon, tops in stock buybacks, now saving its cash. Available at: https://www.reuters.com/article/us-exxon-mobil-results-buybacks-idUSKCN0VB1W6. Accessed 6/14/2019.

Jia, L. and Winseck, D., 2018. The political economy of Chinese internet companies: financialization, concentration, and capitalization. *International Communication Gazette,* 80(1), 30–59. Available at: https://doi.org/10.1177/1748048517742783

Nasdaq, 2018. ExxonMobil institutional holdings. Available at: https://www.nasdaq.com/symbol/xom/institutional-holdings. Accessed 1/26/2019.

Piketty, T. 2014. *O Capital no século XXI.* Rio de Janeiro: Editora Intrínseca.

Srnicek, N. 2016. *Platform Capitalism.* Cambridge: Polity Press.

Statista, 2020. Number of employees at Exxon Mobil since 2002. Available at: https://www.statista.com/statistics/264122/number-of-employees-at-exxon-mobil-since-2002/. Accessed 7/15/2019.

12 Conclusions

The results obtained so far by our research demonstrate a wide range of situations experienced by the ten companies analyzed. The financialization process proved to be more dynamic and heterogeneous than one might think at the beginning of the investigation. In one of the main indicators used by us (dividend payments to shareholders), companies almost split in half in this regard, with four companies out of ten not paying dividends to their shareholders, just to illustrate what happened in this indicator. This is an important fact because it would question the assumption of dividend payments to shareholders as a *sine qua non* condition for financialization. Our work has demonstrated that financialization is not so linear and not all companies behave the same way. We will now proceed to resume the indicators.

12.1 Sources of profitability

When we study the companies' financialization process, the main bibliographic references remind us of the need to analyze the companies' balance sheet and financial statements, through their annual reports and check the composition of the business's profitability. Froud et al. (2006) drew attention to the existence of a productive sector and a financial sector in companies in the automotive industry. In the case of Ford, the company's financial sector (leasing, financing, Ford Credit) had a proportionally much higher profitability than its productive sector (production in factories and facilities). Our first book, published by Routledge (Carmo et al., 2021), analyzed the five largest automakers worldwide and confirmed the thesis of Froud et al. (2006), not only at Ford, but also at GM, Volkswagen, Toyota, and Hyundai, each with a different performance in each indicator.

Now, in this book, the ten companies chosen by us do not have separate sectors, as their products are different from the automobiles produced by the automakers, and their acquisition is also different (most of the time they do not need banks to finance the purchase of products), but even so they present segments on their balance sheets that demonstrate an evolution in the composition of profit in line with the financialization process, such as servitization, attempting to lengthen the production chain to appropriate greater profits,

DOI: 10.4324/9781003309536-12

outsourcing, aiming to save as much as possible in manpower with a view to greater profits, and the use of click-counting algorithms, widely used by Facebook, Google, and Tencent Holdings, for example, extracting value as their wish.

But one might question whether wanting to always maximize profit would be characteristic of financialization as the search for greater profits has always been the objective of capitalism, in all previous conceptions of control. If this happens, at present, profit maximization aims at the shareholder first, leaving all other business stakeholders in the background. Moreover, what we see about employee salaries, compensation paid to CEOs and dividends paid to shareholders, in addition to stock repurchases, makes it clear that the financialization process of companies is in full force.

We can see how financialization affects companies, in terms of the sources of profitability. Table 12.1 shows the fast growth of services and confirms the trend to servitization as coexisting with financialization, both feeding each other.

While revenue from the sale of iPhones grew from US$ 78,6 billion in 2012 to US$ 191,9 billion in 2021, an increase of 245%, service revenues grew from US$ 12,8 billion to US$ 68,4 billion in the same period, leading to an increase of 535%. This expansion of service revenues constitutes an aspect of financialization as it proportionally decreases the profitability of the productive sector (outsourced manufacture of iPhones, iPads, Macs) vis-à-vis the services sector. "Services net sales include sales from advertising, AppleCare, cloud, digital content, payment and other services" (Apple *Annual Report*, 2021, p.21). This distancing from production is a characteristic of financialization, also verified here in the case of Apple.

At Google, the situation is different because it is a profitability based on revenues over users per month and per year as it is the largest search platform on the Internet.

Revenue from Google properties is comprised of Advertising, Android, Chrome, Commerce, Google Cloud, Google Maps, Google Play, Hardware, Search, and YouTube. Google generates revenue primarily from advertising,

Table 12.1 Apple's profitability

	2012	*2013*	*2014*	*2015*	*2016*	*2017*	*2018*	*2019*	*2020*	*2021*
iPhone in billions of US$	78,6	91,2	101,9	155	136,7	141,3	164,8	142,3	137,7	191,9
% of revenue	50.3	53.4	55.8	66.3	63.4	61.6	62	54.7	50.1	52.4
Services in billions of US$	12,8	16	18	19,9	24,3	29,9	39,7	46,2	53,7	68,4
% of revenue	8.2	9.4	9.9	8.5	11.3	13.1	14.9	17.7	19.5	18.7

Source: Apple *Annual Reports*, several years

app sales, in-app purchases, hardware and digital content products, licensing, and service fees, including fees received for Google Cloud offerings. Table 12.2 presents the substantial operational profit and percentage return on revenues.

That is, with this entire range of products being offered to customers, which grow by the millions every year, Google has achieved an average of 25% return on revenue, and much of the increase in these revenues is due to the collection of fees of all nature, and the company seems to be a tax collector in terms of using its platform. The collection of fees of the entire order was analyzed by Ertürk (2015) in banks. It also proves to be a characteristic of financialization. Although there is a substantial difference between the banking sector, which charges fees and thereby escapes the core business (bank spread), at Google, there is the possibility of high profits arising from the core business itself, through all types of fees of using the platform.

Regarding fees, we can observe a typical case in the banking sector, through JPMorgan Chase & Co, as can be shown in Table 12.3.

The case of JPMorgan Chase shows that the financialization process is a phenomenon that also affects banks since revenues from interest-related activities (core business) were lower (in four of the five years shown in Table 12.3) than those revenues from non-interest-related activities, that is, fees of all kinds on asset management, investment banking, mortgages, etc.

To substantiate the thesis of Froud et al. (2006), that the profits from productive activities are much lower than the profits from financial activities, we can see in the cases of Exxon Mobil, Berkshire Hathaway, and Amazon

Table 12.2 Google's profitability

	2013	*2014*	*2015*	*2016*	*2017*
Revenues in billions of US$	55,519	66,001	74,989	90,272	110,855
Operational Profit	15,403	16,496	19,360	23,716	26,146
% return on revenues	27.74	24.99	25.81	26.27	23.58

Source: Alphabet *Annual Report*, 2018, p.25. Available at: https://abc.xyz/investor/pdf/20171231_alphabet_10K.pdf. Average 25.67% return on revenue, from 2013 to 2017

Table 12.3 JPMorgan Chase & Co's profitability

	2014	*2015*	*2016*	*2017*	*2018*
Total revenues in billions of US$	95,994	94,440	96,569	100,705	109,029
Net profit	21,745	24,442	24,733	24,441	32,474
% net profit on revenues	22.65	25.88	25.61	24.26	29.78
Revenues related to interest	43,634	43,510	46,083	50,097	55,059
Revenues non related to interest	51,478	50,033	50,486	50,608	53,970

Source: JPMorgan Chase & Co. Annual Report 2018, pp.40-48; 2017, p.44; 2016, p.40

(when comparing Amazon Web Services with other sources of profitability). ExxonMobil is one of the largest oil companies in the world but has a return on revenue of 7% on average per year, much less than the return of all the companies selected here, such as Apple (20–25% return on revenue), Google (25%), Microsoft (30%), Amazon Web Services (25%), Facebook (28%), Tencent Holdings (32%), JPMorgan Chase (26%), and even the pharmaceutical company Johnson & Johnson (average 20% return on revenue over the past five years). Table 12.4 shows the low profitability of company ExxonMobil.

The case of ExxonMobil is the most typical of financialization when comparing the sources of profitability, as we see that a manufacturing company, old and mature, similar to the automotive industry (Carmo et al., 2021), has low returns on revenues, as Ford and GM showed. Exxon does not have a financial sector, but it illustrates well what we have been arguing for some time, that productive activities are much less profitable than financial and service activities. Another company that exposes these same facts is Berkshire Hathaway, an insurance company that has diversification in its activities and also operates in the railway and energy sector. Table 12.5 shows that in two segments of the company, the question of profits from financial activities versus profits from productive activities is clear as daylight.

The sales and service revenue segment has a return on revenue of more than 50%, while the Railway and Energy segment gives a return of around 20% on the total revenue. This is evidence from Froud et al. (2006), which is based on observable and empirical data that we find everywhere.

At Amazon, this is also evident when comparing the three segments of the business. The North America segment is still the one that, in absolute

Table 12.4 ExxonMobil's profitability

	2014	*2015*	*2016*	*2017*	*2018*
Total revenues in billions of US$	385,481	249,248	208,114	244,363	290,212
Net profit	33,615	16,551	8375	19,848	21,421
% net profit on revenues	8.72	6.64	4.02	8.12	7.38

Source: ExxonMobil *Annual Report*, 2018, p.93

Table 12.5 Berkshire Hathaway's profitability

	2013	*2014*	*2015*	*2016*	*2017*
Total revenues in billions of US$	182,412	194,699	210,943	223,604	242,137
Sell and Services revenues	92,993	97,097	107,001	119,489	125,963
% return on revenues	50.97	49.87	50.72	53.43	52.02
Railways and Energy revenues	34,757	40,690	40,004	37,542	39,943
% return on revenues	19.05	20.89	18.96	16.78	16.49

Source: Berkshire Hathaway Annual Report 2017, p.K-31 (63)

Table 12.6 Amazon's profitability

Total revenues in billions of US$	*2015*	*2016*	*2017*
North America	63,708	79.785	106,110
Operational profit	1425	2361	2837
% return on revenues	2.23%	2.95%	2.67%
International	35,418	43,983	54,297
Operational profit	−699	−1,283	−3,062
% return on revenues	−1.97%	−2.91%	−5.63%
AWS (Amazon Web Services)	7,880	12,219	17,459
Operational profit	1,507	3,108	4,331
% return on revenues	19.12%	25.43%	24.80%

Source: https://ir.aboutamazon.com/static-files/917130c5-e6bf-4790-a7bc-cc43ac7fb30a, pp.25 and 69

numbers, has greater participation in the set of revenues, but has a return on revenues of just over 2%. The International segment, although responsible for increasing revenues, has been making losses for three years, from 2015 to 2017. Losses of US$ 3 billion in 2017 cast doubts about the continuity of this business. What saves the company are the internet services, cloud infrastructure etc., concentrated in the Amazon Web Service (AWS), whose revenue is the lowest in absolute numbers, but the highest in the percentage of return on revenues, reaching 25% in 2016, as we can see in Table 12.6.

In summary, each company presented a characteristic sign of financialization when it comes to comparing the sources of profitability, whether due to the increase in services in terms of revenue, the high profitability of non-productive sectors, through fees, and the persistent low return on manufacture. In the cases studied in the automotive industry (Carmo et al., 2021), we had already demonstrated multiple dynamics of financialization in that sector and we can now affirm that there are also different trajectories exercised by the largest contemporary companies in the current financialization process.

12.2 Shareholding composition

In this indicator, we can see that the largest shareholders of the ten companies analyzed here are practically the same: large investment funds, pension funds, hedge funds, investment banks, among other financial institutions. The highlight is the so-called Big Three (Fichtner et al., 2017) of North American funds, which are among the biggest investors in all the companies we analyzed. Table 12.7 shows how well positioned are these biggest institutional investors in the corporate ownership of the ten largest companies in the world in 2017. Furthermore, they continue until today, as we will see in the appendix of this book.

Table 12.7 shows that the three largest US investment funds, The Vanguard Group, BlackRock Inc., and State Street Corp. are the first shareholders in the ten companies. The Vanguard Group is the first in all companies, except

Table 12.7 Major shareholders in the ten companies analyzed

Companies	*The Vanguard Group*	*BlackRock Inc.*	*State Street Corp*
Apple	1st	2nd	3rd
Google	1st	2nd	4th
Microsoft	1st	2nd	4th
Amazon	1st	2nd	5th
Berkshire Hathaway	1st	2nd	3rd
Facebook	1st	2nd	4th
Johnson & Johnson	1st	2nd	3rd
JPMorgan Chase & Co.	1st	2nd	3rd
Tencent Holdings	3rd	4th	-
Exxon Mobil	1st	2nd	3rd

Sources: http://www.4-traders.com/TENCENT-HOLDINGS-LTD-3045861/company/; http://www.nasdaq.com/symbol/aapl/institutionalholdings

for Tencent Holdings, in which it appears as the third-largest shareholder. BlackRock is second in all but Tencent, and State Street Corp in third and fourth in almost all companies as well.

This fact reinforces the thesis that more and more large financial groups acquire shares in manufacturing companies, but also in technology, communication, banks, among others, to use vast amounts of capital awaiting appreciation (Chesnais, 1996) in companies that will return their investments in the form of dividends and stock repurchases. Here, it is seen that the intertwining between the "real" and the financial economy (which would be speculative and "fictitious") is much more complex than one imagines. The idea that there would be separate dimensions between the productive economy and the financial sphere is weakened since production only exists because of the capital coming from these financial type institutions that are invested in these productive operations. In a previous moment, the company simply went into debt with the banks to raise capital and produce. It was the debt phase. With financialization, there is a development of the equity phase, by which large financial groups participate directly as owners of companies' shares, through the stock market. The debt/equity ratio of a company that tends to increase its equity share is also a symptom of financialization.

12.3 Mergers and acquisitions

Mergers and acquisitions are being practiced quickly by the largest contemporary companies. Mainly, the acquisitions of companies have been carried out by the ten largest companies that we are studying. Since 1972, in the case of Berkshire Hathaway, companies have been acquiring others to increase access to markets and develop their skills. At least and what is stated in their annual reports when they are accountable to shareholders. In fact, this vertical integration process, which was being put aside due to the need to emphasize the core business (by most conglomerates), has been happening normally in

Table 12.8 Companies acquired by the ten companies analyzed

Company	*Number of companies purchased by*	*Period*
Google	233	1998–2018
Microsoft	214	1987–2018
Apple	102	1988–2018
Amazon	82	1998–2018
Facebook	77	2007–2018
Johnson & Johnson	28	1994–2018
Berkshire Hathaway	13	1972–2017
Tencent Holdings	13	2011–2018
JPMorgan Chase & Co.	9	1999–2018
Exxon Mobil	5	2009–2018
Total	776	1972–2018

Source: www.crunchbase.com

recent years, albeit in a different way, so that it privileges the core business. In general, the acquired companies are complementary, sometimes competing, and it is more advantageous to incorporate this company into a business than having to outsource actions or operations, for example. Table 12.8 shows the number of companies that were bought in the last forty years by the ten largest companies in market capitalization.

We can see that 776 companies were bought by the ten largest companies we are studying. The largest amount was concentrated in the information technology or communication sector, as are the cases of Apple, Google, and Microsoft. Together, these three companies acquired another 549; Microsoft and Apple, in a period of thirty years (1987–2018), bought 316 companies and Google, in twenty years (1998–2018), bought 233 companies. This movement of mergers and acquisitions reinforces the reconcentration (Davis, 2008) of companies in even larger groups, leading to capitalism led by finance, which, for us, is synonymous of financialization.

12.4 Origin of company managers

According to Neil Fligstein (1991), the professional and personal trajectory of each manager of the companies speaks volumes about their decisions. Depending on their origins, this is their entire way of life and their worldview. If a manager came from the world of industry, it can be considered that his/her inclinations will be more related to issues of production, markets, among other metrics and expectations. If the leader comes from the world of finance, having belonged or passed through financial organizations, it appears that his/her concerns are more in tune with financial metrics, which are quite different from metrics and industrial and productive strategies. Table 12.9 shows the companies´ board of directors' members.

Table 12.9 Directors' professional trajectory

Company (Board of directors members)	*Financial organizations*	*Non-financial organizations*
Apple (10)	1	9
Google (8)	1	7
Microsoft (11)	5	6
Amazon (9)	4	5
Berkshire Hathaway (6)	5	1
Facebook (10)	6	4
Johnson & Johnson (10)	3	7
JPMorgan Chase & Co. (10)	7	3
Tencent Holdings (10)	0	10
Exxon Mobil (12)	2	10
Total	34	62

Source: Authors, based on previous tables of each company

In Table 12.9, we selected 96 members of the boards (out of a total of 124) from the ten largest companies that we are analyzing in this work. Around two-thirds of the total number analyzed, 62 members had no experience in financial organizations, having worked in large manufacturing companies or civil society institutions, such as clubs, foundations, and universities. The other thirty-four board members went through financial organizations such as banks, investment funds of all kinds, and insurance companies.

What can we infer from these data? That, although we agree with Fligstein (1991) on the issue of professional and educational trajectories, we cannot affirm today, thirty years after Fligstein's text was written, that only the origin of the professional had a definite meaning for the inclination to take this or that decision. Because among the companies analyzed, we will soon see that most of them (6) paid dividends to shareholders and practiced stock repurchases in billion-dollar amounts, meeting the interests of investors and complying with the maximization of shareholder value. These are companies that add board directors who come from both the world of industry and the world of finance.

In fact, what we can translate from the data found is that, also in this aspect of the origin of the managers, what happens are different dynamics of the financialization process, in which the worlds merge, intertwine, the managers are part of several boards at the same time, and most of them acquire a mentality aimed at maximizing shareholder value. We can also conclude that, if there are still leaders committed to the industrial metrics and the production processes, referring to the industrial conception of control (Fligstein, 1990), they should probably be voted down in the meetings where the main decisions are taken. This leads to the belief that more research should be carried out in order to assess, with greater precision, through surveys and other investigations, what the real correlation is between the origin of the leader and the decision taken by him/her.

12.5 Compensation to executives

The indicator that analyzes the compensation paid to the executives of the ten largest companies in market capitalization can be considered largely supported by the data found in our research. The real numbers allow us to corroborate the definition that more and more companies pay millionaire amounts to their CEOs, and this contributes to the creation of a layer of very rich executives, while the vast majority of workers receive salaries below the average salary for all ethnic groups in the United States, for example, where nine of the ten largest companies studied by us are located. Table 12.10 shows the compensations paid to CEOs.

Table 12.10 shows the period between 2015 and 2018 and the amount of total compensation paid to executives. At Google and Apple, there have been compensations paid in excess of US$ 100 million in at least two years. These compensations, in their majority, were paid through stock options, which are a tactic to increase the value of the shares, since a wide buying movement increases their price. In addition, it involves the executive (a high-level employee) to become a shareholder, blurring the boundaries between ownership and control. The only exceptions were for Amazon and Berkshire Hathaway, which pay lower compensation to their CEOs, who are also the oldest owners of the business and holders of a large number of shares.

In the United States, mainly, in many companies, there is the phenomenon of accumulating functions between the CEO and the Chairman of the board, which does not occur in Europe (Webber, 2018). This accumulation of functions has been considered to favor the millionaire earnings of the CEOs since the CEO him/herself is also the chairman of the same board that will define the compensation to the main executives. This strategic positioning of the CEO as chairman of the board implies enormous power (Bebchuk & Fried, 2004), as the body that should supervise the executives is chaired by an executive, obviously very interested in setting his own remuneration in stratospheric values (Webber, 2018). However, this did not happen in Amazon and

Table 12.10 Compensations paid to the CEO. Annual salary in US$

Company	*2015*	*2016*	*2017*	*2018*
Google	100,632,102	199,718,200	1,333,557	1,881,066
Apple	10,281,327	145,000,000	12,825,066	15,682,219
Tencent Holdings	n/d	n/d	37,750,000	n/d
JPMorgan Chase & Co.	18,221,060	27,205,551	28,278,278	30,019,840
Microsoft	18,294,270	17,692,031	20,014,152	25,843,263
Johnson & Johnson	21,081,598	21,207,949	22,843,420	20,097,572
Exxon Mobil	24,261,291	25,144,225	14,140,354	15,800,290
Facebook	5,037,841	5,765,832	8,852,366	22,554,543
Amazon	1,681,840	1,681,840	1,681,840	1,681,840
Berkshire Hathaway	470,244	487,881	100,000	388,968

Source: www.salary.com
*n/d: not disclosed

Berkshire Hathaway. Perhaps because in these two companies, the CEOs and presidents are also former shareholders and holders of significant shares in the total of the business, and they are interested in better managing their money, thus paying much lower compensation to their CEOs. However, in other companies, the accumulation of the position of CEO and the chairmanship of the board (Rex Tillerson at Exxon Mobil until 2017) greatly favored the payment of millionaire compensation to the CEOs of these huge companies, such as JPMorgan Chase & Co. (Webber, 2018, p.120).

12.6 Dividend payments to shareholders and stock repurchases

This financialization indicator, which is considered by many authors already mentioned in this work as the main characteristic of the current conception of control, (maximization of shareholder value) presented different behaviors in each analyzed company. Table 12.11 shows the issues of dividends and repurchases.

Not all companies paid dividends to shareholders or made stock repurchases. Amazon and Berkshire Hathaway did not pay dividends to shareholders or repurchased shares. Google and Facebook did not pay dividends but repurchased shares. ExxonMobil paid dividends and stocked repurchases. We did not obtain data from the Chinese company Tencent Holdings. Apple, Microsoft, Johnson & Johnson, and JPMorgan Chase & Co. paid dividends and practiced stock repurchases, fulfilling these requirements equally.

This information portrays different behaviors of companies in the financialization process, which is complex and heterogeneous, as we have been arguing since the beginning. For those who think that in order to experience the financialization process the company would need to fulfill all the requirements, in a mechanical and repetitive way, the data we found allow us to verify a much richer and more dynamic socioeconomic process, in all dimensions and in all indicators.

Table 12.11 Dividends and Stock Repurchases by the ten companies – 2015–2018

Company	*Dividends*	*Repurchases*
Apple	Yes	Yes
Google	No	Yes
Microsoft	Yes	Yes
Amazon	No	No
Berkshire Hathaway	No	No
Facebook	No	Yes
Johnson & Johnson	Yes	Yes
JPMorgan Chase & Co.	Yes	Yes
Tencent Holdings	n/a	n/a
Exxon Mobil	Yes	Yes

Source: Previous tables of each company
n/a: not available

12.7 Employee salaries

In the indicator that deals with employee salaries, we saw that the lowest initial values are well below the average for all ethnic groups in the United States, as reported by the US Census Bureau, an agency of the United States Department of Commerce. The average was at US$ 61,000 annually in 2017. Table 12.12 presents several salaries in the companies.

Except for the Software Engineer role in Beijing, which starts earning a miserable US$ 2,000 annually, but which reaches an average of US$ 30,000 a year (in fact a very low salary) all the other starting salaries for the ten companies are low, starting at around US$ 15,000 annually. This figure represents a quarter of the average American income, paid by billionaire companies and who are world leaders. The wage issue nowadays reaches noticeably clear contours, with a decrease in the value of remuneration, but it also admits contradictory signs. While income for all ethnic groups has been increasing over the years, the salary values of the main professional categories, once well paid, have been falling. This is what we found when we studied the automotive industry and saw wage values that were much lower than the North American average (Carmo et al., 2021).

Wartzman (2017) verified the same trend, stating that General Motors paid much more than the average salary of all workers as early as 1947, paying more than US$ 3,000 annually while the average American wages was US$ 2,700 that year (Wartzman, 2017, p.47). That is, there was a time of great appreciation for some professions in the United States, but today this situation has been changing.

When compared to the total earnings of the CEO's, the salaries in ten companies showed a huge disparity in the salary ranges, as can be seen in Table 12.13.

The ratio established between the CEO's earnings and the workers' wages is a powerful indicator of inequality between income groups and, therefore,

Table 12.12 Value of the lowest starting salary in the ten companies analyzed. Annual salary in US$ – 2018

Company	*Professional*	*Annual starting salary in US$*
Tencent Holdings	Software Engineer- Beijing	2000
Amazon	Cashier	15,825
Exxon Mobil	Cashier	16,352
Apple	Mc Specialist	18,000
JP Morgan Chase	Bank teller	18,000
Google	Customer Service Representative	18,074
Microsoft	Sales Associate	19,354
Berkshire Hathaway	Realtor	20,424
Johnson & Johnson	Intern	27,200
Facebook	Customer Service Representative	28,168

Source: Authors, based on the companies' tables

Table 12.13 Ratio between compensation to CEO/lowest starting salary

Company	*Professional*	*CEO/lowest starting salary*
Tencent Holdings	Software Engineer – Beijing	18.875*
Amazon	Cashier	106
Exxon Mobil	Cashier	864
Apple	Mc Specialist	8.055
JP Morgan Chase	Bank teller	1.571
Google	Customer Service Representative	11.050
Microsoft	Sales Associate	1.335
Berkshire Hathaway	Realtor	5
Johnson & Johnson	Intern	713
Facebook	Customer Service Representative	314

Source: Authors, based on the companies' tables, presented throughout this work
* This starting salary does not represent the totality. It is around 1020 times the earnings of the CEO to the salaries of Beijing Software Engineers not starting

an indicator of financialization as it prioritizes the financial pole of operations and not most human resources. In 1965, the ratio of the CEO's earnings to the worker's wages was only twenty times. In 2015, this ratio rose to 303 times (Webber, 2018, p.145). In our research, we found more than 18,000 times the total earnings of the CEO and the less paid worker at the beginning of his/her career. This number does not represent the totality because it is limited to a Chinese company and a specific professional from a specific city. If we take the average, it will pass 1,000 times, reaching 8,000 times at Apple and 11,000 times at Google, in a year in which CEOs received compensation greater than US$ 100 million. In normal years, the CEO / Employee ratio was more than 800 times in several companies, even higher than what was found in the work of Webber (2018).

In summary, the difference in earnings between the CEOs and the group of workers of a certain company has been getting bigger and bigger, and in this regard, all the companies studied by us behaved similarly, explaining hundreds and even thousands of times the ratio between the total earnings of the CEOs and the salaries of the groups of workers.

12.8 Employment

In the last financialization indicator, we discussed the issue of employment. Table 12.14 shows the evolution of the number of employees in the ten companies analyzed, from the beginning of the 2000s until 2018.

It can be observed in Table 12.14 that all companies increased their number of employees, with the sole exception of ExxonMobil, which employed 97,900 in 2001 and dropped to 69,600 workers in 2017. The other nine companies significantly increased the number of employees, such as Amazon, for example, which went from 17,000 in 2007 to 566,000 in 2017,

Table 12.14 Employment evolution in the ten companies analyzed

Company	*Number of employees T1*	*Number of employees T2*
Apple	14,800 (2005)	123,000 (2017)
Google	16,805 (2007)	88,110 (2017)
Microsoft	61,000 (2005)	131,000 (2018)
Amazon	17,000 (2007)	566,000 (2017)
Berkshire Hathaway	288,462 (2012)	377,291 (2017)
Facebook	7 (2004)	25,105 (2017)
Johnson & Johnson	119,200 (2007)	134,000 (2017)
JP Morgan Chase & Co	224,961 (2008)	252,539 (2017)
Tencent Holdings	6,194 (2008)	44,796 (2017)
ExxonMobil	97,900 (2001)	69,600 (2017)
Total	846,329	1,810,841

Source: Previous tables of each company, throughout the text

a jump of more than 3000%. Apple also showed a considerable leap, from 14,000 employees in 2005 to 123,000 in 2017, the same movement of Tencent Holdings, which went from 6,000 employees in 2008 to 44,000 in 2017, growth of more than 700%. Others grew relatively little, such as J&J and JPMorgan Chase & Co.

This indicator shows that the financialization process does not necessarily destroy jobs, as one might suppose. We might think that, because it is a process that prioritizes the financial pole of the business, to the detriment of the physical, human and productive pole, it would inevitably assume a linear cut in jobs in all sectors of the economy. Not quite. As Cushen and Thompson (2016) remembered well, work processes still matter, and a lot.

What we can deduct from the financialization process in the biggest companies is that even with the massive creation of jobs in the last decades, this job is qualitatively different from the job created in previous times. Lower wages, more intense work hours, part-time jobs, little or no incentives, such as decent and attractive retirement plans and health plans. It was what Wartzman (2017) called "the end of loyalty", which was responsible for "the fall of good jobs in America".

Another dimension of the employment issue in the era of financialization is that the "platform capitalism" described by Nick Srnicek (2016) has so far failed to show itself as a salvation from the problem of unemployment and the transformation of the classic industry into industry 4.0, as much was expected. The ten largest companies in market capitalization employed just 1.8 million workers worldwide in 2017–2018, a fraction only when compared to entire sectors, such as automotive, construction, petrochemical, among others. This shows that financialization, also in the indicator that deals with employment, is full of specificities that come to the fore when we carefully analyze each company.

12.9 Final remarks

We have reached the end of this book, seeking to analyze the financialization indicators in the ten largest companies in market capitalization worldwide. We use categories of analysis, which we can also call indicators, which were responsible for trying to materialize the abstract economic concept of financialization. Comparison between sources of profitability, shareholding composition, purchase and sale of shares, mergers, and acquisitions, the origin of company directors, dividend payments and stock repurchases, compensation to executives, employee salaries, and employment were the indicators found in the literature on financialization, with several authors participating as developers of these indicators. The main authors were Froud et al. (2006), Lazonick and O'Sullivan (2000), Ertürk (2015, 2020), Piketty (2014), Bebchuk and Fried (2004), Wartzman (2017), Webber (2018), Van der Zwan (2014), among many others that provided us with the theoretical basis for the development of analysis categories and indicators.

Our aim was to carry out exploratory research in order to understand how the financialization process in the largest world companies takes place, since we had studied the automotive industry and found significant data of the growing process of financialization of the production that reflected on that sector. And now, to our surprise, we find in the ten largest companies in the world a much more complex and heterogeneous process than that found in automakers.

12.10 Financialization is not a homogeneous process

What was noticeably clear in our research is that financialization is not a linear process, homogeneous and equally applicable to all companies, manufacturers, financial or not, but in each company the indicators found were quite specific. Some companies paid dividends and practiced repurchase of shares, others that did neither. Some companies paid dividends but did not repurchase shares, in addition to others that repurchased shares but did not pay dividends. That is, in one of the essential financialization indicators, related to the principle of maximizing shareholder value, at least four types of conduct took place. Unlike the automotive sector, as demonstrated by our study, even with different intensities, all five automakers paid dividends to their shareholders (Carmo et al., 2021). Furthermore, the main shareholders are the same, both in the automotive sector and in the ten largest companies by market caps. Why is there a different posture in the face of large investment groups such as The Vanguard Group, BlackRock Inc., and State Street Corp?

When studying the literature on the primacy of shareholders in the 1980s and 1990s, Ismail Ertürk (2020) says that it focused on the

> transformation of Chandlerian managerial capitalism into shareholder primacy capitalism where firms compete in stock markets. In such a

> capitalism stock markets have become bubble producing giant financial mechanisms, making long-term shareholder value creation a rhetoric rather than a realizable managerial goal and, at the same time, undermining wage-led sustainable economic growth.
>
> (Ertürk, 2020, p.46)

And the

> survival of the shareholder value primacy after the burst of the dot.com bubble and the scandalous collapse of Enron in 2001, after enriching managers and destroying shareholder value, has directed corporate financialization research into mostly empirical investigations on the gap between the rhetoric and the reality in financialized firms.
>
> (Ertürk, 2020, p.46)

That is, just like Froud et al. (2006) stated even before, there is a narrative, a rhetoric on the one hand, and a completely different number, a different reality, on the other. Although all companies are under the aegis of the conception of control of maximization of shareholder value and long-term value creation, we do not see this happening in this way. The principle of maximizing shareholder value is seen as the objective of the firm, but this principle is a matter that is contested in studies of corporate law and economics. "In this context a stakeholder perspective defines the purpose of the firm to equally serve employees, owners, customers, and the wider society" (Ertürk, 2020, p.43).

This fact is corroborated when we analyze the rise of the working-class shareholder (Webber, 2018), which practices financial activism through workers' pension funds, such as CalPERS, (California Public Employees Retirement System) maintained by California public employees, with 1.3 million members and estimated at US$ 323 billion in 2018, the largest pension fund in the United States. These funds (which bring together more than US$ 5 trillion) operate in the financial market investing the resources of workers and have already been responsible for several political struggles, such as the introduction of the proxy statement, which is a voting process for the board of companies considered more democratic than the previous method (which made it difficult for some shareholders to participate) and succeeded in replacing board members of companies that fired employees, chased unions and acted unfairly, companies in which these funds were major shareholders, such as Walmart promoting various divestments and punishing, in their view, capital unfair to the interests of workers. Moreover, they fight for the separation between the CEO and the Chairman of the board, positions that in the United States have been accumulated by the same person, giving him/her enormous decision-making power, mainly regarding the fixation of compensations and those of executive colleagues.

The investments made by the workers' pension funds have already been victims of the executives of the Hedge Funds, who promise to "beat the market", with performances superior to the more conservative investments and of lower risks, but in fact, such a promise does not occur in practice, because this type of risky investment has been beneficial only to the managers of these Hedge Funds. They charge higher fees, higher commissions for executives and give the same or less return on investments, compared with other passive funds, according to research from the historical series (Webber, 2018, p.81). In other words, this observation goes in the same direction as the conclusions of Froud et al. (2006) and Ertürk (2020) in the sense that these investment fund´s executives have a rhetoric of creating shareholder value, but in practice they are destroying value, for their benefit. This is one of the most perverse aspects of the financialization process, which is the transfer of high values to a layer of executives who say one thing and do something completely different.

The rise of the working-class shareholder, as classified by Webber (2018), was considered the "last and best weapon for workers" to be used in favor of workers at a time of predominance of the principles of maximizing shareholder value, represented mostly by large financial institutions and large fortunes. This rise is a great novelty in the financialization process, since it brings with it a new shareholder, who is the pension fund acting also politically within this financial game. Although the creation of the joint stock company is old and open to everyone who wants to be investors, including the simplest worker, we now have a more politically powerful layer to overcome the stock dispersion and act in gigantic funds too, to mitigate the effects of financialization in that category that the fund represents.

To continue to demonstrate the difference between rhetoric and reality, in other indicators, we have seen throughout our work that reality is quite different from the scenario that narratives seek to portray. According to the current narrative, communication and information technology companies are the big dream and a great opportunity when it comes to work. Work and wages are two categories that make up our concerns from the start. Through wages and benefits, we can see in which situation of inequality the production system is found, how much of it is destined for workers and how much goes to profit, interest, dividends, etc.

Regarding the situation of the wages of workers in communication and information technology companies, the companies belonging to platform capitalism (Srnicek, 2016), what we saw was a real depreciation of the workforce and very low wages compared with the size of companies such as Apple, Google, Amazon, Microsoft, and Facebook, for example. Lower wages, part-time work, forcing the worker to have more than one job, making life more difficult, longer hours in many countries, outsourcing all production in developing countries as a way to reduce labor costs (Apple in China, for instance), among other painful and less valued working conditions. In 1947, General Motors paid 20% above the average salary of all North American ethnic groups. Today, it pays 60% of the average for most of the initial workers and with the lowest wages. This represents the end of loyalty between companies and employees in various sectors of the economy (Wartzman, 2017).

Meanwhile, executives are increasingly well paid in all the companies analyzed in our work, with few exceptions. Millionaire compensation helps to create a layer of wealthy executives, increasing inequality between income brackets and social strata. Compensation payments through stock options make the tax on income lower (leading to losses to public coffers) since cash wages are small compared with earnings on shares and other bonuses. At the same time, stock options cause their price to rise artificially and make the agent also a shareholder, blurring the line between ownership and control. Our study found a difference of thousands of times the ratio between the CEO's earnings and the average employee salaries, for the most part. This ratio has been increasing at an impressive speed, going from just 20 times in 1965 to 303 times in 2015, but we find even greater differences. In other words, financialization is a conscious process carried out by companies and managers who could certainly have a different approach, acting differently.

If fewer dividends were paid, less compensation paid, and less stock repurchases carried out, there could certainly be better wages, more jobs and fewer factory closures, at a time when there is dramatically a lack of work for all and a lack of an economy that includes more people in its mechanism, overcoming historical problems still unresolved such as hunger, misery, and the deprivations of a time that seemed to be left behind.

Considering this work, our objective was to contribute to the research agenda of economic sociology and finance, seeking to understand the financialization process in the largest global companies. We hope to have added to this process and that our reflections and findings can contribute to public policies that make our world economically better and more sustainable for all.

References

Alphabet *Annual Report*, 2018. Available at: https://abc.xyz/investor/pdf/20171231_alphabet_10K.pdf. Accessed 10/25/2019.

Apple *Annual Report*, 2021. Available at: https://s2.q4cdn.com/470004039/files/doc_financials/2021/q4/_10-K-2021-(As-Filed).pdf. Accessed 03/17/2022.

Bebchuk, L.A. and Fried, J.M. 2004. Pay without performance, the unfulfilled promise of executive compensation, part II: power and pay, draft of the book *Pay without Performance, the Unfulfilled Promise of Executive Compensation*. Available at: http://www.law.harvard.edu/faculty/bebchuk/pdfs/Performance-Part2.pdf. Accessed 09/10/2021.

Carmo, M.J., Sacomano Neto, M., and Donadone, J.C. 2021. *Financialization in the Automotive Industry: Capital and Labour in Contemporary Society*. London and New York: Routledge. Available at: https://www.routledge.com/Financialisation-in-the-Automotive-Industry-Capital-and-Labour-in-Contemporary/Carmo-Neto-Donadone/p/book/9780367751395

Chesnais, F. 1996. Os grupos industriais, agentes ativos da mundialização financeira. *A mundialização do Capital*. Editora Xamã: São Paulo.

Davis, G.F. 2008. A new finance capitalism? Mutual funds and ownership re-concentration in the United States. *European Management Review*, 5, 11–21.

Ertürk, I., Froud, J., Johal, S., and Williams, K. 2005. Pay for corporate performance or pay as social division: re-thinking the problem of top management pay in giant corporations. *Competition and Change*, 9 (1), 49–74.

Ertürk, I. 2015. Financialization, bank business models and the limits of post-crisis bank regulation. *Journal of Banking Regulation*, 17(1/2), 60–72.

Ertürk, I. 2020. Shareholder primacy and corporate financialization. *The Routledge International Handbook of Financialization*. Philip Mader, Daniel Mertens and Natascha Van der Zwan (eds.). Available at: https://www.routledge.com/The-Routledge-International-Handbook-of-Financialization/Mader-Mertens-Zwan/p/book/9781032174631

Exxon Mobil *Annual Report*, 2018. Available at: https://corporate.exxonmobil.com/-/media/Global/Files/annual-report/2018-Financial-and-Operating-Review.pdf. Accessed 11/28/2019.

Fichtner, J., Heemskerk, E.M., and Garcia-Bernardo, J. 2017. Hidden power of the Big Three? Passive index funds, re-concentration of corporate ownership, and new financial risk. *Business and Politics*, 19(2), 298–326.

Fligstein, N. 1990. *The Transformation of Corporate Control.* Cambridge, MA: Harvard University Press.

Fligstein, N. 1991. The structural transformation of American industry: an institutional account of the causes of diversification in the largest firms, 1919–1979. *The New Institutionalism in Organizational Analysis.* Paul J. DiMaggio and Walter W. Powell (eds.), 311–336. Chicago, IL: University of Chicago Press.

Froud, J., Johal, S., Leaver, A., and Williams, K. 2006. *Financialization and Strategy: Narrative and Numbers.* London: Routledge.

JPMorgan Chase & Co. *Annual Report*, 2018. Available at: https://www.jpmorganchase.com/content/dam/jpmc/jpmorgan-chase-and-co/investor-relations/documents/annualreport-2018.pdf. Accessed 08/28/2019.

Lazonick, W. and O'Sullivan, M. 2000. Maximizing shareholder value: a new ideology for corporate governance. *Economy and Society,* 29(1), 13–35.

Piketty, T. 2014. *O Capital no século XXI.* Rio de Janeiro: Editora Intrínseca.

Srnicek, N. 2016. *Platform Capitalism.* Cambridge: Polity Press.

Van Der Zwan, N. 2014. Making sense of financialization. *Socio-Economic Review,* 12, 99–129.

Wartzman, R. 2017. *The End of Loyalty: The Rise and Fall of Good Jobs in America.* New York: Public Affairs.

Webber, D.H. 2018. *The Rise of the Working-Class Shareholder: Labor's Last Best Weapon.* Cambridge, MA: Harvard University Press.

Appendix

Five years later

Most of the data we used in this book were frozen in December 2017. Now, in 2022, almost five years later, we would like to know what the current situation of these companies is like. The ten largest companies by market capitalization analyzed by us, whose table was presented in the introduction and whose reference year and month were December 2017, are now no longer the same. Five years later, ExxonMobil, Johnson & Johnson, JPMorgan Chase & Co, and Tencent Holdings are no longer on the list of the top ten companies by market capitalization in which they appeared in 2017. Instead, we find Saudi Arabian Oil Co., also known as Saudi Aramco, an oil company valued at US$ 2.4 trillion in market capitalization, ranking second in 2022; Tesla, with a market capitalization of US$ 864 billion; NVIDIA, a US company that develops graphics processors with a market capitalization of US$ 570 billion; and TSMC, Taiwan Semiconductor Manufacturing Company with a capitalization of US$ 556 billion as of March 3, 2022; all these companies climbed to the top ten ranking (Johnston, 2022).

The companies that have remained firmly in the best positions are Apple, which went from a market capitalization of US$ 752 billion in 2017 to US$ 2648 trillion in 2022; Microsoft, which had a market capitalization of US$ 507 billion in 2017 and went to US$ 2.1 trillion in 2022; Google (Alphabet), from US$ 579 billion in 2017 to US$ 1.7 trillion in 2022; Amazon, which went from US$ 427 billion to US$ 1.5 trillion in 2022; Berkshire Hathaway (up from US$ 409 billion to US$ 723 billion) and Facebook, which changed its trade name to Meta Platforms Inc., going from a market capitalization of US$ 407 billion in 2017 to US$ 545 billion in 2022, the lowest growth among the companies that continued in the ranking of the ten most valued ones.

The most interesting fact when we analyze these numbers is that they show a growth of technology companies, which belong to platform capitalism or the new economy of the fourth industrial revolution, which has tripled (Google, Amazon, and Apple) and quadrupled (Microsoft), market capitalizations, in a space of less than five years. This exponential growth can be seen in a context of corporate financialization in which the largest shareholders of companies, those who actually decide the directions and strategies, continue to be the large passive investment funds, the new permanent universal owners in the current configuration of the international economy. In 2017, the fifteen largest institutional investors held 53.64% of Apple's institutional shares, for example. In 2022, these same fifteen largest institutional investors increased their fraction to 59.62% of Apple, among 3944 institutional investors (Nasdaq, 2022), less than 0.5% of investors, demonstrating how values are becoming increasingly concentrated. The data allow us to affirm that the reconcentration of property in the hands of a few and gigantic groups continues to grow, day after day.

Regarding dividend payments to shareholders, values have been continuously increasing, always favoring shareholders more and other stakeholders less. In 2017, Apple paid dividends and repurchased shares worth US$ 45 billion, and in 2021 that number jumped to US$ 95 billion (more than doubled in four years). Stock repurchases also experienced increases at Google, from US$ 4.8 billion in 2017 to US$ 31.1 billion in 2020, growing sixfold in three years (Macrotrends, 2022; Ycharts, 2022). On Facebook, stock repurchases were even higher, rising from US$ 1.9 billion in 2017 to US$ 44.5 billion in 2021, a twenty-two-fold increase in four years. In all the other indicators we used in this book, there was an increase in the values that were meant for shareholders and the most important executives. All these data reflect the core of the financialization process, which is the growing importance that the financial pole of society acquires in the economy as a whole, dictating its strategies and the destinies of all humanity.

Total assets of global financial institutions

The growth of financial assets around the world has been happening extremely fast, far above the speed of global GDP growth. As we discussed in the introduction to this book, the data provided by Thomson and Dutta have already shown an exponential growth in financial assets since the 1980s. Financial assets reached US$ 12 trillion in 1980 – 120% of the world's GDP; US$ 56 trillion in 1990 – 263% of world GDP; US$ 127 trillion in 2002 – 320% of world GDP; US$ 219 trillion in 2010 – 316% of the world's GDP; US$ 325 trillion in 2015 – 400% of world GDP and US$ 468 trillion in 2021, 500% of world GDP, which reached US$ 90 trillion in 2021 (Thomson & Dutta, 2015; Norrestad, 2021). That is, financial assets are already more than five times larger than all fixed assets, human capital, facilities, and everything that is produced in goods and services over a period of time.

In 2022, all the values found were much higher than those in 2017, indicating that it is not just a quantitative increase in the same economic reality, but the qualitative changes in contemporary capitalism have been causing these exponential increases in the financial pole of society. Hence, we can say that some trends are solidifying in this new socioeconomic environment, such as the following:

1. A significant increase in the share of services and financial activities in the total contribution of manufacturing companies, leading to a decrease in the profitability of the productive sector.
2. An increase in the participation of large groups of institutional investors in the shareholding composition of companies, as well as an increase in the concentration of shares in a few hands.
3. An increase in company mergers and acquisitions, mainly acquisitions that concentrate the market more, harming the economy and working against competition, strengthening monopolies and oligopolies.
4. An increase in dividend payments to shareholders and stock repurchases in most companies listed on the stock exchange, reinforcing the policy of maximizing shareholder value, central to the understanding of financialization.
5. An increase in the payment of million-dollar compensation to corporate executives, reaching millions of dollars every year, and the increase in compensation payments through stock options.
6. Salary stagnation in most companies, with starting salaries paid to workers well below the average salary for all ethnic groups in the countries, mainly in the United States.
7. An increase in the tendency to close job positions in rich countries and create jobs in poor or developing countries, as a way to save on labor costs; an increase in deindustrialization in many countries in favor of targeting resources to shareholders.
8. An increase in job instability and a lack of security regarding the future.
9. An increase in wage, economic, and social inequality between income groups, concentration of capital in a few hands, and return to the inequality patterns of the early twentieth century.
10. An increase in the power of investment funds, companies, and economic groups over the sovereignty of countries and the interests of people, making these economic actors more geopolitically important than the majority of the population, exacerbating the harmful aspects of globalization.

Finally, we can say that in a short period of less than five years, the companies studied by us increased their financialization indicators with full force, depicting a rapid transformation process that brings with it all the negative consequences that we have already noted. Hopefully, based on the broader knowledge of people in general about the phenomenon of financialization, we can propose measures that mitigate and reverse the process of financialization and deindustrialization that countries and the entire world economy are going through.

References

Johnston, M. (4 Mar 2022). Biggest companies in the world by market capitalization. Available at: https://www.investopedia.com/biggest-companies-in-the-world-by-market-cap-5212784. Accessed 03/18/2022.

Macrotrends, 2022. Apple dividends. Available at: https://www.macrotrends.net/stocks/charts/AAPL/apple/total-common-preferred-stock-dividends-paid. Accessed 3/19/2022.

Nasdaq, 2022. Apple institutional holdings. Available at: https://www.nasdaq.com/market-activity/stocks/aapl/institutional-holdings. Accessed on 02/22/2022.

Norrestad, F. (21 Dec 2021). Total assets of global financial institutions from 2002 to 2020. Available at: https://www.statista.com/statistics/421060/global-financial-institutions-assets/. Accessed 3/18/2022.

Thomson, F. and Dutta, S. 2015. *Financialisation: A Primer.* Amsterdam, NL: Transnational Institute.

Ycharts, 2022. Apple stock buybacks. Available at: https://ycharts.com/companies/AAPL/stock_buyback. Accessed 3/19/2022.

Index

Note: **Bold** page numbers refer to tables.